Radicals Against Race

Radicals Against Race

Black Activism and Cultural Politics

Brian W. Alleyne

Oxford • New York

First published in 2002 by
Berg
Editorial offices:
150 Cowley Road, Oxford, OX4 1JJ, UK
838 Broadway, Third Floor, New York, NY 10003-4812, USA

© Brian W. Alleyne 2002

Berg is an imprint of Oxford International Publishers Ltd.

Library of Congress Cataloging-in-Publication Data
A catalog record for this book is available from the Library of Congress.

British Library Cataloguing-in-Publication Data
A catalogue record for this book is available from the British Library.

ISBN 1 85973 522 3 (Cloth)
1 85973 527 4 (Paper)

Typeset by JS Typesetting, Wellingborough, Northants.
Printed in the United Kingdom by Antony Rowe, Chippenham, Wiltshire.

For Cristina, *zia* Pearl, Sean, Sherwyn, Wayne

**In memory of Ellis Alleyne and
Janet Griffith Alleyne**

Contents

Acknowledgements   ix

Introduction   1

1   Beginnings: The Politics of the Word   21

2   Cultural Revolutionaries   51

3   Activist Work and the Workings of Activism   79

4   Slow Builder and Consolidator: A Life History of
        John La Rose   111

5   'Life Experience with Britain'   145

6   Radical Lifework   171

Appendix I: New Beacon Publications, 1966–1999   183

**Appendix II: Scope of the George Padmore Institute's
Archive**   189

**Appendix III: Activist Network centred around New
Beacon**   193

Bibliography   197

Index   211

Acknowledgements

This book is an attempt to hold a political conversation across space and generation. It is also an attempt to objectify some of the excitement I first felt on discovering the sociological imagination, under the guidance of Susan Craig (who frequently reminded me that I had to do some work). I am grateful to my other early tutor and mentor – Maureen Cain. Keith Hart supervised the doctoral dissertation which was in a sense the earliest draft of this book. As academic guide, his challenging and sometimes unsettling questions helped me to develop a research area and strategy; he kept me always aware of broader reality. Susan Benson helped me through the difficult period of starting to write after initial fieldwork and she saw me to that vital first draft; her substantive and theoretical inputs have been and remain invaluable.

Time spent at the C.L.R. James Institute in New York (1994–1995) was vital to my own development – I was able to expand my knowledge of the vast literature on migrant writers and activists, and through studying C.L.R. James's life and work, to begin to grasp the complex social and cultural relations that connect Britain, the English-speaking Caribbean, and the USA. Jim Murray, who runs that Institute, has consistently given me intellectual and personal support, and is himself an outstanding cultural activist.

I am grateful to Kathryn Earle and the staff of Berg for their deft handling of this book. This work has greatly benefited from the comments of Berg's anonymous reviewer and the careful input of their copyeditor. Pat Caplan and Nigel Rapport read and commented on early versions of several chapters; both encouraged my efforts to use personal narratives. Various members of my research-student cohort at Cambridge gave intellectual input and friendship, as did the other participants of the writing-up seminar of 1997–1998. Of my Goldsmiths colleagues, Suki Ali, Les Back, Chetan Bhatt, and Kirsten Campbell, sometimes without realising it, helped me to work through some of the ideas I was trying to get down on paper.

Throughout the period of time objectified in this text, Cristina Chimisso read my many drafts. The rigour of her intellectual input was matched always by the generosity of her emotional support. I deeply value the

Acknowledgements

inputs of my friends and comrades. Riccardo Vitale, Brett St Louis, Knut Nustad, Nicole King and Terrance Roopnaraine offered comments and criticism at numerous junctures. *La lotta continua.* During the early stages of fieldwork, I received financial backing from the following Cambridge funders: the William Wyse Fund, the Richards Fund, The Holland Rose Fund, the Smuts Fund, the Lundgren Research Fund, the Ling Roth Fund, and also from Queens' – my Cambridge College. The Errol Barrow Memorial Fund awarded me a writing-up grant. The Institute of Commonwealth Studies, University of London, granted me a stipendiary junior research fellowship for 1998–1999, along with work space and collegial support. A Wingate Scholarship awarded in 1999 facilitated the final preparation of the book.

For most of the three-and-a-half years that I worked on the first phase of this project, my main source of financial support was my family: chiefly Pearl Eccles and Errol Eccles in New York. Pearl Eccles has been the main pillar of this project, in so many ways. Wilma Alleyne-Bostic and Oscar Trotman also held up the trans-Atlantic support net. I hope I have rewarded their confidence. This book is in part my recognition of their own Atlantic crossings.

It remains to acknowledge the help of my field interlocutors. Throughout the book I name persons whom I interacted with, but I must mention specially some individuals here. John La Rose, my key informant, gave his time and knowledge generously from the beginning, always responding to my many prying and sometimes inept queries. The same holds for Sarah White, who shared her immense technical and political knowledge as an activist, and as a bookseller and publisher. Their shared passion for social transformation and justice was a source of inspiration. The following persons also greatly assisted my research: Michael La Rose; Roxy Harris; Janice Durham; Akua Rugg; Joan Goody; Irma La Rose; Leroy Coley; Claire Shepherd and Lawrence Scott. Margot Rodway-Brown and Zuleika Dobson provided me with London lodgings. Though they are too numerous to list here, I am grateful to all the other people, some associated with New Beacon, some not, who made their time and knowledge available to me. Though it is not often done, I would like to say of the few individuals who declined to assist my research that their refusal was nonetheless revealing.

I was given extremely helpful advice throughout the course of writing this book. I have not always followed that advice. What appears herein is entirely my own responsibility.

Introduction

We can live together only if we lose our identity.

Alain Touraine

New Beacon bookshop is situated, in June 2001, on the ground floor of a
four-storey building at number 76 Stroud Green Road, a five-minute walk
from the Finsbury Park underground station, north London. The bookshop
has been at that location since 1973. New Beacon was started as a
publishing house in August 1966 by John La Rose with the support and
assistance of Sarah White. A survey of the '50 Best Specialist Bookshops
in the UK', carried out by *The Independent* (22–28 July 2000), refers to
New Beacon as 'Britain's oldest black-interest bookshop'; this is true
but indicates only part of the work which is the subject of this book.
New Beacon's reputation and clientele extend beyond Britain, including
the Caribbean, North America, continental Europe, and parts of English-
speaking Africa. New Beacon is a publisher, and specialist bookseller,
concentrated in the areas of Black British, Black American, Caribbean
and African fiction and non-fiction. Apart from serving the general public,
the shop caters to the needs of students of all ages, teachers and researchers,
and librarians.

The people who form the subjects of this book are engaged with a
wider network of social-movement organizations which operate both
within and against the dominant paradigms of race and ethnic/community
relations deployed by the British state and media. Much of their activist
work has centred around imagining and mobilizing toward a radical-
democratic, post-racist and post-'classist' Britain. In representing the ideas
and projects of these people as I do in this book, I construct a narrative
that is part of larger narratives on the post-war history of migration and
settlement in Britain, the cultural politics of anti-racism and the New Left
from the 1960s, and beyond to various strands of socialist politics that
span the Atlantic part of the world system. People who have been involved
in some or all of these projects, and who have remained in close association with John La Rose and Sarah White, constitute what I term the
New Beacon circle. This is my own rubric, not theirs; I use the term New
Beacon, because New Beacon Books book shop was in a sense the locus

around which I came to learn about the people and their projects. They constitute a circle, I argue, because they came together on various projects, sometimes because of prior friendship or kinship links, but other times meeting for the first time because of these projects; they have remained in contact through friendship, kinship, professional, and 'comradely' links. There are both historical and contemporary dimensions to the account which follows.

The historical dimensions consist in: first, my collection and analysis of life histories of selected members of the circle; secondly, my re-presentation of oral and archival accounts of a number of cultural and political projects in which my interlocutors have been involved over the past two decades. The contemporary dimensions consist in my recounting my own involvement and documentation of various projects organized by the circle.

The cultural and political activities of the circle – book publishing and selling, community education, and organizing legal defence campaigns and more – constitute a strategy intended to combat a form of cultural hegemony that my interlocutors believe is exercised in Britain to attempt to marginalize the working class, and Caribbean-, African- and Asian- descended elements within it. Their activism is thus not only built around resistance, but seeks actively to create alternative systems of value and communication. In building their activist praxis,[1] the New Beacon Circle are making history and making political-historical subjects in an 'interactive' fashion. In producing historical and biographical narratives they bring a political subject into being; in turn, that new political subject, which exists in the identities and sense of community that the circle construct in their activist work, facilitates the continued production of historical and biographical narratives. This dialogue among persons and across time is at the heart of this book.

Social Movements and Activism

I use the term activism to refer to a type of politically-oriented action that is conceived and deployed largely outside of established state structures, especially legislative assemblies (della Porta and Diani 1999: Chapter 1). The type of political activity that is most often indicated by this term in highly industrialized societies of the world system is mainly that connected to the so-called new social movements, which have had a major impact on politics in Western societies: concerned with gender, ethnicity, the environment, sexuality, globalization and more (Castells 1997a; Diani 1995; Green 1997; Melucci 1996; Starr 2000; Touraine 1977). These are *social* movements because they operate on the terrain of civil society. Their aims are political insofar as they are about wanting to bring about shifts in the balance of power; they have sought to politicize aspects of social existence – race, gender, sexuality for example – that have not been seen as expressly political in both liberal and some forms of conservative political theory and practice. But activism is broader in scope, both temporally and spatially, than is implied by the strictest meaning of *new* social movements. There is some overlap between old and new social movements, best exemplified by the long tradition, in Western countries, of left-wing activism – itself exemplified by the labour movement – where the class structuring of society has been contested by agents employing tactics from outside of the established arrangements (Calhoun 1982); this is sometimes overlooked by students of and participants in new social movements (Eyerman and Jamison 1991: 78–88).

Social movements, whether thought of as old or new, are by no means unique to the West (Tarrow 1998). In what are now the (officially) excolonial parts of the modern world system, there have been myriad challenges to the existing orders that can be termed activism; some such challenges, perhaps most famously the anti-colonial struggles of Gandhi and his followers (Fox 1989), were direct action *par excellence*. In the South of the world system, yesterday's anti-colonial struggle mobilized many ideas and actors similar to today's struggles for the rights of indigenous peoples or against destruction of the environment by multinational corporations. The anti-capitalism, anti-globalization movements see activists in the North and South of the world system making alliances (Starr 2000). The anti-slavery movement and the women's suffrage movement were two examples of activist movements that spanned long periods and were truly international in scope; more recent struggles against racism and patriarchy span old and new social movements. Blackburn's (1988) account of the late eighteenth- and early nineteenth-century British and French anti-slavery movements describes methods that are strikingly similar to those of 1990s social movements – the abolitionists employed the printed media, lobbied officials, mobilized intellectual resources and built coalitions of interests. D'Anjou (1996) makes the case for seeing the British abolition campaign of the late eighteenth century as an instance of a social movement simultaneously caught up in and affecting cultural change. He demonstrates that while there were pockets of resistance to Atlantic slavery from its very inception, it was only when the abolitionists were able to articulate their campaign with social and cultural changes in British society which saw the spread of ideas of possessive individualism, a gradual opening up of democracy, and the growth of liberal ideas on trade and production, among other factors, that they began to make inroads against the institution of the slave trade.

Though they share some characteristics, old and new social movements are not reducible to one another. One relatively clear distinction between the two types of movement is in the scope of their guiding narratives: old social movements – trade unions, women's suffrage, anti-slavery – were articulated in the form of universalist grand narratives; while new social movements – ecology, local autonomy, body politics – are mistrustful of grand narratives and speak their desires from the standpoint of specificity, from carefully crafted *petit* narratives. The new social movements are organized around different conceptions of political subjects from those of older social movements.

Cultural Politics

There is little benefit in making too sharp a distinction between cultural and political activity: the distinction is one which reductive Marxists in particular have been prone to making, seeing the cultural as relating to the superstructure while the 'real' business of politics arises out of the relations rooted in the economic base (Williams 1977). There is also little benefit in making too strict a separation between the state and the rest of the social order. After Gramsci (1971), we should be more attuned to look for ways in which state and civil spheres overlap and interpenetrate in modern capitalist societies.

Cultural politics as a label has come to increased prominence in political discourse since the anti-war, student, women's, and Black power movements came to the fore in the 1960s (Caute 1988; Harman 1988). Cultural politics is definitively the politics of these new movements, for which alienation was perceived as the greater threat to human happiness than exploitation, thus shifting the focus of revolutionary thought and action from the strict economic domain of society to its interconnected cultural formations. A consequence of this shift was the constitution of a kind of politics that attacks, for instance, the exclusionary distinction of high and low culture, and further, foregrounds the way in which elite groups value the cultural capital which they possess while devaluing that of those subordinate to them in a given social formation. This kind of politics opens up to contestation the way in which cultural products are consumed and how cultural artefacts are produced and interpreted. An important site of cultural politics has been struggle over the representation of persons, their histories, and social relations. Another has been struggle over socialization and cultivation of human subjects. These two strategic sites are interconnected.

Introduction

The activism which is characteristic of new social movements, imagined and realized often as and through cultural politics, seeks to go beyond the accepted terms of engagement of bourgeois political discourse. Direct action – the most visible and most strident manifestation of social-movement activism – as a form of cultural politics is well suited as a label for post-1968 groupings fighting corporate and state bureaucratic power structures in the advanced capitalist world (Beck 1992). Advocates of direct action in this context seek to create spaces for individual and group autonomy from late modern technological and bureaucratic mega-structures that colonize increasing aspects of their life-world (Melucci 1989). In contrast to direct action, new social-movement activism is considerably broader in scope, as is cultural politics; indeed, activism and cultural politics are truly global even though they are most visible locally.

However we imagine society, we necessarily imagine the subjects and relations which constitute it. Cultural politics, on an initial working definition, would emerge from struggles over these very imaginings, representations and control of human subjects and social relations. On this broad definition cultural politics could be said to be as old as society itself. Arguments over the genesis of society, whether taken as concept and/or thing, affect the way we imagine and conceive cultural politics, without denying the usefulness of the *idea* of cultural politics itself. Cultural politics is a fundamental sociological category, but how we conceptualize and go about studying it will vary with our sociological standpoint. We must now turn from these conceptual generalizations to the specific context of this book – the settlement of large numbers of non-White people in post-war Britain, and the transformations which ensued.

The Empire Comes Home, and other Sociological Discontents

The contemporary Black and Asian population in Britain was constituted mainly as a result of post-war migration. The body of work done by sociologists and anthropologists on this migration has tended to view migration to and settlement in Britain in terms of persons moving in order to better their life-chances (Harris 1993; Miles 1982; Patterson 1969; Peach 1969; Rex and Tomlinson 1979; Thomas-Hope 1992). During the heyday of African, Caribbean and Asian migration to Britain (roughly from 1948 to the mid-1970s) most migrants were of working-class or peasant background; they took jobs in the openings at the lower end of the British labour market, openings which had been created by the post-war labour shortage and economic boom.

Though post-war migrants to Britain came from European as well as non-European homelands, in the post-war period it is migrants who were 'non-European' who came to be seen as constituting a migrant 'problem' and requiring special policy and legislation. The arrival of large numbers of Black and Asian people after the Second World War created problems for the notion of British identity, as well as complicating the identity of those Black settlers themselves.

Through the period of political ferment over race of the 1960s and 1970s, the race-relations 'industry' was the preferred site for state intervention into a 'racial' politics which was widely held to have been the result of the Black and Asian settlement. It remains so to the present. The two main weaknesses of the race-relations framework were (and remain), first, its failure to problematize the category of 'race' itself; and secondly, its relative disregard for the constraining effects of the political and economic structures and processes which set the terrain on which non-Whites settled in Britain.[2]

The move from race-based thinking to seemingly more sophisticated imaginings of 'ethnic communities' is one which was made first by social scientists in the 1970s and early 1980s, after which it became more widespread in popular, policy and media discourse. The shift began when a number of anthropologists rejected the race-relations framework in favour of one based around ethnicity (Ballard 1992; Watson 1979). They argued that so-called racial minorities in Britain may be more fruitfully studied as 'ethnic communities' with distinctive social structures and cultural patterns. This approach did have the virtue of taking on board classical anthropological issues of kinship, language, and religion, but as Benson (1996) notes, the study of non-Whites in Britain became dichotomized between that of Asians, seen as possessing 'deep' culture, on the one hand, and that of Black West Indians, seen generally in terms of social and family dysfunction, on the other.

The ethnic community approach may be seen as 'culturalist', in that it resorted to ideas of cultural variation to account for (mainly socio-economic) differences between human groups. This culturalism was vulnerable to attack from Marxists,[3] as well as from the structuralist/social-constructionist perspective of the Birmingham school of cultural studies (Centre for Contemporary Cultural Studies 1982). The social-constructionist approach seeks to ask a number of searching questions about how people come to be racialized, i.e. socially constructed as being a member of a racial category. It sees racial discourse as constantly being constructed and reconstructed on an everyday basis, and is sensitive to changes in the way racial identities are mapped and negotiated; generally, persons working in this perspective have been more aware of gender as a fundamental structuring aspect of social reality, and have brought this awareness to ideas of racial and ethnic construction. The shifting and permeable boundaries between concepts of race and ethnicity are centrally addressed by much work in this perspective. From this standpoint, the 'coping' of people within a racialized social reality is an everyday accomplishment, constantly renewed. And, learning from the migrant labour and relative autonomy perspectives, the social-constructionist approach often tries to hold the structural context as a field against which racial and ethnic identities are imagined and deployed (Alexander 1996; Alexander 2000; Back 1996).

Social constructionism (and Marxism) notwithstanding, both the race-relations and ethnic-community approaches to the social study and policy-making on behalf of non-Whites have overwhelmingly informed official and popular discourse in contemporary Britain. The simplistic categories of race relations have to some extent given way in the media and popular discourse to more ostensibly sophisticated discourses of cultural difference, but the notion that identifiable groups of persons may be fairly easily mapped into ethnic communities is still (too uncritically, in my view) held. Mainstream media and policy officials continue to speak of race relations and/or ethnic communities (few bother or perhaps are able to make distinctions between the two terms), as if official categorization were enough to bring such things into social being. Though vulnerable to the criticism that they are reductionist and theoretically naive, ideas of race relations and ideas of bounded ethnic communities remain important parts of many people's self-representation and identity. Perhaps unsurprisingly, such ideas have been quite successfully used by official agencies to govern and also to colonize the lifeworlds of British citizens.

Redressing Omissions and Absences: Reconstructing the Lives and Work of the 'Heroic Generation'

Notwithstanding the fact that most Black migrants to Britain after the Second World War were working class, it is also the case that a minority of migrants from the New Commonwealth, including those from the Caribbean, were well-educated persons seeking intellectual careers either through the route of higher education or as freelance creative artists. Less attention has been devoted to this subset than to the overall group of migrants. This lack of interest in the *intellectual* activity of Caribbean migrants to Britain stems partly from forms of Eurocentric reluctance to grant Black people (as other historically subordinate people in the world system) the social and cultural complexity which is reserved for people of European descent (Wolf 1982). The anthropologists have been most often guilty in this regard (Rigby 1996), but the sociologists are not blameless, as Benson (1996) reminds us. Even students of British cultural studies – a field willing to see Blacks in Britain as more than a labouring mass – have shown little interest in the cultural and political activity of the adult Black population of Britain. Instead, they have focused on the more rebellious and visible Black male youth population (Hebdige 1987; Jones 1988): this may be partly explicable by the fascination of cultural studies with popular culture and youth, and its relative disinterest in more 'dated' forms of resistance such as trade union activity. A related explanation may be rooted in the assumption by many students of political activism that as people grow older they become less politically active (Andrews 1991).

One consequence of these tendencies in the literature on Black social and cultural formations in Britain is that insufficient attention has been paid to the work of those Black (and White) activists who deployed a praxis that was self-consciously informed by an anti-racial-essentialist cultural and historical understanding of the Atlantic world system, and who employed forms of activism which, while they often included popular expressive cultural forms, are not reducible to them.

In a review of the development of British Cultural Studies (BCS), Roxy Harris (1996), himself a member of the New Beacon circle, has pointed out that while BCS opened spaces for cultural analysis it has overlooked the achievements of the adult Black working-class population of Caribbean descent in Britain – what he calls the 'heroic generation'. Harris commends BCS for recognizing that the British-born children of Black migrants, frustrated as they are by relatively limited opportunity for socio-economic advance (as are all working-class youth) and also by discrimination/marginalization, constitute – along with elements of White working-class youth – a potentially revolutionary force, but that recognition has been gained at the price of overlooking the activism of the parents of these Black youth.

For Harris, the omissions and absences have occurred for three reasons: first, as noted above, BCS work on Blacks in Britain has centred on the visible, rebellious youth; secondly, and as a consequence, the adult Black population are deprived of a sense of agency and come to be seen as a reactionary force in Black communities; thirdly, the concentration on Black youth has obscured the concrete contributions made by their elders in contesting racism and classism (Harris 1996: 339). In this regard it must be borne in mind that the Black people who fought racists in Notting Hill in 1958 were parents by the time the 1981 Brixton riots occurred: action at street level against racism did not begin in 1981. Relatively over-looked too has been the political and cultural work, less visible than rioting youth and less exciting perhaps than Black popular music, of Black migrants and their descendants in community groups, trade unions, churches, and supplementary schools.

This book is intended to address these omissions through constructing an ethnographic-biographical account of the ideas and practices of a group of socialist intellectual-activists who have struggled to open cultural, political and social space within the British nation for those who arrived after the Second World War.

Critical Humanism

I have written from the standpoint of a critical humanist sociology (Plummer 2001: esp. chapter 1).[4] It may appear strange to invoke the term humanism in the social sciences, given that so much intellectual energy since the 1960s – and not only in France – has been devoted to challenging its claims and proponents. In doing so I do no more than indicating that my commitment is to a focus on human beings as agents, though structurally and historically constrained, who seek actively, through culture, to feel at home in the world (K. Hart, personal commun-ication). Persons are to an extent shapers of their worlds, but not always in ways they fully understand or are in control of; while pursuing this perspective we need to be critical of people's own claims of agency.

In the second edition of his widely-read book on the life-history method in social science, Plummer (2001) articulates a set of five central criteria for a critical humanism:

> (1) attention to *human subjectivity and creativity;* (2) concern with concrete human experiences through their *social and economic organization;* (3) 'natur-alistic *intimate familiarity'* with such experiences; (4) self-awareness of moral and political role in moving towards a social structure in which there is less exploitation, oppression and injustice and more creativity, diversity and equality; (5) an epistemology of *radical, pragmatic empiricism* (Plummer 2001: 14; emphasis in original).

My conception of a critical humanism is a modest one. It is a form of humanism because it assumes that persons can and do imagine projects intended to transform their social world, that such projects may be collectively worked out, and such projects may sometimes succeed. The critical elements inhere in my not taking it as given that people always get what they intended, or are always certain what they intended, or better, are always capable of articulating this to other people. My idea of critical humanism is not based in a naive empiricism, but I do insist on humans as agents and as ends in themselves, though not the ends of sociological inquiry. In trying to write a person-centred sociological account (Bowring 2000), I am not dismissing the post-structuralist attack on humanism and ideas of the subject (Poster 1984), but merely taking a pragmatic position within a range of possibilities.

While taking aboard the many trenchant criticisms of humanism, especially its historical failure to universalize its human subject in line with its own prescriptions, I hold that in terms of social-movement activism, much can be achieved by persons who work from a humanist and inclusive standpoint, who try to construct an inclusive political subject. Such persons and their projects, especially their personal narratives, are central to this book.

Allied to my construct of a critical humanist sociology is my use of a dialogical model of research. I conceive of the activist dialogically constructing his or her knowledge and politics; I further imagine and implement my own sociological account as the outcome of a second dialogical process, casting myself as an interlocutor with living activists on the one hand, and with texts which account for activist projects outside my sphere of direct human contact, on the other.

Though I write about small collectives, individuals, and their bio-graphical self-representations, the social movements with which they engage are broad in scope. The power constellations which they challenge have been long dominant in Western capitalist societies: Eurocentric White racism; imperialism and neocolonialism; exploitation and domination.

The type of autonomous radical cultural activism I discuss in this book is a voluntary engagement based around aims conceived outside of the dominant rationality of market society and founded on a principle of solidarity other than that of work-based late capitalist society.

Biographical Narrative

In his 'ethnographic biography' of the Greek socialist and novelist Andreas Nenedakis, Herzfeld (1997) writes that his focus on biography seemed apt to capture the issue of motivation, from which anthropologists have tended to steer clear. For Herzfeld, while one cannot get at the inner private motivation of the subject, one can set stated motivations into the social field of the subject, and in so doing gain some insight as to what it meant *socially* for the subject to articulate and seek to realize a set of desires in a given time and place.

As it is a central concept in my work, an elaboration of the personal narrative is in order. As all typologies, the following is a relatively crude heuristic device, but it will serve to indicate the various forms which personal narratives may take. The **biography** is essentially another person's reading, and inscription, of the life in question; the biographer decides what to write, and how to write it. The **autobiography** is an inscription of a life, as remembered and written down by the subject him- or herself (generally the case, but some autobiographies may be *assisted* [Lewis 1968; Radin 1925] whereby the subject was helped in creating the text; assisted autobiographies blur the boundaries between categories in this typology[5]); St Augustine's *Confessions* (fourth century AD) is one of the earliest examples and has provided the model for much subsequent writing. The autobiography's limitations as a research resource are obvious: except for a minority of assisted autobiographies, its author was by definition literate, so a critical reading of an autobiography requires us to consider the social significance of being literate in the author's time and place, which is especially relevant when reading autobiographies of those oppressed and socially marginalized. The **life story** is a narrative of a life as related by the subject himself or herself. The life story is an important means by which we express our sense of self and communicate and negotiate that sense with others (Linde 1993). Anyone can tell a life story, he or she need not be literate nor possess the time and resources to produce an autobiography. The **life history** can be thought of as a life story plus a superstructure of analysis and commentary. The life history is a narrative of an individual life that may draw upon multiple resources: it may employ biography, autobiography, life stories, journals, written and oral histories in its constitution. The life history inscribes the individual life and attempts to account for why that life unfolded in the way it did; it has been extensively employed in anthropology, social work, sociology and psychology (Plummer 2001). While in many respects similar to biography, the life history *always* foregrounds the explanatory dimension, which is perhaps why it is the favoured form of personal narrative employed by social scientists in their own work. It is the product of an encounter – whether contemporaneously or historically – between the subject of the life history and an interlocutor/researcher (Crapanzano 1980); the researcher's interpretations are properly part of the final product (Caplan 1997). Theoretical issues of interpretation are made explicit in life histories in a way that they may not in a biography, autobiography, or transcript of a life story. The life history places the subject's life story or autobiography into a social and historical context. For Kohli, the use of the life history is accompanied by three sets of expectations: 'to get access to social life (1) as comprehensively as possible, (2) "from within", i.e., in its meaning and subjective aspects, and (3) in its historical dimensions' (Kohli 1981: 63).

Personal narratives may be constituted from many different sources: diaries, journals, letters, photographs, official records, and oral testimony; in the case of the autobiography, the subject takes it upon him- or herself to write down his or her own memories. However, much of the life histories produced by historians, anthropologists and sociologists have employed techniques of oral history in collecting their data. For these personal narratives, the material did not exist in written form until an ethnographer/historian transcribed the oral testimony of the subject. For Paul Thompson, oral history is 'the voice of the past', and the subjects of oral histories are living, breathing sources (Thompson 1978). For research work in non-literate communities or, more commonly, for work with social groups or persons who, though literate in the formal sense, have not kept any systematic documentation of their lives, oral history is an important research tool.

Two notions were especially important in my work because they connect my attempt to work as a critical humanist with my use of biographical narratives; the two concepts are *imagination* and the life seen as a *project*. The exercise of imagination is critical to any ethnographic work, as is the willingness to take our interlocutors as ends in themselves, even though we know that their knowledge and skills – as our own – are sometimes incomplete and inadequate to the tasks at hand.

C.W. Mills wrote of what he termed the 'sociological imagination' that it 'should enable its possessor to understand the larger historical scene in terms of its meaning for the inner life and the external career of a variety of individuals' (Mills 1959: 5). Mills held that the central problem to which social science should address itself is that to do with the relation between 'private troubles' and 'public issues'; this relation had become sharply problematic owing to modernity's strict separation of public from private spheres. Mills analysed the rise of bureaucratic and technical structures in modern society, showing that while on the one hand they permitted great improvements in the material well-being of most people in the developed world, on the other they had the unfortunate effect of isolating the individual amid impersonal processes and organizations. This contradictory experience of modernity ought to be addressed, according to Mills, by an imaginative standpoint that sought to understand how the individual biography was related to social structures and historical processes.

The question of locating the human subject in the structures of modern society was also a central concern of Jean-Paul Sartre (Sartre 1963). He wrote of the 'project', of the individual life seen as a project, involving the striving of the individual to realize a self within the possibilities and constraints of modern society. To write a meaningful biographical study for Sartre was to seek to understand life projects; in this regard he proposed the 'progressive-regressive method'. The progressive dimension of this method looks forward to the conclusion of a set of acts or actions, it relates to the desires of the subject. For Sartre, it is essential in order to understand the individual life that we can give some account of what the subject desired, of how the subject sought to shape his or her own life. The subject is generally able to articulate this progressive dimension in terms of desires, but in order to address questions of 'why' the subject conceived and sought to realize *this* and not *that* other life-project, it is necessary to construct a regressive dimension to the life history. This regressive dimension looks back to historical, cultural and biographical conditions that moved the subject to take actions, and that shaped the context in which life projects emerged. Sartre's notion of the project and of progression-regression provides an approach to the conceptualization and study of human agency in a given social structure which complements Mill's sociological imagination.

On Ethics and Knowing

There is affinity between the approach I seek to develop by drawing on Mills and Sartre, and the autonomous and culturally-sensitive Marxism of C.L.R James (Buhle 1989). Hovering over all is the benign ghost of Antonio Gramsci (Davidson 1977; Femia 1981). While these writers and tendencies are quite distinct and complex and certainly did not agree on many issues of theory and practice, I do see them as sharing a common focus on understanding people as agents in social life, constrained *and* empowered by various structures. They have in common too a socialist commitment to social transformation.

The issue of ethics cannot be avoided by any field researcher in the social sciences, especially one who was as closely involved with field respondents as I was. I tried to avoid using interlocutors as objective data sources. I do not judge the morality of their projects or of their representations. Indeed, this account would have been very different if I did not have some theoretical and political affinity for their work. They made it clear to me that they would not be willing to work with any researcher who did not empathize with their politics. I am aware that making this admission means that I am greatly distanced from the objectivist model of scientific enquiry. But such were the conditions of my research. Had they not been met I would not have been able to work with the people I did. In short, I was allowed access to their milieu because they were assured that I was to some degree supportive of their projects, and to some degree I came to share their political imagination.

To write as a sociologist is first of all to make a move toward constructing a sociological object or set of objects (Bourdieu and Wacquant 1992): in this case activism, activists, social movements and so on. Moreover, activism as a sociological object does not simply exist out there to be captured in a sociological text. There is no neat separation of the ideas of activism held by persons self-described as activists, and the object(s) constructed by the sociologist to study these. Even more importantly for my approach in this book, I take the position that activists' and sociologists' knowledge of activism are constructed necessarily – that is, *always* – in social interaction which takes place in historical – that is, *contingent* – contexts. (The meeting of contingency and necessity here is both provocative *and* productive, setting up a conceptual conflict which I note without attempting to resolve.)

The conception of activism I propose here tries to capture the interactive character of knowledge generation in activist praxis, be it through my own interviews and observations or reading of material on past projects with which I had no direct acquaintance. The dialogical appears in two senses: that among activists themselves, and that between texts and actors and myself as a researcher writing an account of them. Activism is a form of collective action and social knowledge construction. My method has some elective affinity for this conception of activism because I become as researcher part of a collective ongoing exercise, a social movement, yet I stand back somewhat as that same researcher. This book is the result of a dialogical process: my interaction with the classic ethnographic figure of the field informant or interlocutor forms one element; another is that of myself as a political subject, feeling some affinity for the independent radical democracy which I came to see as underlying the work of the New Beacon circle.

Plan of the Book

Chapters One and Two introduce the New Beacon circle – its key members and early projects. What ties all of the circle's projects together is the bringing of a radical political consciousness to cultural – literary as well as vernacular – form and production. This narrative of activist projects constitutes also the empirical basis for understanding cultural politics 'on the ground', in the broad space of anti-racist and multicultural politics and policy in Britain since the 1960s. The complex history of Black settlement in Britain and the zones of conflict and alliances which ensued form the backdrop for the discussion.

This book is partly an exercise in translation: I attempt to translate among activist, sociological and various political discourses. The work of Chapter Three is partly to begin translating the projects of the circle into sociology of social movements. I discuss the deployment and management of informational, social and cultural resources by the circle. A key social resource is the range of connections and memberships of the individuals who make up the circle. I then consider the activist work of the circle as cognitive praxis (Eyerman and Jamison 1991): the constitution of a world view and a related set of technical and organizational strategies by means of which activist ideas are translated into action.

Chapters Four and Five are connected ethnographic-biographical[6] discussions. In both, I have followed Sartre's (1963) approach to doing life history; he advocated that we ask: what kind of person can the subject of our interest be in order to produce the personal narrative before us? In seeking to answer this question, Sartre advocates that we examine, where available, personal narratives written by the subject's contemporaries, and attempt to connect these to other social and historical writing on the subject's milieu. In this way we can construct a plausible and suitably nuanced representation of our subject as an individual in history and within society.

Apart from these considerations, there was one major 'on-the-ground' reason for my employment of biographical representation: when I first came to know them in 1996, most of the core members of the New Beacon circle were middle-aged or nearing retirement age, and as such were given more to reflection and consolidation than to vigorous militancy. In a sense, I met them when their 'streetfighting years' were over. This does not mean they were inactive by any means, just that their activism was more laid back than it would perhaps have been if I had first met them in 1966 or 1976, rather than 1996. According to their own testimonies and other documentary sources, in years past they were quite militant and often active at the level of street protest – some of them even faced arrest. My understanding of where most of them were in their life cycles – middle age to early retirement – conditioned the way I went about constructing this account.

Chapter Four elaborates an interpretative mini-biography of John La Rose. The focus on La Rose is justified because he is the leading figure of the New Beacon circle and has had a major influence in formulating the circle's ideas and practices. I show that La Rose's life story is dialogical: his present life narrative speaks to his remembered past in colonial Trinidad, from which he draws rhetorical resources to elaborate and justify his self- conception as an activist. His conceptions of the capacity of culture to effect social change are important elements in his personal narrative; his cultural praxis is made visible by his own theorizing of politics and also at those points when he reflects on his own roles in various projects of the circle. I do not present his subjective account of his lifework as a history of radical Black politics in Britain over the last four decades, nor even as a partial substitute for such a history. Rather, I explore activist ideas and practices from the vantage point of the life history because that point offers possibilities of engaging the question of *why* people chose to engage in activist work, in La Rose's case virtually full-time for a life in its seventh decade at the time of writing.

In Chapter Five I widen the focus out from one individual to several, necessarily having to sacrifice biographical depth for breadth of coverage. I demonstrate how personal narratives have been used as a political and cultural resource by the circle, building the discussion around two series of public life-story presentations organized by the circle in 1997 and 1999. My account of these presentations looks at the way personal achievement and race/class identity are constructed in the narratives. I also consider the narrative presentations as 'performances of the self' that combine elements of pedagogy, entertainment and testimony. In Chapter Six I conclude the book.

On Terminology

While conceding its widespread current use in British media, popular and policy discourse, I dislike and do not use the currently popular term 'Afro-Caribbean', which is often used as a generic marker for anyone of 'Caribbean ancestry'. This label implies to my mind ignorance of the fact that many thousands of British nationals of Caribbean descent are mis-categorized, in the sense of the region from which they or their forebears migrated to Britain, as 'Asian' because of their phenotype (Vertovec 1993).

One of my motivations in pursuing this research was a felt need to challenge currently fashionable discourses of 'cultural difference' which totalize people into 'communities', and serve to reinforce historically and theoretically untenable notions of immutable difference between things called 'cultures', 'communities', 'ethnic groups' and 'races'. In talking about my work, I have frequently had to disabuse persons of the notion that I had carried out research on or in 'the Afro-Caribbean community in London'. While such an entity certainly exists in many persons' minds (and may even exist in London) my research as reported here has very little to say *directly* about it.

Not being able to steer clear of the minefield of racial, ethnic and national identity, I do the following: I use the terms 'Caribbean', 'West Indies' and 'West Indian' to refer to the English-speaking or Commonwealth Caribbean; African-, Asian-,[7] and Caribbean-heritage (sometimes West Indian) to refer to persons living in Britain who trace their ancestry to Africa, Asia and the Caribbean respectively. While I would have preferred to avoid their use altogether, I do write about 'Black', 'White' and 'Asian' when referring to individuals and groups.[8] The boundaries of these terms are unclear and my work did nothing to make them any clearer. It is my hope that these terms will make sense when considered within their overall structural relation to my narrative. These race-colour terms – particularly Black and White – are manifestly imprecise and even confusing, often conflating notions of phenotype, putative genotype, nationality, race and ethnicity (there are, for example, Black Europeans and White Caribbeans and Africans); but they are nonetheless socially grounded and widely used in myriad situations. None of these terms is fixed – each is a contested identity and some persons among my field informants do not fit neatly under any of these rubrics. Nonetheless, I use these terms because they remain those with which many if not most people in contemporary Britain identify themselves and others.

Notes

1. I employ the term 'praxis' to refer to practice which is informed by reflection on the best way to achieve a desired goal. Praxis is theoretically-informed (not only high theory, but the everyday reflection that is part of being human in the world), reflective practice; practice which aims to transform ideas, people, social relations, representations and the material world, and which in so doing, is itself transformed. I understand praxis to be recursive as well as reflexive.

2. These weaknesses are clearly seen a classic study of this genre, Patterson's *Dark Strangers* (Patterson 1963). This study is well documented, dealing with questions of assimilation from the perspective of the classic race-relations problematic. There is a wealth of statistics, individual profiles, interviews, and reference to debates in the print media; but 'race', around which much of the analysis is based, is accepted as a given, almost natural category. The problems of assimilation experienced by the West Indian migrants are seen to stem from their racial and cultural difference from the host population; the social and historical constructions of these differences are not foregrounded. The differences are employed to explain, more than being themselves explained. Patterson fails to problematize the post-war political economic environment, which saw Western Europe's leading industrial nations encouraging the immigration of needed labour, while simultaneously allotting most migrants to the lower reaches of the economy. In 2001, the British state and much of the media remain wedded to the race-relations problematic; though now one is more likely to hear of 'ethnic communities', to which racialized minorities are seen naturally to belong. The racialization of immigration, vividly highlighted in 1968 by Enoch Powell, lives on in the xenophobic pronouncements on asylum seekers and the harsh policies supported by both major political parties in 2001.

3. Scholars and activists working from a Marxist position have attacked the race-relations approach for its almost total oversight of both the structural determinants of post-war migration and the composition of labour markets in Western Europe (Castles and Kosack 1985 [1973]; Harris 1993). From this perspective, Black workers were systematically at a disadvantage not because of their skin colour but because they originated in underdeveloped and often colonized or ex-colonial parts of the modern world system, which in turn lowered their bargaining power on the labour market.

4. In *Between Camps* Gilroy (2000) called for a planetary humanism as a way out of the dead-end of race-based thinking. While I fully endorse Gilroy's call to move beyond race-thinking, my aim here is more modest in scope. C. Wright Mills in his *Sociological Imagination* (1959), set the scene for the kind of humanistic sociology I am pursuing. Charles Lemert's (1997) wonderfully engaging humanist introduction to sociology is what I would aspire to. While I would not commit myself fully to Rapport's (1997) individual-centred anthropology, I am guided by his injunction not to let structures subsume individuals, as was the case for much of the history of social anthropology and sociology.

5. Fiction and auto/biography may overlap (Brodber 1994; Eco 1984; Yourcenar 1955).
6. I borrow the term from Herzfeld (1997).
7. With the rise of identity politics and the campaigns to assert 'difference' since the late 1970s in Britain, 'Asian' has been split off from 'Black'; now the formerly Black as including Caribbeans, Africans and Asians, is replaced by 'Black *and* Asian'.
8. There is instability in the capitalized 'Black' and 'White' that serves to keep us alert to the historical and social fluidity of these terms. I generally use the capitalized versions of these terms (which should always be read as if they are in quotation marks), thus implying an appropriate distancing from the logical and historical fallacy of treating 'racial' terms as if they were natural categories (Guillaumin 1995).

–1–

Beginnings: The Politics of the Word

Introduction

The projects in which the members of the New Beacon circle were, and in some cases still are, centrally involved form the subject of this chapter and the one following. The Caribbean Artists Movement, New Beacon book service, bookshop and publishing house, the George Padmore Supplementary School; the Black Parents Movement, Peoples War Sound System and Carnival Band – among others – were intended to organize people around cultural projects mainly in order to build politically effective identities that transcended the confines of 'race' and ethnic community in an environment where racialized/ethnified understandings of human difference were dominant. I will first introduce key persons and then discuss two important early projects, the Caribbean Artists Movement and New Beacon Books. Both of these projects set the scene for an approach to literary (and artistic and musical) culture which was informed by a radical democratic politics. That politics was aimed to confront elite discourse that stratified cultural production and consumption along class, racial and national lines. It emerged out of the internationalist vision of a group of Caribbean educational migrants to Britain in alliance with progressive persons already settled in Britain.

I created the concept of the 'New Beacon circle' to represent the group of people who were most integrally involved in the milieu of cultural politics to which I was introduced through John La Rose in 1996. The concept makes sense mainly from my perspective as a field researcher. I will use it throughout the book as a shorthand term. I must confess to some uncertainty as to whether I should use it as a collective noun: sometimes I say the 'circle is' and at other times I say 'circle are'. Rather than go for grammatical correctness or at least consistency and chose one over the other, I have decided to leave both usages in because sometimes in the text I am thinking of the circle acting as a corporate body and use singular verbs, at other times I imagine the circle to be several individuals at work and use plural verbs. The infelicity which results is I hope compensated for by the preservation of nuances which are important for my account.

In discussing the New Beacon circle as an activist grouping, I will distinguish what I term 'core members' from 'close associates'. Core members are persons who were either founding members and who remain intimately (i.e. involved in planning and decision- making) and regularly involved in the work of the circle, or persons who have come to be intimately and regularly involved. Close associates are persons who are associated with the circle but not involved in planning and decision-making during the four-year period of my engagement with the milieu. Such persons are also deemed by me to be associates because they were so described by one or more core members. I further distinguish core members and close associates by differentiating those whom I met and came to know during field work, and those whom I met only briefly or not at all. I must emphasize again that these terms are my own, as part of my overall organizing narrative.

John La Rose and Sarah White are, from my perspective, at the core of the core members. They have been and remain my two key interlocutors and I have been introduced to virtually everyone else in the milieu by either of these two. Janice Durham is also a core member. Irma La Rose, John La Rose's ex-spouse, and Michael La Rose and Keith La Rose – their two adult sons – are also core members. Other core members are: Akua Rugg, currently teaching English at Brixton College; Ian Macdonald, Scots-born attorney and a trustee of the George Padmore Institute (GPI; I discuss this organization later) who has been a close friend of John and Sarah since the late 1960s; Aggrey Burke, Jamaican-born psychiatrist, also a GPI trustee; Gus John, Grenada-born educational administrator and consultant, one-time Director of Education in Hackney, is another trustee of the GPI. Both Gus John and Ian Macdonald had relocated to Manchester by the time of my fieldwork; I did not get the opportunity to interview either, nor did I interview Aggrey Burke. Gus John and Aggrey Burke appear in a later chapter in this book, narrating their life stories. Roxy Harris and Pat Harris were the other two core members whom I came to know. Roxy was born in Britain of parents from Sierra Leone; he currently (2001) teaches at King's College, London. He has been part of the circle since 1974/75. Pat Harris is of Scottish heritage; she teaches in a North London infant/junior school and works closely with Sarah White on various projects. Though I never formally inter-viewed Roxy, we had numerous conversations on the ideas and work of the circle which proved invaluable to my work, and a publication of his (Harris, 1996) was crucial in helping me to shape the standpoint from which I wrote this book. There are quite literally dozens of persons to whom I was introduced, who were described as close associates of John and Sarah. This is not a complete list of persons who would be seen by John or Sarah as core members of my imagined circle, but is restricted to those persons with whom I became personally acquainted over the four years. And there were dozens more whom I did not meet but was told about: an indication of the expanding concentric circles and widening networks in which my interlocutors are located.

Taken as a group, these persons are a mix of ethnic background: Sarah White, Ian Macdonald and Pat Harris are White, the others are Black. Some have origins in Britain, some in the Caribbean, two in Africa. Those born outside Britain have spent the greater part of their adult lives in Britain. Some are professional, university-educated. Some have been largely self-educated beyond high school. John La Rose is noteworthy because he is not university-educated while much of his life has been engaged in work that was partly intellectual in nature. He is an activist-organizer-intellectual, with a vast knowledge acquired through self-study and as part of groupings engaged in cultural and political work, as we will see in the chapter on his life history. What the core members all have in common is that they have been engaged in the political or cultural activism with which this book is concerned.

Sarah White was my other main interlocutor apart from John La Rose. She pointed out to me more than once in conversation that over their more than thirty-year partnership, she and John La Rose played complementary roles in their work – he tackles talking and political issues and she does administration; this is borne out by my own observation. Sarah runs New Beacon Books, with the assistance of Janice Durham; she sits on the board of the George Padmore Institute.

From a middle-class British family, Sarah read Russian and history of science at Leeds University, and there became involved with the Communist Party of Great Britain. She worked for a short time in a voluntary capacity for the African National Congress. At the time of meeting La Rose in 1965, she was writing a doctoral dissertation on the history of Russian science. After taking her PhD at Imperial College, University of London, Sarah moved into science journalism.

During the early years of the publishing and bookselling business, Sarah worked as Soviet science specialist for the *New Scientist*, until retiring from that journal in 1985:

> I could have pursued an academic career, but by the time I finished my
> doctorate I was tired of university life . . . When the chance to write for

the *New Scientist* came up I took it . . . it was interesting work, and convenient, it helped to pay bills and allowed me time to work in the book service and later the shop, especially when I had Wole [her son with John] (Conversation between author and Sarah White).[1]

Sarah entered radical and Black radical politics while at university:

It was at university in Leeds that I met people from the Communist Party; I was involved with a student branch of the party for a period. That led on to meeting people from the ANC . . . I did some work as a volunteer for the ANC in Britain for a while. I was doing that when I met John, and then became involved in all the business about West Indian politics . . . I hadn't known much about this before I met John.

Janice Durham currently assists Sarah White in the running of New Beacon bookshop. Janice was born in Grenada in 1957. At the age of twelve, she moved to England to live with an older cousin of her family, Millicent, who adopted her. She completed her O levels and an introductory course in nursing at a local college. Her intention was to go on to full training as a nurse. She met Michael La Rose at a party, and they began a relationship under the watchful eye of Millicent, who was 'very very strict' about Janice's social life. In 1979 Janice gave birth to a son, fathered by Michael:

I got into Epsom, a teaching hospital, to do my nursing . . . and after that . . . during that time I got pregnant with Renaldo [her son with Michael] . . . that was 1979 . . . but in between that, when I was at Epsom, during my weekends I used to come down [to London] and Michael was in the bookshop; and I used to come and help him. He used to work on Saturdays . . . I used to come here, just to be with him, and while I was there I used to help in the business . . . then obviously I met John and Sarah. And [after getting pregnant] my mom was not very pleased, obviously with me deciding to leave Epsom, to leave nursing. I moved back in with my mum. I had no work. So then Sarah said to me one day: would you like to come and work on the weekend? So I said fine, I'd do it until the birth of Renaldo and then obviously see what happened. But since then I've stayed, obviously I've stayed on (interview with author).

In 1983, after John La Rose suffered his first heart attack, Michael took over his father's work at the bookshop. It proved convenient for Michael and Janice to move into a flat above the shop. That flat now forms part of the premises of the George Padmore Institute. Michael never intended to stay on permanently at the shop, and after a while Janice took over as the other person working normally there with Sarah White. At the time I met her, Janice and Michael were no longer living together. She lives with their two children in her own home. Her main occupation is her work at the bookshop.

Janice came to Black politics as a consequence of her relationship with Michael. I asked Janice if she could specify her initial exposure to Black politics, whether it was through working at New Beacon bookshop. She replied:

> No, it was through meeting Michael. Because I met Michael at the age of sixteen, and then Cliff [2] got beaten up, and then I got involved in the BPM (Black Parents Movement), so it was through my relationship with Michael that I was more or less exposed to the black community, because my mother was never that way inclined, and the people I used to go around with, like two girls from college, I was just thinking about how to escape from my mum's house on a Saturday night, we weren't thinking you know, anything too political or anything like that. Through Michael I met his dad and his mum and the political arena where it started.

Irma La Rose, another founding member of the circle, is from a joint Trinidadian-Venezuelan family. In her personal narrative, Irma was influenced by an anti-colonial and proto-nationalist movement that engaged the imagination of many young people in Trinidad in the post-war decade. She was a member of the Trinidad and Tobago Youth Council, 'which tried to bring young people together to discuss a future outside of being British colonials'. She told me: 'we wanted to learn more about Trinidad's history and culture . . . the folklore, the music, the carnival'.

After high school in Venezuela, she moved to Trinidad where she met John in the course of work with the Trinidad and Tobago Youth Council. They were married in 1953. In that same year she went as one of the delegates to the International Youth Festival in Romania, also taking the opportunity to travel through Eastern Europe; that trip was to have serious repercussions for Irma. She came under increasing pressure for her political work, which was labelled as 'communist and subversive' by the conservative economic and social elite of colonial Trinidad. John La Rose went to Vienna in 1953 to attend an international conference of the World Federation of Trade Unions. She and John tried their political luck by contesting an election from a socialist standpoint. They lost, as a result of which they found themselves with debts and poor employment prospects in Trinidad, so they decided to go to Venezuela. There, Irma taught at night school and worked with Mobil Oil as a secretary. She and John moved to Britain in 1961.

Soon after the move to Britain, 'things did not quite work out, the marriage broke up', she told me. While raising Michael and Keith, her two children with John – who by then had started a second partnership with Sarah White – Irma went to work at the University of London in a clerical and later administrative capacity; that went on for twenty-five years. While working and raising her sons, she gained two degrees from the Open University, one an MA with a thesis that looked at the educational functions of the Caribbean-descent carnival in Britain. Education played an important role in her self-representation, this being exemplified by her telling me:

> It was not a question of, as most people say, what are you going to do with your degree after you retire. You don't have to do anything with a degree . . . You can't be the same person after you embark on a course of study, I think you will find that too. You will find the areas of study to which you are exposed make a big difference in your life as person. I found it so. And that was the purpose of my exercise. I don't care whether I could use my degree or not; it is not a question of having letters after your name, it is the experience of going through that whole area of study (interview with author).

At the time I interviewed her in September 1997 she was retired and living in Hornsey, North London; her two sons, Michael and Keith, share the home with her.

A main structuring characteristic of the circle is that John La Rose is in several senses the leading figure. He has been a key initiator in all of the circle's projects, and he was the founder of several. A large part of the circle's collective political strategy is constituted under his influence. During interviews, other people would frequently defer and refer to John's knowledge and acknowledged leadership. A common exchange went something like: 'Of course you spoke to John about that . . . John is the one who knows most about that', to which I often had to respond 'yes, but I'd like to get your view on it'. Six months into the first fieldwork period, in early 1997, when I began to have regular conversations and then interviews with other members of the circle, it had become generally known that I was doing an extended series of life-history interviews with John; people would sometimes skip over an issue, on the assumption that I would get the story from John. In that early stage I tried always to encourage people to talk about topics even when they knew I had discussed these with John.

John La Rose is the oldest and most experienced member of the circle. He is the managing director of New Beacon, chairman of the George Padmore Institute, was a co-director, then director of the International Book Fairs; he also served as chair of a number of projects, such as the New Cross Massacre Action Committee, which are no longer in operation. A man who looks considerably younger that his seventy-two years, he is a fluent and engaging public speaker; he has a good memory and the ability to improvise speech based on circumstances. What I observed of his manner in dealing with others was that of a polite man, who, while possessing the ability to talk at length on a wide range of topics, was also a keen and attentive listener.

As my two key interlocutors, John and Sarah are represented differently in this book; the difference is an indication of my relationship with each. With John I spent a lot of time talking, most often in his sitting room with books and papers close to hand. For most of our meetings in 1996/ 1997, which numbered about twenty-five, I had a tape recorder running. Sometimes we would talk for more than three hours. These formal sessions were outnumbered then and since by meetings when a structured conversation was not on the agenda. Sarah and I have had only one formal interview, and while over the two years from late 1999 to mid-2001 we have talked a great deal, it was often in the context when either she was working in the shop, or we were both doing something together, such as working on organizing the circle's archives. So John often appears in this text through distinct blocks of long quotation; Sarah also appears through quotation but more often as part of an account of how something was done.

There is a division of labour between John La Rose and Sarah White. She exercises executive power in the running of the shop and the trust. To use a corporate analogy, if John were the chair of the board, Sarah would be the managing director. In fact that is precisely the division of responsibility at New Beacon Books. This division does not appear to be strict: John shares some of the administrative work while Sarah deals with some public relations. John has had to reduce his workload since his 1983 heart attack, which has thrown greater responsibility onto Sarah.

Black Activism in Britain

It is part of my overall argument that despite a tendency among researchers to reduce any political activity involving at least some Black people to

'Black politics', the work of the New Beacon circle cannot be understood solely in terms of Black politics. Nonetheless, their work does stand in various relationships to a history of political activity involving Black people in post-war Britain. That activity ranged from initiatives that worked strictly within parameters laid down by the British state, through community-based activity in both secular and religious forms. In addition there was labour-oriented organization (Ramdin 1987), feminist initiatives (Brah 1996) and radical politics in both nationalist and leftist variants. Political identities represented through culture were significant for many young Black politically active people in the 1970s and 1980s, as well; chief among these was rastafari and reggae music. A brief sketch of this field is necessary here.[3]

One of the earliest attempts by Black immigrants to Britain to deal with 'race-relations' problems was that of Henry Sylvester Williams with his inaugural Pan-African Conference in 1900 (Mathurin 1976); Williams sought to appeal to the liberal instincts of the British, and he called for equal treatment of Blacks under the aegis of the British Empire. Harold Moody too, was a pioneer, with the League of Coloured Peoples (Fryer 1984). After the 1958 Notting Hill Riots, West Indians formed the West Indian Standing Conference, to agitate for a better deal for West Indian immigrants and to co-ordinate and advance the general interest of West Indians in British society. Out of these beginnings grew the Community Relations Councils, the Race Relations Board and Act, and the present Commission for Racial Equality. Many Blacks made efforts to join the existing political parties, trade unions and other institutions of civil society. Often these efforts at integration were rebuffed by an establishment sometimes disinclined to accept Black people as full citizens.

A more radical tendency than that of the Community Relations Councils is that represented by left-wing activists. Around the same time as the West Indian Standing Conference was established in 1958 to respond to growing tension over immigration, the *West Indian Gazette* was started by Trinidadian-born Claudia Jones. The *Gazette* was a newspaper targeted toward the Black community (then understood to include Caribbeans, Asians and Africans), with a distinct socialist and anti-imperialist perspective. Jones had migrated to Harlem, New York as a child, going on to become a labour organizer and leading figure in US Communist Party politics. She was a campaigning journalist, in some ways a pioneer in connecting race, class and gender struggles. She was deported to Britain in 1955, because of her radical politics and not being a US citizen; a similar fate had befallen C.L.R. James in 1953.[4] Jones continued her radical political work in Britain, starting and editing the

West Indian Gazette, launching a carnival which has grown into the current Notting Hill event. She was a leading figure in organizing people of Caribbean descent, until her death in 1964 (Johnson 1985; Sherwood 1999).

In the aftermath of the worldwide cultural upheavals of the late 1960s, and especially following the rise of the ideas and politics of Black Power, a younger generation of Blacks in Britain were radicalized, but not in the classical Left pattern of someone like Claudia Jones. These younger radicals developed a more confrontational style of politics and were wary of the apparatus of race relations, but were also wary of the established anti-racist politics of the labour and socialist left. Like so many social movements arising from the late 1960s, British Black Power activism constructed a new identity – Blackness – and imbued it with a radical and sometimes revolutionary tone; unlike their parents, many of these younger Blacks were not inclined to combat racism solely or even mainly through the established channels. The *Race Today* collective, of which Darcus Howe (in 2001 a *New Statesman* columnist and sometime television journalist) was a leading figure, well exemplifies this style of politics. Their journal of the same name was a campaigning publication, while the related *Race Today Review* published in-depth critical discussion of Black literature and arts. One of *Race Today*'s mentors was C.L.R. James (1901–1989), senior Marxist and innovator in thinking-class politics with a racialized awareness. (In fact, James spent his last years in a small flat in a building in Brixton that housed the *Race Today* collective.) Howe and others were involved in a number of high-profile campaigns and court battles in the 1970s that brought the politics of Black Power to the attention of the wider British public.[5] The symbols of rastafari and reggae music were key elements in these oppositional Black identities; but, as I noted in this book's introduction, expressive forms of youth culture have come to occupy too large a space in the sociological imagination of Black identity and activism.

The 1970s and 1980s also saw alliances forged between the established (largely White) left on the one hand, and the more radical tendencies of Black politics on the other. This is not the place to go into the complex issue of how race and class articulate in left-wing politics; all I will do is to note that there were both failed and successful attempts to make the articulation. Sometimes a shared commitment to anti-racist politics would see joint campaigns, but the alliances were never without tension, as for example when some White leftists constructed the struggle against racism on the foundations of anti-fascism (Gilroy 1991). A minority of Black radicals did see themselves as leftists first, but in the main, there was never any mass recruitment of Black people into the established left. What should not be overlooked in this discussion is that many thousands of anti-racist Whites, some left-wing, many not, gave support to struggles against racism across the institutions of civil society.

Rather than a reductive positioning in Black politics, the framework within which the ideas and work of the New Beacon circle should be placed initially is one where relationships between anti-racist and left/ radical politics in Britain were built, a space where the classic Old Left met the New Left and the different tendencies of Black radicalism which arose in the wake of Black Power. This was a space often fraught with conflict, especially between younger Black radicals and the established left, but it is not a simply dichotomized space where young Black radicals are pitted against White radicals.

Another zone of encounter was one where left-wing anti-racism's ideas and policies for social change resonated with the anti-colonial perspective which some Black migrants brought with them from the Caribbean (also Africa and Asia), as exemplified by one account of a Black Caribbean migrant who worked with the Communist Party of Great Britain. In a semi-autobiographical account of his work as an activist and educator, Trevor Carter (who came to Britain from Trinidad in 1956, and has been involved in anti-racist and left-wing politics since) criticizes the labour movement, Labour party and the left in Britain, for racism, but still argues for Blacks as integral to class politics (Carter 1986). Soon after his arrival in Britain, Carter joined the Communist party, because he saw it as an organization that could potentially integrate race, class, and anti-colonial struggles; but he writes that the Communist Party of Great Britain (CPGB) did not address itself to the specificities of racism in Britain: 'In spite of the handful of faithful survivors, it cannot be denied that the stubborn class-before-race position of the [Communist] party during the fifties and sixties cost the party dearly in terms of its members' (p. 62). Carter sees this as a squandered opportunity by the Communists in Britain to make links with the Black working class.

The context for the myriad anti-racist projects and campaigns organized in post-war Britain, sometimes in conjunction with and other times in opposition to the established Left, is delineated by the structural problems of race and class discrimination which confronted non-White immigrants and their offspring. For many Blacks in Britain, these matters came to a head with intensive policing that targeted young Black males from the late 1960s. Black youth in Britain were thrust into public attention as a problematic social category by the mainstream media during the moral panic over 'mugging' in the early 1970s, but so-called 'racial' tensions in Britain have a considerably longer history.

By the early 1970s many Black migrants to Britain and their offspring had become disillusioned with their adopted society. Many British young people of Caribbean, African and Asian descent eschewed the assimilationist attempts of their parents and turned to increasingly militant expressions of the alienation they felt in the society, sometimes leading to public clashes between themselves and the police. These confrontations were differentially interpreted: for Black youth the clashes were the result of the draconian measures adopted by the police in the city, best exemplified by the notorious 'SUS' police procedure, under which a person could be stopped, searched and detained by the police on suspicion of being about to commit an offence. Black youth were disproportionately affected by 'SUS'. From the point of view of the police, Black youth were a minority with a high propensity to commit crime and as such were to be kept under close surveillance (Hall 1978). 'Riots' (for the police and British state) or 'rebellions' (for young militants), erupted during the 1976 Notting Hill carnival; among South Asian youth in Southall in 1979, and most famously, in 1981 in a number of English cities: London, Manchester, Liverpool, Leeds.[6]

While some Black youth did turn to crime, Blacks as a whole, but especially the 'proletarian respectable' elements among them, strongly objected to the criminalization of all Blacks by the British police. There was inter-generation conflict between Black British youth and their parents over the appropriate response to police repression. Although many of the older generation of Black settlers had fought both police and racists on the streets, for example in Notting Hill in 1958, most parents of Black youth felt that their children were best advised to keep a low profile and avoid confrontation with the police; at the same time, these parents resented the rough handling of their children by the police. (While racism remains an urgent problem in British society, the broader situation has changed, particularly in terms of greater awareness and perhaps sensitivity to institutionalized racism on the part of the broad British public).

The initial impetus behind the New Beacon circle was not organizing against police repression, but was instead proactive, aiming to intervene into the spheres of education and literary/artistic culture in Britain. My account of their projects will begin with the post-war migration of intellectuals and artists from the West Indies to Britain.

The Caribbean Artists Movement

I think artists together means that they develop a vulnerable interaction on the basis of where they wish to go with their ideas. And that they expose themselves to one another much more intimately than other groups of people expose themselves to one another, by virtue of the kind of truth and honesty they are seeking to encounter, to search for.

John La Rose[7]

I never realised I was lonely. I never thought I was in exile . . .
It was Eddie that made me realise this, and John. I was just a guy,
and in love with reading . . . just loved to have a book open.

Andrew Salkey[8]

A significant group of writers and artists moved from the Caribbean to England in the post-war period (Walmsley 1992). I consider them a cohort because they came from societies quite similar in the sense of being small colonies of Britain situated in the Caribbean; they shared a similar educational and cultural background. They were all part of the post-war migratory wave from the Caribbean; however, by virtue of their advanced education and career goals they were not typical of that largely proletarian resettlement in Britain. The most available outlet for their work was in Britain. The writers had in common the BBC *Caribbean Voices* pro-gramme, through which they came to know one another's work (Lamming 1992 [1960]).

The cohort made the move to England so that they could pursue intellectual careers as writers, artists, academics, painters and poets. The necessary infrastructure of intellectual work was not present to a sufficient degree in the colonial West Indies: libraries, galleries, publishing houses and studios. It was necessary to migrate in order to have the possibility of making a living by their pens and brushes.

Many, but by no means all of the cohort, were in favour of some form of self-government for the West Indian territories. Walmsley (1992) notes that most of the cohort were influenced by the pioneering work of C.L.R. James on West Indian self-government (James 1933). They were mostly people of colour, educated and working in English, but concerned to express, through the established media, a reality of the region which was richer than that of colonialist discourse. A major breakthrough achieved by a number of the writers was in giving voice to the West Indian masses, hitherto overlooked as literary subjects. While they were often pushed to migrate, these writers and artists were not leaving a cultural wasteland: from at least the nineteenth century there are records of continuous activity in the areas of literature and the arts in Jamaica, Barbados and Trinidad, but never sufficient to sustain most persons wanting careers in these areas.

An anti-colonial and cultural nationalist outlook was typical of these artists and intellectuals. Bolland (1992) has argued that most Anglo-Caribbean intellectuals are cultural nationalist in orientation, and that 'creolization' – a notion of a syncretic process of cultural and social development – is their operating ideology. Against this view, however, Harney (1996) cautions that for many Anglo-Caribbean intellectuals, migrant or not, nationalism – cultural or political – is an ambivalent text and state; his work on Trinidadian writers sees them as imagining nationalism and identity in varied and often contradictory ways. He contrasts the pessimism of V.S. Naipaul toward the post-colonial Caribbean, with C.L.R. James's enthusiastic imagination of a new and vibrant nation. Both of these writers migrated to Britain to develop their writing careers.

The cohort strove to express their visions of post-colonial Caribbean society through a European language and European creative forms. In this they faced the dilemma of employing dominant cultural forms to express a counter-hegemonic vision. It was no easy task, as is testified by the intense discussion and debates which form part of the archive of proceedings of the Caribbean Artists Movement (CAM), a project which I have chosen as the opening point for my narrative on the New Beacon circle.

By the early 1960s writers, artists and students from the Caribbean were well established in Britain, particularly London. After the initial impact of the novels of George Lamming, Roger Mais, Samuel Selvon and Vidia Naipaul in the 1950s, there was something of a lull. John La Rose came to Britain in 1961 to study law, but soon got involved in activism; he met Edward Brathwaite and Andrew Salkey, the first a poet and research student in West Indian history and the second a poet, novelist and BBC journalist, from Barbados and Jamaica respectively. They all felt that something needed to be done to place Caribbean arts and letters into the British cultural spotlight. Brathwaite recalled:

> We also felt that the kinds of things that were being said about West Indian immigrants on the BBC and on TV were coming from people who were inarticulate immigrants, when in fact there was C.L.R. James, George Lamming, and so on, who we felt were much more representative of what we were about. And also since at Cambridge, I had been in touch with people like Ted Hughes, Edward Lucie Smith. My argument was: Why is it that our literature is not being treated as literature, instead of being marginalised into West Indian or black literature?[9]

Brathwaite, Salkey and La Rose decided to start a forum for the meeting of Caribbean-descent writers, artists and students in Britain. Out of this the Caribbean Artists Movement (CAM) was born. Its heyday was 1966 to 1972. CAM was a forum for discussion, work was presented and discussed, regular meetings were held, a number of conferences were organized. The journal *Savacou*, brainchild of Brathwaite, emerged out of CAM as an interdisciplinary review, publishing fiction, poetry, reviews, journalistic and scholarly pieces.

The motivation behind starting CAM is quite clear in the accounts of the early CAM meetings (Walmsley 1992; CAM archive held at the GPI). That motivation bears further examination because in its political standpoint and its reading of the relations between mainstream and minority cultures, it took a view that is quite exotic in our contemporary cultural politics, where identity conceived as immutable difference is given greater prominence than identity conceived as hybridity and inclusion in a cosmopolitan shared culture. It was this second sense of identity which was elaborated in CAM's overall vision. In addition to its central aim of bringing Caribbean artists and writers together, CAM wished to have Caribbean arts recognized by the mainstream public in Britain, and importantly, as arts without the qualifiers of 'black' or 'West Indian'. The CAM conception of culture was of multi-culture, of interpenetrating influences and ideas; the members acknowledged, to varying degrees, the European influence on Caribbean cultural formations, and appeared to want to constitute a space where Caribbean culture in turn could enrich modern European literary and artistic culture. CAM wished to make an entry into the existing metropolitan system of artistic production, consumption and criticism; this aim led them toward a direct engagement with the politics of literary and artistic canon formation.

What is canon formation? I use the term here to indicate the constitution, always contested, of a body of works (i.e. the canon) which form the core of a 'proper' education (Bloom 1995). It is actually located in concrete social relations and histories, but is most often discussed in terms of transcendental value (Guillory 1993). In contemporary battles over the composition of the literary canon, exemplified by the US case, the argument is made by radical critics that the literature of the canon represents and or reflects the values of those dominant in US society, that is to say, White middle-class heterosexual men. It is further argued by radical critics of the canon that literature by people of colour, women, the working class has been systematically excluded from the canon because such literature represents an alternative set of values, and not just alternative, but threatening to the dominant position of privileged

White males. (This is a necessary simplification of a complex set of arguments.) This form of multiculturalist cultural politics holds that aesthetic value is indeterminate outside of particular communities of interest, and indeed, its proponents would argue that discourses of universal value, indeed of aesthetics itself, are no more than the values of privileged groups disingenuously articulated as universal. The strategy which follows from this reading is that excluded literatures, and the communities to which they are seen to be organically connected, must construct alternative communities of value, with alternative readerships, publishing and critical apparatus. From the 1960s onward, this strategy spawned whole new fields in the academy and in intellectual culture, in Women's Studies, Black Studies, Gay and Lesbian Studies and more. The 1960s also saw the establishment of 'Commonwealth Literature' as a discipline which was concerned with the vast and growing body of writing in English produced outside the USA, Britain and the largely White dominions of Canada, Australia and New Zealand.[10] Struggle for and colonization of new academic and artistic space for formerly excluded cultural products and identities is now the dominant mode of bottom-up and anti-establishment cultural politics, at least in the Atlantic or Western part of the world system. At its core is an assumption of the relativistic, non-hierarchical value of cultural form, production and consumption.

In contrast to this relativist strategy, CAM pursued a policy of inclusion, aiming to achieve the infiltration of works of English Caribbean literature into the canon of twentieth-century literature in English (then called English Literature). Their strategy was to argue that such works had sufficient of that presumed transcendental value which is mandatory for canonical inclusion. They contended that these works spoke to a 'general human condition', albeit from a place – the English-speaking Caribbean – which had hitherto been overlooked in mainstream criticism. In arguing that English Caribbean literature had a value to persons outside its region of origin/inspiration, CAM was simultaneously arguing for value which transcended specific times and places. CAM also built up links with the British literary establishment, with publishers and critics. In so doing they were entering the game of canon formation as savvy 'outsiders' who believed that they were as significant for the field as any of the 'insiders'. Even further, their outlook was characterized by a rejection of the very distinction between insiders and outsiders.

In order to understand the context of cultural politics in which the formation of CAM took place, we need to imagine a different scenario from that of the canon wars and multiculturalist politics and policy of the past two or three decades. Third World and indeed any other forms of nationalism are generally viewed with suspicion by progressive intellectuals. Revolutionaries are out of favour. To understand an initiative such as CAM on its own terms, we must imaginatively suspend our relationship to the global world system as currently constituted under market principles, and think back to a time – the 1960s – when capitalist hegemony was under threat from Third World, Second World and leftist First World political challenges (Harman 1988). In this scenario revolutionary ideas were more widely held and inspired many more people than at present. In the 1960s formal independence from colonial domination was a dream that was in the process of being realized in the English-speaking Caribbean, as it had been in much of Africa and Asia. The social movements for independence in Jamaica, Trinidad and Tobago, and Guyana were revitalized in the aftermath of the Second World War (Hart 1998); they were inspired by the moves to decolonization in Africa and Asia which had built up enormous momentum by the early 1960s. There was tremendous hope for the future of newly independent nations. This spirit of new-found independence suffused the 1967/1968 Havana Cultural Congress (Salkey 1971). For many on the Left in the industrialized countries, Castro's Cuba was a pointer to a future free from capitalist exploitation and colonial rule over the Third World. Ernesto 'Che' Guevara was an icon for the youth of the counterculture in Western Europe and the USA. The New Left looked increasingly to the Third World for the impetus of revolution, largely but not completely abandoning faith in the revolutionary potential of the working class at home. The figure of the oppressed in the Third World, well exemplified in Frantz Fanon's widely read works (Fanon 1967b; Fanon 1967a), was an important element in the imagining of radical political projects and subjects by the New Left, especially in Western Europe. And following the examples set by Fanon and 'Che' Guevera, New Left activists often sought to make concrete links with social movements in the Third World (Ali 1987). Cultural exchanges were seen as vital to supporting these links, which from the perspective of the New Left was entirely in keeping with the greater emphasis given to culture in New Left theory and practice (Dworkin 1997). It is in this context that the Havana Cultural Congress must be understood. It took place just before the 1968 peak of the 1960s worldwide upheavals.

As narrated by Andrew Salkey in *Havana Journal* (Salkey 1971) – an account of his attendance at the conference – a number of Anglo-Caribbean intellectuals resident in Britain were present, among them C.L.R. James and John La Rose. CAM was, in a sense, well represented in Havana: La Rose and Salkey were two founding members of the

Caribbean Artists Movement, and C.L.R. James was a featured speaker at a number of CAM events. The Havana conference was an event that emerged out of a general concern with the role of culture in national development, seen mainly from the perspective of emergent Third World nations and progressives in the developed societies. A similar constellation of concerns was articulated and acted on in London in 1966, by La Rose, Salkey and others in the CAM's formative period. CAM was a creature of the cultural and political ferment of the 1960s.

The idea of forming CAM was born in a meeting at the London flat of Edward Brathwaite and his partner Doris, in December 1966. Subsequently, the first meeting of CAM was hosted by Orlando Patterson, Jamaican-born sociologist, novelist and member of the editorial board of *New Left Review*.[11] A number of Caribbean-descent intellectuals were present, as were British intellectuals interested in Caribbean culture. The topic of discussion was 'dialogue on the West Indian aesthetic'. There was considerable variety in terms of ideology and standpoint from the very inception. Patterson rejected the notion of the African roots of Caribbean culture, and indeed, was sceptical of any notion of cultural tradition in the Caribbean. In contrast, Brathwaite, historian and poet, was concerned to develop a uniquely Caribbean aesthetic which he saw as primarily derived from Black Diaspora cultural forms such as jazz and calypso (Torres-Saillant 1997: chapter 3). Kenneth Ramchand, a Trinidadian graduate student working on the history of West Indian fiction, criticized the early stated aims of CAM for being too elitist, and not connected to the lives of most Caribbean people, whether in the Caribbean or living as migrants in Britain. Nonetheless, Ramchand was involved in several subsequent CAM projects. The discussions held under the umbrella of CAM were aimed at formulating a Caribbean aesthetic. In that sense CAM can be seen as a cultural nationalist project.

On 3 March 1967, Edward Brathwaite gave a public reading of his epic-length poem, *Rights of Passage*, at the Jeanetta Cochrane Theatre (now the Cochrane Theatre) in the Holborn area of London. The reading had been organized by John La Rose and Sarah White and harmonized with the prospective public launch of CAM. The event was a success and inspired the artists and intellectuals who were at the same time forming CAM; most of them attended the event and were 'excited by the poetic innovation', according to La Rose and White (personal communication with author). It also had the effect of bringing New Beacon's first two publications – a book of poems by John La Rose, *Foundations*; and Adolph Edwards's *Marcus Garvey 1887–1940*, to a receptive public. It was New Beacon's first major public exposure. Out of the early public

CAM forums which immediately followed Brathwaite's reading and performance of *Rights*, New Beacon's bookselling service was to grow, as a response to the growing demand for Black, Caribbean and other Third World literature.

CAM was not only concerned to bring about change in the field of arts and letters in Britain. Indeed, its founders and many of the subsequent participants in its activities were involved with the issues of West Indian independence. With the gaining of independent status by increasing numbers of Anglo-Caribbean territories from the early 1960s onward (Jamaica and Trinidad and Tobago became independent nation states in 1962), and with the growing worldwide momentum of decolonization, the locus of artistic efforts shifted from the metropolises to the former colonies. This shift affected CAM. A number of key Caribbean writers had left Britain by 1972. Brathwaite returned to the Caribbean for good at the end of his research; Selvon would soon leave for Canada. CAM propagated a branch at the newly established Centre for Creative Arts at the Jamaica campus of The University of the West Indies. In 1972 it was not so much that CAM came to an end as that it evolved and spread out over a wider geographic area to match the wider possibilities and spaces made available to Caribbean writers and artists by decolonization. Some left Britain in order to engage more directly with the nation-building efforts in the fledgling Commonwealth Caribbean nation states.

CAM inspired a number of cultural activist projects in Britain. *Creation for Liberation* was formed in 1978 by persons active in the *Race Today* collective; it was a grouping of creative people with activist aims, in a direct descent from CAM. Their aim was to involve creative artists in bringing about political and social change in the conditions of Black and working-class people; their activities centred around encouraging the work of minority creative artists and writers and organizing outreach in the form of fund-raising concerts and exhibitions.[12] The South East London Parents Organisation (SELPO) was formed out of CAM influence; the same was the case for the Nigerian Society of African Artists. Christopher Laird, a Trinidadian of White ethnicity, was a student in London in the early CAM years.[13] He recalled CAM being one inspiration for the Banyan company – an independent television production house based in Trinidad – which has produced a number of well-received programmes, the most famous of which is *Gayelle*, which ran on Trinidadian television in the 1980s to local and international critical acclaim.[14] *Gayelle* was in the CAM tradition of seeking to broaden ideas about cultural value, in this instance in a context where most Trinidadians held local television programming to be of lower value than (mostly North American) imports.

Banyan continues to resist the domination of North American televison programming in Trinidad, which was heightened by the introduction in the early 1990s of cable television.

Unsurprisingly, not all those active in the same cultural and political space as CAM take a positive view of its aims or influence. Amon Saba Saakana (Trinidadian born, formerly Sebastian Clarke, currently active as a Black publisher in London), who was active in radical Black politics in the 1960s, felt that the CAM founders were mainly interested in integrating themselves into the British establishment and were speaking to a middle-class audience; he felt his own efforts to publish Black literature had no support from CAM's founders.[15] He expressed the view that there were alternatives to the mainstream publishing outlets which were not exploited by the CAM generation. He also made clear that his influences were primarily Afro-American; from 1970 to 1974 he lived in the USA, 'exclusively among the Afro-American community' and had very little contact with the 'Afro-Caribbean community' in America. This period he remembers as having had a pivotal influence on his own political formation and his perspective on Black cultural politics. Saakana speaks, in the interview, from an Afrocentric/Black nationalist perspective; this may explain his distanced stance vis-à-vis the CAM founding members, who were at ease with the overwhelmingly White and middle-class British cultural establishment of journals, publishers, critics and such. Marc Matthews, Guyanese-born and active in the radical Black politics of the late 1960s in London, recalled of the CAM milieu:

> I suppose I was younger in generation to John [i.e. John La Rose] . . . they [CAM] were very active, but it seemed to us were overly intellectual about things and we were of that period . . . They did their thing, they had their books and they organized their things, but we were looking for action, we wanted to burn, we were caught in that, we were of that generation, we wanted to burn . . . (Interview with author, February 1997)

The views expressed by Saakana and Matthews are indicative of a generational and ideational difference highlighted by the 1960s rise of Black Power in the USA, which had the effect in the British context of dividing a younger generation of militant activists, for whom Black identity was central to their politics, from an older generation exemplified by the CAM founders, for whom Black politics was an important part but not the most important part of their overall vision for social transformation. Those closely involved in CAM, and especially the New Beacon circle, while they kept abreast of and supported the Black Power struggles taking place in the USA, maintained an autonomous outlook through which they conceived their work in Britain and the Caribbean as connected to but by no means derived from the US situation. They did not look for intellectual or political leadership or inspiration to the US Black Power struggles, or to national independence movements. Autonomy and self-generation of ideas and analysis were key elements of their praxis.

Notwithstanding the differing emphasis in politics outlined above, it would be a mistake to overstress this generational difference in outlook: first, a number of younger artists and writers were involved in CAM, and secondly, the New Beacon circle would become involved in more direct campaigning activity in the 1970s, which were centrally about Black politics in Britain. Second, and more importantly, as we will see in subsequent chapters, the generation of activists following John La Rose's cohort were not all Black nationalists. Indeed, in the later discussion of the Black Parents Movement and Black Youth Movement, we will see younger activists trying to augment with a class and internationalist perspective a Black politics that was by the early 1970s showing self-referential and nationalist tendencies. This widening out of the terms of Black politics is typical of the New Beacon circle.

It is precisely the attempts to widen the terms of debate over cultural value in Britain, by directly engaging with the settled creative and critical establishment, which make CAM in many ways special, when viewed through the lens of contemporary Black cultural politics in both the USA and Britain, where creating alternative space is accorded at least as much importance as storming the ramparts of the majority cultural establishment. Though the movement lasted seven years strictly speaking, its impact has been long-lasting. CAM widened awareness and reception of Caribbean arts and letters in Britain and the Caribbean; it fostered important exchanges and nurtured early careers. It opened up dialogue among Caribbean artists and writers; and between them and the British literary, artistic and critical establishment. The meetings, conferences and the journal *Savacou* constituted and sustained a network which linked people in Britain, the Caribbean and further afield. CAM was influential in shaping the then emergent fields of West Indian literature and literary criticism. Its three founders, John La Rose, Andrew Salkey and Kamau Brathwaite, each made major contributions to the expansion of Caribbean literature in English: La Rose as poet, publisher and bookseller; Salkey as a critic, novelist and anthologist; Brathwaite as historian and innovator in creative writing.[16] While the inputs of these three were invaluable, CAM's impact extends beyond that of the work of its founding trio. It was in the creation of space where creative people could meet and exchange ideas, engage in debate; it was in the creation of a public sphere for Caribbean arts and letters in Britain that CAM had its greatest influence.

New Beacon Publishing House, Book Service and Bookshop: A Short History

I had been thinking about getting into publishing for quite some time, even before coming to England [in 1961]. But there was the problem of money . . . it was costly to get started . . . Sarah and I talked a lot about starting a publishing house after we met, but nothing happened right away. Then around the time of getting CAM going, I was working part-time on a construction site as a brickie's labourer . . . I had to stop when I got a back injury, but the compensation provided the money we needed to start up in publishing (John La Rose, interview with author).

La Rose and White started the publishing arm of New Beacon from their flat in Hornsey, North London in 1966. Demand for books that came out of the first meetings of the Caribbean Artists Movement (CAM) would galvanize La Rose and White to expand from publishing into bookselling. The venture into book publishing and bookselling would see La Rose directly engaged with the radical intellectual tradition of his native Trinidad. I will return to important persons and texts from that milieu throughout this book, but a brief outline is in order at this point. New Beacon Books is descended from a venerable tradition of radicalism, one which has socialist, anti-colonial and internationalist lines. That many people know New Beacon only or mainly as a 'Black Bookshop' is indicative of the reductionist way in which everyday as well as socio-logical understanding of radical political activity involving any significant number of Black people is often transformed into 'Black politics' and the radical element is jettisoned. To understand the space from which New Beacon emerged we must turn to the intellectual history of colonial Trinidad, from which John La Rose as founder of New Beacon Books drew important symbolic resources for his work in Britain.

A high point in the development of the native intellectual tradition in Trinidad (Cudjoe 1997) was the 1920s, when a group of local intellectuals started two pioneering literary and cultural journals: *Trinidad*, and *The Beacon* (Sander 1988). These intellectuals, of which C.L.R. James was one, were not merely 'non-whites seeking their way in a white literary world' as suggested by Buhle (Buhle 1989: 26), but were descended from a history of struggle against colonial domination and hegemony that goes back to the beginning of the nineteenth century. They attacked the Eurocentricism, arrogance and anti-intellectualism of the Trinidadian middle and upper classes from a liberal humanist standpoint. These 1920s Trinidadian intellectuals often expressed contradictory positions, but were nonetheless consistent in their drive to counter White supremacist and colonialist thought and practice in the Caribbean, as elsewhere in the Black Atlantic (Alleyne 1998a; Bogues 1997). By the 1920s, then, when *Trinidad* and *Beacon* were formed, the local intellectual space was comparatively well-developed, with a network of literary and debating societies, and several short-lived attempts to produce literary journals. Further development was greatly hampered by limited access to secondary schooling and no local university or established publishing house.

The choice of name for La Rose's and White's publishing house and later book shop – New Beacon – was meant to evoke the *Beacon* journal from Trinidad in the late 1920s. New Beacon's first publications were: *Foundations*, a volume of poetry by La Rose himself; *Marcus Garvey – 1887–1940*, by Adolph Edwards; *Tradition The Writer and Society*, by Wilson Harris; and *Caribbean Writers – Critical Essays*, by Ivan Van Sertima. These were all aimed at bringing Caribbean history and letters to a reading public in Britain. In 1969 New Beacon republished two books, both written by a nineteenth-century Trinidadian autodidact, John Jacob Thomas: *Froudacity* (Thomas 1969 [1889]) and *Theory and Practice of Creole Grammar* (Thomas 1969 [1869]). Thomas, a Black rural school-teacher, wrote his pioneering Creole grammar in 1869; in it he sought to formalize the structure of the (Afro-)French *patois* spoken then by most people in Trinidad. *Froudacity* was a response to eminent Oxford historian James Anthony Froude, who, after a visit to the West Indies in 1887, wrote *The English in The West Indies* (Froude 1888), a text highly critical of the capacities of the formerly enslaved to govern themselves. Froude wrote as a defender of the British Empire and its ideology of White supremacy. Thomas countered by demonstrating the great advances made by Blacks in the decades following emancipation in 1838, and he docu-mented the many obstacles set up by the British colonists in order to prevent Blacks acquiring land and education.

Republishing Thomas's work in 1969 was a strategic move by New Beacon in that it was making available to a new readership the early anti-colonialist, and what we would now refer to as anti-racist, work of a Black intellectual who wrote in the nineteenth century. The value of Thomas's work lay not only in his critical scholarship and the quality of his writing, but also in establishing that there was a tradition of scholarly writing by Black people in the colonies. In part because of its historical *gravitas*,

Thomas's work potentially provided literary ammunition for those engaged in struggle against a dominant view (in the late 1960s) that Black children in Britain were underperforming because they were intellectually inferior to their White counterparts. Racist folk explanations of this alleged inferiority ranged from the crudely biologistic to ostensibly more sophisticated notions of the Caribbean or Africa as spaces where literary culture was historically thin on the ground. Thomas's work, that of an early Black anti-racist writer, fitted well in a context where many Black people in Britain were seeking a literature in which they could recognize a positive construction of a Black political subject.

Another important early publication was *Marcus Garvey 1887–1940* (1967) by Adolph Edwards; that small book came out of a paper Edwards had presented to a discussion group hosted by C.L.R. James. It was the first publication on Garvey in the post-war period and was widely read and discussed among Black and anti-racist groups and in student reading groups in high school and at higher levels. It was reprinted three times and a French edition came out in 1983. Garvey was arguably the major political figure in the Pan-African movement of the early twentieth century, and an essay on his life and times met with a willing readership in the climate of a resurgence of Black politics in the late 1960s and early 1970s in Britain.

New Beacon's early publications also included works by Wilson Harris, *Tradition the Writer and Society: Critical Essays* (New Beacon, 1967) and Ivan Van Sertima, *Caribbean Writers: Critical Essays* (New Beacon, 1968). Both of these can be set in the vein of CAM's strategy of seeking to create space for the critical reception of Caribbean literature in the wider world of letters, while at the same time introducing this literature to a wider audience than that of critics and students of English. Both volumes were collections of critical essays, intended to build up the necessary base of analysis on which a 'new' literature must depend in order to break into the canon. Also at this time Kenneth Ramchand was working on a doctoral dissertation at the University of Edinburgh that would eventually be published as the first major study of West Indian literature (Ramchand 1983); Ramchand participated in early CAM meetings, and would later be a pioneer in introducing West Indian literature as a distinct field of study at the University of the West Indies.[17]

John La Rose stated in a 1977 published interview that he recognized that the 'breaking of continuity' caused by colonialism, which he conceived as impacting negatively on the self-understanding of Blacks in Britain, could not be easily counteracted:

It can't be done totally because we are not in control of the schools, we don't have control of media, we are not in control of everything that impinges on a person's life in the society. However, you can break some elements of that discontinuity and give people some sense of what is important, so that they get some sense of what they need to know to transform their lives. This was my conception of publishing (Beese 1977).

The formation and growth of New Beacon Books has in sum two aspects: first there is the primary influence of the formation of the Caribbean Artists Movement and consequent demand for 'alternative literature'; then there is La Rose's and White's channelling of their political vision into the sphere of literary culture as independent book-sellers and publishers. These two aspects could be seen roughly as objective and subjective, respectively, or structural and individual. The overall context for the formation of New Beacon Books is that of a heightened anti-racist and anti-colonial politics, the rise of the new left, anti-war and women's liberation movements, that set the political tone of the late 1960s. Specifically, the development of Black-consciousness movements meant that there was growing demand for specialist book-sellers and publishers dealing with radical Black materials.

In 1969, La Rose and White moved from their flat in Hornsey to no. 2 Albert Road, off Stroud Green Road. They had bought a house and the bookshop and publishing operation moved with them. The needs of the bookshop were a major consideration in their decision to acquire a (large) house:

> We had some difficulty explaining why as two people we needed such a large house. Of course we couldn't tell them that we wanted enough space to do bookselling and to hold meetings . . . a large house would be flexible enough to allow us to do various sorts of things (Sarah White, conversation with author).[18]

In 1973, New Beacon moved to number 76 Stroud Green Road, about five minutes' walk from the house at 2 Albert Road; the shop has occupied the ground floor of that building from then to the time of writing in June 2001. John La Rose told me how he and Sarah White managed to obtain the building on Stroud Green Road where the shop is located:

> It was that time in the early seventies when there were a lot of Asian people coming over . . . especially from East Africa . . . they had money and were looking to invest in property on high streets so that they could start businesses. We had to move quickly when we found out that the

building at number seventy-six [Stroud Green Road] was up for sale. There were several Asians interested and they were willing to pay in cash . . . So we had to come up with cash somehow. It was Sarah's parents who helped us. They provided the funds for us to pay for the building straightaway. Otherwise we would not have got it (reconstruction from author's notes).

In 1991 Sarah White donated the building at 76 Stroud Green Road to the George Padmore Institute (discussed in Chapter Three), which in turn leases space in it to New Beacon bookshop.

New Beacon books is a family firm. One of the reasons New Beacon has survived through a period in the 1980s and 1990s which saw increasing consolidation in the bookselling business in Britain, with large chains coming to dominate the market, is that it is able to draw upon a network of family and friends to provide skills and labour at times of peak needs. As we saw earlier, Sarah White manages the shop with the assistance of Janice Durham. Michael La Rose (who is John La Rose's son by his first partner, Irma) himself worked at the shop for several years; Michael and Janice formerly lived together and have two children. Sarah and John have one son, Wole, who works part-time at the shop.

With just one or at best two persons attending to customers, New Beacon bookshop has an intimate atmosphere. There is an air of informality that differs from the engineered relaxation of the large chain bookstores with their me-too coffee bars. Holding books for customers has a special meaning at New Beacon; not just holding a book for a few days for a customer – which most bookshops will do – but actually allowing a customer to make a small down-payment and then pay off the remaining balance in small instalments, until the full price is paid and the book turned over to that customer. This is not a conventional credit system, Sarah explained to me. New Beacon has got the normal system of credit accounts for many of its customers, allowing them to pay by invoice. The 'lay away' plan means that people with very little money can still afford to buy books, even if they cannot take them away directly.

For Sarah White and Janice Durham the bookshop is their place of work. They run the entire operation – bookshop and international book service – between the two of them. Both have different days-off each week, and on some days they are both at work in the shop. Here they are talking about their work:

Sarah White: I wouldn't be interested in making more money doing something else . . . we didn't get into the book business to make money, even though the shop is now in a position to pay a modest salary . . . John and I had to subsidize the operation in the earliest days . . . New Beacon makes a special kind of cultural intervention . . . we introduced literature in the 1960s that no one else was supplying in Britain – Caribbean literature, other black literature . . . I like to think that we can supply material that a person could not get at one of the large chains.

Janice Durham: Sometimes when teenagers come in to look for sort of . . . romance literature or best-sellers, I try to point out to them some of the Caribbean or African novels . . . they think that these novels are only for reading in school . . . we have a few of the X-Press series[19] because many young black people are interested in reading them, and it's good that young people read something at least, but we always encourage people to read a wider range . . .[20]

In 1996/1997, the bookshop was a stopping-off point on my way to Wednesday afternoon appointments for biographical interviews with John La Rose at his home; it was where I met several people I would later interview; from time to time I made appointments to meet people there. In 1999 I moved from Cambridge to live in the Finsbury Park area, which greatly facilitated my ability to attend meetings and maintain close contact with the circle's activities. For members of the circle the bookshop is a meeting place in addition to a source of information. I was introduced to a number of John's and Sarah's associates in the shop itself. Meetings were sometimes planned, and several actually took place there, during business hours. The bookshop does not only sell books. It is also a venue for readings and book launchings. It is a clearing house for people interested in radical literature of all types, in education, in activism of various kinds; but it is also a place for people who just want to buy a book.

New Beacon's stock in mid-2001 stood between 17,000 and 18,000 items, grouped under the following categories: radical politics; Caribbean non-fiction (history, politics and social sciences); African-American non-fiction; African non-fiction; (mostly Black) British non-fiction; Caribbean, African, African-American, Asian, Black British fiction and poetry; Cultural Studies and Women's Studies; with smaller sections on Latin America and Asia, art, literary criticism; sport; music; theatre; media; language; and education. There is a large selection of children's literature from around the world, some in languages other than English, and an education section. According to Sarah White: 'We do not rely on walk-in business . . . that varies. Our main business is in supplying schools, libraries and college and university students. We also sell internationally as well.' The shops's operators review the categories in light of changes in publishing and book-buying tastes: for example, in early 2000, Sarah

White was considering adding a separate section on philosophy, to hold the growing numbers of titles of non-traditional, non-Western philosophy, targeted toward a Black readership. Mail order is a large part of New Beacon's bookselling business, with customers on all continents. New Beacon produces a ten-page monthly catalogue which is sent out overseas as well as to interested parties in Britain.

While smaller in scope than previous years, New Beacon's publishing arm remains active. The most productive year was 1988, when eight titles were brought out. At June 2001, New Beacon had published sixty-five titles in total (see Appendix I). Sarah White explains that some early print runs of 3000 copies were overly optimistic, leaving them with a large unsold inventory; however, this was more than balanced by several very strong sellers which went into multiple printings. Among New Beacon's publications, those works most successful in terms of sales are:

With around 5000 copies sold:

Being Black: selections from Soledad Brother and Soul on Ice, edited by Roxy Harris (1981).

With more than 10000 copies sold:

Jane And Louisa Will Soon Come Home by Erna Brodber (1980, reprinted 1988, 1993, 1998);
Marcus Garvey 1887–1940 by Adolph Edwards (1967, reprinted 1967, 1969, 1972, 1987; French edition 1983);
For The Liberation of Nigeria by Yusufu Bala Usman (1979, reprinted 1980).

Summary

The aims of the Caribbean Artists Movement, and the range of New Beacon's publishing and bookselling activities, while significantly concerned with what would be understood in contemporary discourses of culture as 'Black literature', are more properly analysed in terms of their transformative, universalist and internationalist scope. The crossing of genre is not to be overlooked either. New Beacon have published fiction by established and new Caribbean authors, republished a number of classic fictional works from that region; they have also published works of contemporary Black British fiction, criticism, history, politics. The geographical scope takes in the Caribbean, Africa, and Britain. New Beacon

Books in both its bookselling and publishing arms is directly concerned with promoting and supplying Black and Third world literature, much of which was until quite recently difficult to obtain from mainstream British booksellers. Even with the recent allocation of shelf space to Black literature in the large British chains and the growing virtual shelf space for this literature on online booksellers such as Amazon, New Beacon's specialist knowledge remains in demand. That knowledge is derived from the long personal experience of the firm's principals and associates, and also from the outreach and networks built up from the period of CAM and the International book fairs (discussed in the following chapter). New Beacon's founders' development over decades of expert knowledge of their field, knowledge of lesser-known authors, of small publishers on other continents, and extensive personal contacts, cannot be compensated for by simply substituting the financial and technological clout of the big booksellers. New Beacon's greatest asset in the contemporary knowledge-based economy remains its expertise in assessing, sourcing and supplying Black and Third World literature.

The word – written and spoken – is at the heart of the cultural politics of the New Beacon circle. A desire to make an intervention in the public sphere of literary and artistic culture was a pivotal motivation behind both the founding of the Caribbean Artists Movement and La Rose's and White's initial foray into publishing. The mobilization of CAM opened a space for the emergence of New Beacon as booksellers. From the late 1960s John La Rose devoted himself full-time to cultural activist work, while his partner Sarah White pursued dual careers as a science journalist and bookseller/publisher. The political and cultural upheavals of the 1960s formed the terrain on which the circle was constituted, and on which other campaigns and projects were built, and it is to these we turn next.

Notes

1. I quote statements from conversations and interviews I had with people in this type face. Unless otherwise stated all such quotations are from my own notes and tape recordings.
2. Cliff McDaniel, a youngster whose beating in 1975 by the police sparked the formation of the Black Parents Movement, discussed in the next chapter.

3. For discussions of Black politics in Britain see Bourne and Sivanandan 1980; Centre for Contemporary Cultural Studies 1982; Goulbourne 1990; Solomos and Back 1995.
4. C.L.R. James (1901–1989) is a major twentieth-century Marxist critic, historian and activist. Born in Trinidad, he lived and worked in Britain and the USA. His two best known works are a history of the Haitian revolution (James 1980 [1938]) and a multi-disciplinary work on cricket and colonialism (James 1963). The secondary literature on James's life and work is large and growing, but see Bogues 1997 and Worcester 1996. The website of the New York-based C.L.R. James Institute is also a good resource (http://www.clrjamesinstitute.org).
5. The ideas and activities of this tendency are documented in journals such as *Race Today* and *Black Liberator,* where a race-inflected socialist analysis of political struggles in Britain and overseas was developed.
6. Over the weekend of 26 and 27 May 2001 'the worst riots since 1981' took place in Oldham in the Greater Manchester area of northern England; pitting Asian youth against first right-wing Whites and then the police. Fifteen officers were injured and fifty-nine people were arrested, according to the BBC Online. Following these tensions, in the 7 June general election the far-right British National Party gained more than 12,000 votes in two Oldham constituencies: this was its best result to date.
7. Ann Walmsley interview with John La Rose, 22 Novenber 1985, transcript in GPI archive.
8. Anne Walmsley interview with Andrew Salkey, 20 March 1986, transcript in GPI archive.
9. Anne Walmsley interview with Edward Brathwaite at Irish Town, Jamaica, 15 March 1986, transcript in GPI archive.
10. This field is nowadays better captured by the term 'post-colonial literature' (Ashcroft, Griffiths and Tiffin 1989). It is intriguing to contemplate whether – as former colonies of Britain – the USA, Canada, Australia and New Zealand can be considered 'post-colonial' in the way that India, Nigeria or Guyana are seen in this field of literary criticism.
11. CAM did not have premises of its own. Most sessions were held at the West Indian Students Centre in London (set up by the fledgling English Caribbean states to serve as a meeting place and support centre for West Indian students).
12. Anne Walmsley interview with Akua Rugg, Wimbledon, 1 October 1997, transcript in GPI archive.

13. Anne Walmsley interview with Christopher Laird, Port of Spain, 24 July 1986, transcript in GPI archive.
14. In February 2000, Banyan established the Caribbean Motion Picture Archive, at its offices in Trinidad: 'Banyan's archives have a permanent home in a purpose built environmentally controlled vault and new offices.' For more information see: www.pancaribbean.com/banyan/open2.htm.
15. Anne Walsmsley interview with Amon Saba Saakana (formerly Sebastian Clarke); London, 5 February 1987, transcript in GPI archive.
16. From a wide body of work, see (La Rose 1992; La Rose 1966; Salkey 1967; Salkey 1977; Brathwaite 1967; Brathwaite 1970; Brathwaite 1971).
17. Anne Walmsley interview with Kenneth Ramchand at the University of the West Indies, St Augustine, Trinidad, 29 July 1986, transcript in GPI archive.
18. Of the three floors at Albert Road, one of the two ground-floor rooms is used to store documentation from past campaigns and also serves as the office of New Beacon Books publishing house. Before moving to Stroud Green Road, New Beacon bookshop and publishing house were based at the Albert Road home.
19. The X-Press publishes popular fiction and non-fiction aimed at a Black British readership.
20. The full significance of this statement is indicated by both Janice and Sarah pointing out to me that the Heinemann and Longman lines of Caribbean and African literature do not sell very widely outside of the school and college readership; by contrast X-Press books appeal to the younger Black British reader both in school and out.

–2–

Cultural Revolutionaries

Introduction

We have discussed the formation of the Caribbean Artists Movement (CAM) as part of a strategy to raise the general awareness of Caribbean arts and letters in Britain and to forge links among Caribbean writers and artists in Britain and wider afield, especially but not only in the Caribbean. CAM's aim was also to enter into and seek to transform the terms of cultural discourse in Britain so as to open space for the recognition of Caribbean-heritage people as full cultural and, by implication, political subjects. John La Rose and Sarah White, having started New Beacon in 1966 as a publishing house, were motivated to enter bookselling because of the demand for Black and Third World books created by the general climate of cultural upheaval in the 1960s and by the specific demands generated out of CAM meetings.

I will discuss a range of projects and activities and organizations which were symbolically and sometimes actually centred around New Beacon Books, which were a response to changes in the political terrain of the 1970s and 1980s in Britain, which saw increasing resistance by Black people to their subordination and social and cultural exclusion. Movements of parents, teachers and students, an international book fair and a carnival band and sound system were the projects through which the circle and their political associates took their cultural politics into a new space of engagement. In addition to their work in Britain, they were part of international activities related to the Caribbean and Africa, primarily, but also in Europe.

The Black Parents Movement/Black Youth Movement

The Black Parents Movement (BPM) and Black Youth Movement (BYM) were set up in 1975 following the assault by police on Cliff McDaniel, a Black youngster, outside his school in the Hornsey area of north London. McDaniel was a school friend of Michael and Keith La Rose, the sons of

John La Rose and Irma La Rose, and he was known to many of the parents connected to the George Padmore Supplementary School (to which we will come), which had been started by John and Irma. Many of these parents formed the membership of the Black Parents Movement. Simultaneously with the formation of the BPM, Michael and Keith La Rose were among a group of young people who formed the Black Youth Movement. The original principal aims of the BPM and BYM were to organize defence of Black youth who found themselves without proper reason on the wrong side of the law.

There was a cultural as well as a political agenda to these two organizations. There was first the work around policing. Many of the people involved in the Black Parents Movement took the view that the widespread exclusion of Black pupils was largely unfair and had to be fought by organizing Black parents into groups that could lobby educational authorities for reform. Secondly, they became involved in the expansion of supplementary schools, which had been set up from the late 1960s to help Black children cope with the British school system (interviews with John La Rose and Irma La Rose, London, May–August 1997). Thirdly, the Black Youth movement sought to organize sporting activities such as football, and cultural activities such as carnival masquerade bands, which they saw as a counter to a tendency of unemployed Black youth to drift into street life and sometimes into crime (talk by Michael La Rose, GPI, London, May 1997).

The BPM and BYM emerged out of prior anti-racist and school-reform struggles. By the 1960s, there were already established several organizations concerned with the position of Caribbean migrants in Britain (such as the West Indian Standing Conference, formed in 1958 after the Notting Hill 'race riots' of that year). John La Rose, like many Black parents when they became aware of the procedure, was strongly opposed to the tendency of British schools to direct Caribbean-heritage children into Educationally Sub-Normal (ESN) streams. The parents of the North London West Indian Association (NLWIA) of which La Rose was a member, with the support of the West Indian Standing Conference, vigorously opposed ESN policy in Haringey. Proposals for streaming or 'banding' in Haringey in 1969 prompted the formation of the Caribbean Educationists Association, which became the Caribbean Education and Community Workers Association (CECWA). Caribbean-descent as well as British schoolteachers[1] who were also opposed to banding joined the challenge to the reliance on IQ testing and the assumptions on which these tests and their interpretation were based. The fledgling New Beacon Books joined the initiative of the NLWIA which was organizing meetings of teachers and parents in order to formulate a collective response. New Beacon Books contributed to the response by supplying material for the emergent field of multicultural literature, and also by their publishing efforts, among which was an important work in this area: *How the West Indian Child is made Educationally Sub-normal in the British School System* (Coard 1971). Published for CECWA by New Beacon Books in 1971, this was the work of Grenadian-born Bernard Coard.[2] In this small book, which began as a paper prepared for a 1970 conference organized by CECWA, Coard documented the racist underpinning of the ESN policy, and highlighted ways in which the self-image of Black Caribbean children was damaged by low teacher expectations in an already hostile social environment; he also pointed to the racist tone of much teaching material. Apart from its obvious relation to anti-racist struggles being waged around schooling and in the wider society, Coard's work may be read in the vein of the radical sociology of education which was expanding at the time (Young 1971), produced by teachers and academics who had been radicalized by the 1960s social movements (Illich 1971).

Though most Caribbean settlers in Britain were working-class, they had high expectations of the British education system for their children's mobility, expectations often at odds with the views of officials and teachers in that very system. Far from being unrealistic, however, these expectations were rooted in these parents' experiences of the colonial West Indies, where the main route to social mobility for lower-class Black people was education (Campbell 1996). Though only a handful of students in the colonial Caribbean made it through the hyper-selective system of schooling to finish with a secondary school diploma, the possibility was tangible enough to lend the manifestly unjust system some stability and legitimacy. In Britain, however, Black working-class Caribbean migrants found even that narrow route to mobility blocked, due to an overdetermined class base of schooling where (White) working-class kids were channelled to blue-collar or low-end white-collar jobs, and *Black* working-class kids were not programmed for any jobs at all. One response by many Black parents and teachers was to set up local community schools, which sought to supplement the normal schooling with extra lessons. The period since the late 1960s has seen considerable growth in supplementary schools (Carter 1986; John 1986).[3]

The George Padmore Supplementary School was set up in 1969 by John La Rose, Irma La Rose and others, in order to combat what they perceived to be the negative cultural stereotyping that John's and Irma's two sons and the children of close family friends would face as Black children in the classroom. Apart from supplementing school lessons principally in English, science and mathematics, the Padmore School was intended to expose its pupils to the history and culture of the Caribbean and Africa. John La Rose recalls:

> The first time I gave a talk on African history and civilization to the children at the Paul Bogle Youth Club [which preceded the George Padmore Supplementary School] some of them laughed loudly when I mentioned 'Africa'. I think it was partly a nervous, embarrassed reaction, because they, as black kids in Britain, were used to hearing Africa dismissed as a primitive place, and Africans as primitive people. Africa was something they were a bit ashamed of. So we had to change that. We had to teach them about the civilizations of Africa.

John adds:

> I don't mean we neglected the history of Europe, of classical Greece and Rome; that too was part of our history; it was part of my own education at St Mary's College in Trinidad. We did not neglect European culture – after all, the kids were growing up here in Europe – but we wanted them to learn about and develop pride in the African parts of their heritage.

Part of the curriculum of the Padmore school consisted in sessions of world geography, Caribbean cuisine and music, and talks by African and Caribbean-heritage adults about their lives in Africa, the Caribbean and in Britain. In this the Padmore school was pioneering in the field of multicultural education, which, while it is now accepted by many in the British education establishment, has been the object of a right-wing backlash by those who see multiculturalism as an attack on the integrity of 'British' or 'English' culture. Joan Goody, a close associate of the circle, retired schoolteacher and long involved in issues of multicultural education, wrote in 2000 as editor of a publication by the National Association for the Teaching of English:

> The term 'international/multicultural' as we use it here embraces world literature, literature from parallel cultures, cross cultural literature, and literature which portrays aspects of a multicultural society. At the present time its importance is generally acknowledged amongst teachers and other educationalists, but in practice it still tends to be marginalised, at least in part because it does not yet have an integral place in the National Curriculum and is considered as a separate category of reading (Goody 2000: 1)

The studentship of the Padmore school varied over the years, from as few as six to as many as forty pupils. The school was active for most of the period from its 1969 inception to the time of fieldwork in 1996; by 1997 it had not been in operation for almost a year.[4] The school has had a generation recycling: John La Rose's son Michael himself became a teacher there, and Michael's son in turn was a pupil of the Padmore school.[5]

The founders of the BPM had all been involved in education regarding Black children, whether as teachers themselves, as community activists, or as parents of Black children. Irma La Rose explained to me that while the McDaniel case referred to earlier was a catalyst in starting the BPM, she and the other founders had already developed an analysis of the problems faced by Black children in a racist social environment, and had already developed a response through the Padmore school. So the BPM was intended to concentrate efforts and consolidate prior experience in combating these problems. A Manchester Black Parents Movement was started in 1978 by Gus John and others.

The BPM produced a considerable amount of documentation – position papers, a newsletter, conference proceedings. Several issues of *Battle Front: Paper of the Black Parents Movement* came out as well as other occasional publications, laying out the aims of organization, and presenting information on campaigns. It would appear that considerable care was devoted to producing and preserving this documentation, based on the range of materials on the BPM and BYM held in the archive of the George Padmore Institute. The politics articulated in BPM and BYM publications, and their particular views on organization and membership will all be dealt with in Chapter Three.

The BPM was involved in numerous campaigns: legal defence, anti-deportation, working against racism in education, and contesting suspensions and expulsions. The BPM campaigned in support of dissident groups, pro-democracy initiatives and trade unions in Kenya, Nigeria and the Caribbean. The Committee for the Release of Political Prisoners in Kenya (whose address was the same as New Beacon Books: number 76 Stroud Green Road) issued pamphlets condemning the repression of the Moi regime. One such pamphlet, entitled *Release the Political Prisoners in Kenya,* issued in 1982, opened with an analysis of the current situation, listed seven persons who had been detained by the regime and gave names and addresses to which appeals should be sent.

The BPM gave 'critical support' to the Maurice Bishop government in Grenada during the 1979–1983 revolutionary period (La Rose 1985a).

The membership was instrumental in the work of the Committee Against Repression in Guyana (CARIG), which articulated resistance to the increasingly repressive regime led by Forbes Burnham, in so doing serving as a rallying point for Guyanese in Britain who had fled the harsh political situation in their homeland.[6] The BPM and BYM were among the conveners (along with the *Race Today* Collective) of a public meeting called to discuss events surrounding the death of Walter Rodney[7] in Guyana in 1981. It was widely believed that Rodney's death was orchestrated by the Burnham regime, which had become increasingly concerned by his role in mobilizing opposition as a leader of the leftist Working Peoples Alliance. C.L.R. James was one of the speakers at that event and his talk was published as a pamphlet by *Race Today* (James 1983).

The BPM gave public support to the striking miners of the 1980s. They organized boycotts of British firms which traded with South Africa or sold South African goods. The picket of the Tesco's supermarket branch on Stroud Green Road lasted for two years, taking place mostly on Friday evenings or Saturday lunchtime. But it was not all campaigning and reacting to negative developments: the BPM and the BYM were also involved in organizing social sporting and cultural events; there were several dinners and dances each year, at which the musical entertainment was often supplied by the La Rose sons, who became disc jockeys in the 1970s. The BYM started a football team – Uniques – and were involved in the Carnival movement (discussed later).

The Black Youth Movement saw itself as distinct from the BPM though closely connected. Its social and political analysis paralleled that of the BPM. In a presentation by the the Black Youth Movement at the Annual Conference of the Black Parents Movement, held in October 1979 (GPI archive), the issue is raised of needing to deal with the 'principles of organisation'. The Black Parents Movement had produced their own statement of these principles, and it would be reasonable to assume that the Black Youth Movement was acting in tandem. The BYM as represented in the presentation saw its aims at that 'present stage of organisation' (that is, with expanded and more 'disciplined' youth membership, than at its inception in 1975) as: producing a regular internal bulletin, publishing a paper for the general public; and building organizations around 'our cultural and social activities'. The document then goes on to discuss the school as one of the major institutions of the State, adding that the courts and the police seem to work 'hand in hand'. Both the BPM and BYM, while overtly concerned with issues affecting Black people, developed their analysis and strategies from a broad left standpoint, as we shall see in the next chapter.[8]

One important campaign in which the circle was involved was the result of a tragedy. On 18 January 1981, thirteen young Black people lost their lives in a fire. The venue was a birthday party at a home at number 439 New Cross Road, in south London. It was widely believed, though not by the police, that the fire was the result of an incendiary device thrown by white racists. The New Cross area had seen numerous racist attacks on Black people in the period leading up to the fire and there was a general atmosphere of tension in the area. The parents of the victims were not satisfied with the police response, which seemed intent on blaming the victims. Media reports were divided as to the cause of the tragedy. In light of this, there was established the New Cross Massacre Action Committee, which John La Rose chaired. The Committee set up support and counselling for the bereaved relatives, fund-raising (£27,000 had been raised within weeks of the fire), media relations, and legal support. A commission of enquiry was organized. The mass response to the tragedy was different from that of the police and much of the media. The Black People's Day of Action was organized by the Committee; a march took place on Monday 2 March 1981, moving from New Cross through Fleet Street and ending in Hyde Park. With 20,000 people on the march, it is described by the Committee in a statement released in 2001 for the twentieth anniversary of the tragedy as 'the biggest mobilisation of black people ever seen in Britain'. To date, no one has been brought to justice.

The International Book Fair of Radical Black and Third World Books

> The organisation of this First International Book Fair of Radical Black and Third World Books is intended to mark the new and expanding phase in the growth of radical ideas and concepts and their expression in literature, politics, music, art and social life. (From the brochure of the First International Book Fair)

The International Book Fair of Radical Black and Third World Books took place twelve times between 1982 and 1995 in various venues in London. Smaller offshoot book fairs were held elsewhere in the UK, in Bradford and Manchester. Two Book Fairs was held in Trinidad in 1987 and 1988, co-organized with the Oilfields Workers Trade Union, of which John La Rose is European representative. The Book Fair was a synthesis of the cultural work which had opened up space for Black and non-Western literature in Britain; CAM and New Beacon played an influential part in that work. The Book Fair met a demand that resulted from a heightened awareness on the part of progressives – Black and White – of the need for material to help shape a coherent social-cultural identity for Britain's non-White population. One commentator on the first Book Fair highlighted its comprehensive challenge to stereotypical notions of Black social and cultural deficiency, notions which underlay a host of racist discourses and practices:

> In the face of mainstream white media presentation of the black community as violent, lawless, intimidating to whites, threatening to established order and altogether alien, the Fair and its accompanying events bore witness to a different reality. Everyone knows about the riots; policemen bleeding under their helmets, youths throwing stones and bottles and burning cars have passed into the popular consciousness as images of black resistance. The Book Fair was something else: black people organising peacefully to affirm and celebrate their creativity (Bryce 1982: 26).

New Beacon was one of three organizations which founded the International Book Fair. The other two were Bogle L'Ouverture Books, a publisher of Black literature started in 1967 in London by Guyanese-born Jessica and Eric Huntley, who also ran the Walter Rodney Bookshop; and the *Race Today* Collective, based in Brixton, South London, who put out the journal *Race Today*. Bogle L'Ouverture's publishing was concerned mainly with Afro-Caribbean and African literature.[9] The *Race Today* Collective grew out of a breakaway faction from the Institute of Race Relations (IRR), which comprised young Blacks and Asians who wanted a more direct confrontation with racism in Britain, as against the IRR's practice of working within the existing state structures. Another source of personnel and ideas for the *Race Today* Collective was the British Black Panther Party, modeled on its US counterpart.[10] For the three founding organizations, the Book Fair was a logical step in their radical publishing and campaigning. New Beacon and Bogle L'Ouverture had been pioneers in publishing and bookselling for a largely unserved market of Black readers in Britain, especially in schools.

Sarah White recalls of the first Book Fair, which took place at the Islington Town Hall:

> The first book fair took place in 1982, and the decision to hold book fairs was around Autumn 1981. That was the year of the New Cross massacre and also the Brixton riots, and it really arose out of the work that had been done by the three organizations – Race Today, New Beacon and Bogle L'Ouverture – and we had worked together in the alliance. So it

was a kind of cultural manifestation of the politics that had been going on at the time. That is one way of looking at it. Plus the fact that all three organizations were involved in publishing. New Beacon and Bogle were sort of standard publishers, and Race Today were doing the magazine, and also doing some books as well . . . There was a tremendous enthusiasm for the first book fair. When it took place there were queues outside, it really caught the imagination . . . It was at Islington Town Hall, and on the Saturday it was quite amazing, there were queues waiting to get in. And things like the poetry reading were in the Camden centre, and there had never been a poetry reading like that in London. There had been big poetry readings in the sixties . . . but not one [focused on the work of black and third world poets] . . . in that sense every event was very successful, the book fair was very successful. The publishers who came were very enthusiastic and were pleased to meet the people who were reading their books. So, it really sparked and took off from there.

Margaret Busby, one of the principals of Allison and Busby, an independent publisher started in the late 1960s, attended several of these Book Fairs, and gave the feature address at the 11th; she recalled to me in an interview:

[The Book Fairs] were places where you saw a kind of person engaging with literature who wouldn't have gone to a mainstream British bookstore. Black working-class people were not viewed as readers of literature by the British literary establishment and they were not treated as such: mainstream bookstores and publishers did not cater for their needs and did not make them feel welcome. At the book fairs, however, these people would be there in their hundreds, browsing and buying and meeting authors (interview notes, September 1997).

The International Book Fair was intended to bring together artists, activists and other interested persons from all spheres of culture and politics, drawn internationally (Lloyd 1985). It was organized as a large exhibition of books from independent publishers and those mainstream publishers with radical Black or third-world lines; there were readings; there were discussion forums; an evening of cultural performance was integral to the Book Fair. Each Book Fair was accompanied by a Festival Week which ran from Sunday to Saturday, with events every night and many afternoons. The Book Fair itself ran from Thursday to Saturday inclusive. On the Saturday mornings an event was put on for supplementary school children based around Caribbean music, song, dance and drama (Roxy Harris, personal communication). Though inspired by intellectual production, the tone of the Book Fairs was non-academic, according to John La Rose:

> We discouraged people from presenting papers. We wanted to get away from that one-sided model of academic presentation. The forums were discussions. The panellists were invited to make statements, not read papers. Participation from the floor was integral.

The fact that each Book Fair drew participants from all continents is an indication of the importance these participants attributed to the gatherings, especially given the fact that the organizers did not provide travel grants; participants had to fund their expenses themselves:

> It was for them [i.e. those persons invited to the Book Fair], because of their own conviction that what we were doing was important, to come on the basis of their own resources; but that having come here we would find them modest accommodation in the homes of the black community, and that we would also try to find them bookings as well, to help them defray their costs (La Rose interviewed in Lloyd 1985: 28).

The first International Book Fair of Radical Black and Third World Books took place at the Islington Town Hall, North London from 1 to 3 April 1982. It attracted over 100 publishers from Africa, the Caribbean, North America, Asia and Europe. There were 6,000 people in attendance throughout the festival week; on this basis alone that Book Fair can be considered a success. The opening address was delivered by C.L.R. James on 1 April 1982. James was arguably the leading Black intellectual figure in Britain at that time.

For a sense of the scope of activity we can look at the programme of events for individual Book Fairs; as an example I will list those for the Festival Week of the eleventh Book Fair (21 to 27 March 1993, Camden Centre, London):

- Day Conference: Bigotry, Racism, Nazism and Fascism in Europe: Strategies for Change, 21 March, with speakers from France/Egypt, UK, Ghana/Germany, Germany, UK/India;
- International Poetry Evening, 23 March;
- Restructuring on a Global Scale: Crises, Consequences and the Way Forward, 24 March;
- Malcolm X, Urban Youth and the Direction of Black Struggle, 25 March;
- International Prose Reading, 26 March.

Cultural Revolutionaries

During the actual period of the Book Fair (25 to 27 March) the following daytime events took place:

- Forum on Crisis in the libraries, 25 March;
- Writers days on 26 and 27 March.

In the weeks leading up to the Book Fair, there were three conferences:

- Communalism, Fundamentalism and Secularism, 6 March;
- The Profound Significance of Women's Resistance, 7 March. Both organized jointly with the Southall Monitoring Group and Tabula Rasa;
- Education economy and Society: the struggle for education in Britain, 13 March.

What was significant about the forums and events taken together is the aim to forge a combination of cultural and political analysis, and to reject division between artistic and intellectual work on the one hand and social transformation on the other. There is no simple way to measure the extent to which the Book Fairs achieved their aims, but then a strict empiricist approach to measuring outcomes is perhaps best left to the managerialists: the outlook underlying the Book Fairs was one that was not concerned to achieve results measured on strictly managerial criteria of numbers attended or sales generated or markets conquered. The Book Fairs were intended as an entry into the public sphere and were aimed at radically democratizing that public sphere by breaking down barriers between intellectuals and the public (especially the Black and working-class public) and between genres/fields of intellectual and artistic endeavour. Another barrier attacked by the Book Fair was the racial divide of literary artistic culture, a divide that worked within Britain and between Europe and the Third World. Within the space of Black politics in Britain in the 1980s, where cultural nationalist tendencies were gaining influence, the Book Fairs were notably internationalist in outlook.

The Book Fair marked the emergence into the public sphere of what we may term submerged knowledge. For 'submerged' is what Black and Third World literature was, from the perspective of most mainstream publishers and booksellers in Britain. The Book Fairs, as with CAM and New Beacon, not only made more visible this submerged knowledge, but raised probing questions about the way in which mainstream British and Euro-American culture had been constituted and elevated on the local and global stage, with the suppression of other cultural orientations in the process. Politics was always on the agenda, and it is noteworthy that discussion time at the Book Fairs was often devoted to racism and fascism in Europe. The Book Fairs were never addressed exclusively to Black or third-world concerns strictly conceived, but were internationalist, as indicated for example by the recordings of these forums which have been preserved in the archive of the circle, ranging from 'Transition to Socialism' to 'The Working Day – Technology and Society' to a session on the film 'Battle of Algiers'.

It is impossible to judge the mood of the forums based solely on listening to the recordings which were made. One session from the ninth Book Fair on 'Racism, Nazism, Fascism and Racial Attacks: the European Response' (held on 23 March 1990 at the Camden Centre, London) was fully transcribed and published as a booklet (La Rose 1991). The main speakers presented information on fascist and racist attacks and organization against these in France, West Germany, East Germany and the UK. These were followed by an open discussion. Each of the main speakers was personally involved in organizing the campaigns they spoke about. John La Rose, the chair, in his remarks not only felt that this lent authenticity to the accounts, but he stressed that the presenters were activists first and therefore engaged in a way that academics could not be because of the academic privilege of analysis over action. What emerges from the document is a comparative account of organization in these four countries and a composite picture of the then state of struggles against racism and for social and political equality. Several speakers expressed a concern that the imminent creation of European Union citizenship in 1992 would entail intensified surveillance and exclusion of those persons who were resident in one of the EU nation-states but were not citizens. These concerns have been proven by developments to be well-founded: EU policy on immigration and nationality since 1992 has preserved and at times increased the restrictions placed on freedom of movement for those not fortunate to hold the nationality of one of the member states (Shore 2000).

Sarah White explains that an important aspect to the policy of the Book Fairs was that they were not money-making ventures, indeed efforts were made to make attendance by small publishers as easy as possible:

The Book Fair was one thing, the publishers – we never got any grants – the publishers hired their stalls for three days and sold their books themselves, we never took any percentage of the sales, we decided that was far too difficult, so we just charged a fee, that was it. And we tried to accommodate small publishers as far as we could. Our early pricing system was quite fair – the bigger your [stall] was the more expensive – I mean relatively more expensive . . .

Brian Alleyne: like progressive taxation . . .

A bit like progressive taxation, in the end we didn't do that, we did it on a sort of pro rata basis, but we always had this thing where a stall could be divided up into halves and quarters and then even sort of single titles so that people – small publishers could come in, we tried to make it affordable. But it made it very difficult for the people who had to do the actual layout, all these quarters and these halves and these whatever, and trying to fit everybody into the space that they had booked.

The Book Fairs were imagined and implemented in engagement with what was happening in left-wing and anti-racist politics in Britain at the time. Sarah explained that the Book Fair cooperated with the Socialist Workers Party (SWP)[1] in the early years:

. . . the other thing which I remember now is that at the same time, or maybe a little bit before, there was the socialist book fair, which was run by Bookmarks – the SWP book shop . . . and that was very successful, they used to hold that in the autumn, around October/November . . . in the Camden centre, and that went on annually . . . we used to participate as publishers, we didn't used to sell very much, they were more Marxist-oriented . . . So in that sense we were not the only book fair . . . they were very supportive of us . . . for example, they had probably started in the late seventies, and they loaned us the screens, to have behind the stalls. For two or three years we used to borrow their screens, so we sort of worked together in that sense . . . and we chose our dates so that we were separate from when they were having theirs, so that we wouldn't clash, so that we would both attend each others'. But we had a very different constituency anyway . . .

Brian Alleyne: Did they display at your book fair?

They came sometimes, yes, quite often, but not always. But again quite like us in their book fair, they didn't sell very much in our book fair . . . but one has to remember, in that late seventies period there was a market, there was interest in left-wing Marxist literature . . . things change . . .

The last book fair was held in 1995. By that time there had been a rift between Race Today and New Beacon, and Bogle L'Ouverture had withdrawn from as active a role as previously. The work of organization was proving too much for Sarah, and John La Rose was on a reduced workload due to health problems, so a decision was taken that 1995 would be the last year of the Book Fair. In a January 1997 statement issued by

'The Organising Committee of the International Book Fair of Radical Black and Third World Books', the following was written:

> John La Rose, the Director and co-founder of the International Book Fair of Radical Black and Third World Books has retired. Following extensive discussions with both John and Sarah White, the other main Book Fair Organiser, the Organising Committee has decided not to continue with the book fair in London in its present form.

Not surprisingly, numerous letters and messages of regret were received by John and Sarah, ranging from persons who had been inspired to get into publishing or bookselling by New Beacon, to persons overseas who remember attending past book fairs.

Significance of the Book Fairs

London, as a long-established centre of media, publishing and the arts, has a long history of hosting major international gatherings of writers and artists; it has had major conventions of radicals, Black writers, and of third-world intellectuals and activists. The international Book Fairs were the largest of their kind to assemble a grouping in which all of these currents met. The first Book Fair took place at a time of heightened political tension in Britain, especially following the New Cross fire, the Black Peoples Day of Action, Brixton and other uprisings, all in 1981. The first Book Fair gathered momentum from the previous two decades of struggles against racism, class and social cultural exclusion which had been waged by Black and White progressive activists and many ordinary people whose main concern was fair treatment in the housing market, in schools for their children, and at the workplace. Those persons in what I term the New Beacon circle were active in these struggles and the Book Fairs could thus be seen as a synthesis of their work. The international context was equally important for the three organizers, all of whom had concrete links with political struggles and activists in the Caribbean, in Africa, Asia, North America and Europe. These connections not only facilitated the broad international participation in the Book Fairs, but were themselves sustained and often strengthened by the gatherings in Britain. In the case of New Beacon Books and the Alliance, already existing connections were drawn upon for the staging of the Book Fairs. In light of the resource limitations and grass-roots methodology of organizing the events, it is arguably the case that these personal and political connections and the activist commitments of the persons involved compensated for absent material rewards.

The three founders were all centrally involved with publishing, bookselling and education as sites of political action and cultural transformation. The Book Fair opened up a space where the respective constituencies of the founders could be brought together in real time, making possible the kind of networking on which the success of their often non-waged activities depended. For many of those attending the Book Fairs – and I have in mind especially progressive teachers, small publishers, and writers and artists – their most important resource was the human relationships through which work and ideas were circulated. On these networks many were dependent for earning an income as newcomers and/or to remain relatively autonomous from the cultural establishment.

In political terms the Book Fairs can be understood as strategic campaigns aimed to gain, extend and secure cultural autonomy for radical Black and third-world writers, artists and their work. The Italian Marxist Gramsci wrote in the 1920s on the question of how elites secure their power and position in society without regular resort to force (Davidson 1977; Gramsci 1971). He drew attention to the sphere of culture, introducing the idea of hegemony, through which he sought to render the situation in which powerful elements in a social setting intervened in the spaces of culture and politics to represent their own interests as legitimate, and more importantly, to persuade those politically subordinate to themselves that these interests are common interests in the common good. Hegemony is effective (though never completely so) when an elite world-view and set of interests come to be commonly held, even if political analysis can demonstrate that the interests of the powerful few are in fact in conflict with the interest of the many, or of some excluded minority. The Book Fairs can be read as an exercise in counter-hegemony. They may also be read as attempts to build spaces where a democratic meeting of ideas and experiences could shape the process of knowledge creation.

Despite poststructuralist-inspired critiques of politics based on presumed collective interests (Laclau and Mouffe 1985), I think it can still be shown to be the case that particular cultural products and outlooks are closely associated with powerful groups and serve to reinforce some social positions while excluding or debasing/devaluing others. The marginalization of cultural products produced by women, or working-class or Black people is sustained not usually by brute force or open manipulation but by a sophisticated hegemony constituted in schools, the media and other public spaces. Underlying such hegemony is a history of elite formation and reproduction (Bourdieu 1986a), a history too of the exercise of social and political power to exclude. The political significance of the

Book Fairs lies in this: they were war-machines in a battle to break down the hegemony of a Eurocentric literary, cultural and political establishment.

Peoples War: Sound System to Carnival Band[12]

When we were growing up in this politicized era, there were these people in Mozambique fighting the war of independence against the Portuguese and they had a Support Committee in London and they had a poster with a man looking very serious with a gun and it said 'Victory to People's War'. We were talking about forming a sound system in 1975, all friends together, about eight of us, because we needed more cash within what we were doing to produce a sound system, and we said, 'Yes, that's the one we want, People's War'.

Michael La Rose

The World Turned Upside Down

The Peoples War Sound System and Carnival Band were both closely connected to the Black Youth Movement and indeed to the work of the New Beacon circle. They were projects shaped in the pattern of the circle's strategy of bringing a political consciousness to cultural space; the space in this case was the London Notting Hill Carnival. First some background on the Carnival phenomenon itself: carnival (*carne vale* – farewell to the flesh: flesh as both the human body and meat) in medieval Europe was a public display of passions that Church doctrine held should normally be strictly controlled (Bakhtin 1984 [1965]). It was the big festivity before the austerity of Lent. Gluttony – especially heavy consumption of meat – intoxication, sexual intercourse, loud music and dancing were all prohibited during Lent, when the Christian subject was meant to turn inward and contemplate his or her relationship to God. It is open to debate how many people held fast to these proscriptions, but the pre-Lenten festival of Carnival was a time when these prohibitions were not only relaxed, but indeed the reverse: hedonistic display, was allowed to occupy a public space. Carnival was a period when the world was metaphorically turned upside down: gender polarities were reversed, the poor dressed themselves in the normally exclusive style and colours of the rich, the rich dressed as the destitute, merchants became jesters and clowns.

Documentary evidence exists for the Trinidad Carnival from the early decades of the nineteenth century (Cowley 1996; Hill 1997 [1972]). The festival was introduced by French settlers in the eighteenth century; they brought with them the practice of masquerade on the Monday and Tuesday that marked the beginning of the Lenten season in Roman Catholic parts of Europe. These French settlers tended to be lenient to their slaves at Christmas and Carnival, allowing them some free time and even encouraging them to make their own masquerade bands. The slaves inserted themselves into the turning-the-world-upside-down-for-a-day that was Carnival: they dressed in the cast-off clothing of their masters and whitened their faces. At the same time many Whites portrayed the *Nègre Jardin* – the field slave – in rags and blackface. From the nineteenth century to the present, the Trinidad Carnival has been a space of cultural innovation and hybridization, of political satire and protest, and lately of constitution of national identity. These sedimented layers of politicized cultural formations would inevitably form a part of the cultural apparatus that the Trinidadian segment of the West Indian migration to Britain would bring with them in the post-Second World War period.

The first officially documented encounter of British society with the Carnival tradition of Trinidad occurred with the arrival of the Trinidad All Steel Percussion Orchestra (TASPO) to perform at the Festival of Britain in 1951 (Belgrave 1993). TASPO was a steel drum band; they introduced the British public to this new instrument and its distinctive sound. In informal spaces like their homes and parties, ordinary Trinidadian migrants were also by this time re-articulating the cultural forms that had grown out of carnival – such as the calypso; those with artistic training and access to cultural apparatus in Britain were presenting the folk dances and drama from Trinidad and the wider Caribbean (Connor-Mogotsi 1995; Walmsley 1992).

While there is some difference of opinion as to the 'origins' of the Notting Hill carnival, most of those who have written on the Notting Hill Carnival[13] have tended to take the re-articulation of Caribbean cultural forms in Britain – as outlined above – as their point of departure. They see the development of Carnival in Britain in terms of a struggle by West Indians to make a public expression of a collective identity in the face of a structurally racist and hostile social reality in Britain. They have treated the Carnival as one instance of the ongoing struggle of Black people to forge social and political space in Britain.[14] The account which follows is that of only one participant in the London carnival. Given that the carnival is an issue on which opinions are divided, it should not surprise that Michael La Rose's narrative on the formation of Peoples War Carnival Band is articulated from a particular position. His narrative is important for my overall account because Michael's work is one element of the New Beacon archipelago of cultural activism.

Sound System Business

The Peoples' War Carnival band was formed in 1983 by Michael and Keith La Rose. Both had by that time had a long involvement in the London music scene as DJs (Disc Jockeys). Michael remembers, as a child, 'seeing people liming around a paraffin heater in the cold, listening to Sparrow'.[15] His grandfather always sent to London the roadmarch[16] recording from the Trinidad Carnival. In 1970 Michael made his first visit as a young person to Trinidad, which he had left as a child. In London, the La Rose boys were part of a milieu where carnival traditions were being reconstituted: some people on his street in North London, who were related to his mother, brought out a band for the Notting Hill Carnival in the late 1960s; John La Rose – the father of Michael and Keith – used to take them and their friends to many of the events around carnival.

By 1973 Michael and his brother Keith, in their late teens, were spending time at the Hibiscus club in Stoke Newington, North London, which was run by a Trinidadian; this club played all types of music; according to Michael, 'Trinis [Trinidadians] listen to all music'. After some time Michael and his friends got a chance to try their hand at DJing, when the club's normal DJ fell ill. According to Michael:

It was at this club that the first masquerade bands were planned and subsequently introduced to Notting Hill Carnival. The main Carnival organizer was Lesley Palmer or 'Teacher'. He convinced Lawrence Noel – a mas' maker – to bring a costume band to Notting Hill at the Hibiscus Club.

It was at this time that the idea of putting a masquerade band on the streets of Notting Hill first occurred to Michael and Keith.

The issue of what type of music was to be played in the clubs and parties frequented by Caribbean-heritage youth divided Jamaicans from Trinidadians and others from the Southeast Caribbean. Michael recalls:

there was a lot of strident Jamaican nationalism at the time, they tried to keep other types of music [apart from reggae] out of fetes, so we decided to bus' [bust or break] that, we wanted to listen to all types of music – calypsos, cadance and West African music; the Jamaican-only emphasis was false to ourselves and everything else.

Michael admits that his and Keith's inclusive approach to music was in a sense not in keeping with the dominant trends of Caribbean-heritage youth culture in the 1970s. More than 60 per cent of so-called 'Afro-Caribbeans' in Britain trace their roots to Jamaica; Jamaican speech patterns and popular music in the form of reggae were dominant at that time. This situation would impact on the Carnival. Michael again:

> black youth were attracted to carnival not as a mas [masquerade] thing but as a place where a lot of black people could gather. The carnival movement failed to come to grips with the coming of these black youth – who were chauvinist to [i.e. against] calypso, but still wanted to be part of the carnival; but it was those same youth who fought back and defeated the police in 1976.[17]

Around that time Michael and Keith decided to form their own sound system, which they named Peoples' War 'because we wanted to identify with some of the struggles against oppression that were going on around the world, like in South Africa, in the Caribbean, and here in Britain.' A sound system or 'sound' is a blending of equipment, records and operators that 'plays out' (i.e. provides music, usually for a fee) at clubs and parties. The sound-system phenomenon had its origin in 1960s Jamaica (Hebdige 1987); a number of the famous Jamaican sounds sprung offshoots in Britain, and by the 1970s indigenous British sounds were part of the scene. The world of the sound system was loud, fast, and sometimes dangerous: agents of rival sounds would cut the cables of a system at a 'Blues dance'[18] in order to damage its reputation; occasionally the personnel of a sound would be physically attacked or 'bottled' – have beer bottles thrown at them. The element of danger was increased because the carrying of knives was very popular at this time, according to Michael. Peoples' War often found themselves up against Jamaican music chauvinism: on a few occasions they were threatened with violence for playing music other than reggae. Peoples' War survived, even though Michael recalls 'we had some rough times and a few close calls'.

Following is Michael's account of the formation and policy of Peoples War Carnival Band[19] (the conversation between Michael and myself took place at the Peoples War Mas camp; the narrative picks up just after Michael was talking about his and his brother Keith's early venture into DJing):

> . . . in the meantime [after an initial success playing music at a club] we decided to go on the road, we were with a band called Lion Youth, and they were our friends and they needed a music section and that was when we took the step of going onto a lorry. This was like the first proper sound system, rather than some guy wiring up two PA boxes [loud-speakers], on top of a truck, music for a carnival band in Notting Hill . . .

It was a very fraught and difficult time because it was new ground, nobody knew anything about it, nobody knew how to do it, it was hit and miss . . . you know, the question of generators, the question of fluxes of power . . . it was just a nightmare. And then there was the question of how do you play records on top of a moving truck . . . that was a problem . . . but we got through that carnival, I can't remember . . . maybe '78 or '79 . . . A couple years later we fell out with these people in the mas band, basically we weren't getting paid, and they got somebody else to play for them, this was about maybe four or five years down the road, so everybody knew how to do it now . . . So we decided we're going to bring out a band . . . The basis of that decision was: first of all, a lot of people we brought, because we were playing out all over the place throughout the year, so we used to bring these people to carnival to the band. So that we felt we had a responsibility to the people who would come . . . to us at carnival time, to bring out something . . . so we brought out a T-shirt band;[20] then we had to decide what we were going to do next year, because it's a mas band we want to bring out, not a T-shirt band. But basically, I was saying that I didn't want to make a band that was going to be about butterflies, or fantasy; I wanted to make a band that said something, and I think I'd known enough about carnival at that point to understand the roots of carnival being that kind of commentative mas situation; and I was kind of disenchanted with what was happening in Trinidad at that time, but later on something else happened that would interest me again. I just didn't want to play pretty mas[21] – I just couldn't put my efforts into that, so I said, this is the type of band I want to make, and who was willing to come in with me on this . . . The other thing we thought was important was to explain what the themes were about, whatever constituency we had; one because we were trying to do something with the mas in that sense and first we felt that the only way young black people would, could relate to masquerade – I told you these chauvinisms that existed – was if they understood that it means some-thing, and can say something about their condition here.

Making a political statement is an important part of how Peoples' War seeks to present itself.[22] According to a 1997 Press Release put out by the band:

> The band prides itself on its themes of social commentary and satire. Peoples' War Carnival band makes masquerade that 'says something'. We believe that Carnival masquerade should make a statement. We make 'Radical Mas". (From a Peoples' War Press Release)

A partial list of the band's masquerade themes for previous presentations is as follows:

'Come What may We're Here to Stay';
'None but Ourselves (Black Heroes)';
'There's Something Wrong in Paradise';
'No, Don't Stop De Carnival; Carnival of Resistance';
'Victory at Cuito Cuanavale: Free South Africa!';
'Sparrow's "Jean and Dinah"';
'Black is . . . A celebration of civilisations, inventors, music,
leaders and culture Part I & II';
'Caribbean Festival; We Ting !';
'Untold Stories'.

Anti-racism is evoked in 'None but ourselves' and 'Black is'; anti-
imperialism is evoked in 'Victory at Cuito Cuanavale', and assertion of
the culture of the Trinidad carnival is connoted by 'Jean and Dinah'.[23]
Resistance is a theme that is spread across the themes. The themes suggest,
according to Michael, a critical awareness of social and economic
problems in Britain and beyond. Peoples' War Carnival band can thus be
said to wear its politics on its sleeves.

Masquerade and Politics

Michael La Rose's ideas on cultural activism, as expressed in his personal
narratives, draw upon a number of sources. One is his early exposure to
and later involvement in the political work of his parents and their circle
of associates, exemplified by his role in the formation of the Black Youth
Movement. (While the same may have been the case for his brother Keith,
I interviewed only Michael, to whose narrative I shall confine the
discussion.) The parents and their circle provided a political apprenticeship
for Michael. Another source of Michael's ideology of resistance is the
Black-consciousness movement that made itself felt in Britain in the 1960s
as it did in North America and the Caribbean (talk by Michael La Rose,
London, May 1997).

Michael appears to have grown up with a strong sense of Trinidadian
roots – the London family kept up its connections with the Trinidadian
branches through movement of people, books and records. Trinidadian
and Southeast Caribbean[24] identity was, however, a problem for many
young persons of Caribbean but not Jamaican heritage in the 1970s
because Black youth culture was increasingly defined and expressed
through symbols and forms rooted in Jamaican music and speech. The
tension of having the Trinidadian part of his identity excluded from the
spaces where Black youth listened to popular music was felt strongly by

Michael, as is inscribed in his personal narrative. Faced with the choice of either assimilating into a generic Jamaican-influenced youth culture or resisting, Michael chose to resist. In making this choice Michael was able to draw upon his parents' political work, his own involvement in the Black Youth Movement, his kinship connections in Britain and Trinidad, and not least of all his time as a pupil at the George Padmore Supplementary School.

The Peoples' War Sound System asserted a diverse Black identity by playing a wide range of Black Diaspora music: calypso, soca, reggae, rhythm and blues, funk, soul, 'cadance', hi-life. At the same time it countered the hegemony of Jamaican music in the space of Black youth culture by playing music from the Southeast Caribbean, Brazil and West Africa. Peoples' War Sound System simultaneously supported *and* critiqued the constitution of Black youth culture in London in the 1970s and early 1980s.

The masquerade of Peoples' War Carnival Band sought to give public expression to ideas of anti-racism and anti-imperialism and, like its namesake Sound System, to evoke a Black Diaspora identity. The space for this was the Notting Hill Carnival, an annual event where Caribbean-heritage Britons reproduced and transformed the Trinidad-derived carnival tradition in the contested space they occupied in the new country. As with the Sound System, here again Peoples' War's intervention is both supportive of *and* critical of the wider cultural form – carnival in this case – in which they take part: the Carnival band, by its very presence in the Notting Hill Carnival, supports the public expression of a distinctive Caribbean-heritage identity; at the same time, it sought to bring a political tone to its masquerade by making 'serious' as opposed to 'pretty'[25] portrayals.

This dichotomy may be usefully thought of in terms of the Apollonian/Dionysian contrast made by Nietzsche in his discussion of aesthetics (Nietzsche 1967 [1886, 1888]: 33ff): 'pretty mas' would seem akin to a Dionysian drive to revelry and forgetting of the self in the pleasure of the event, while 'serious mas' suggests the Apollonian state of contemplation. The dichotomy between the pretty and the serious in its starkest form is clearly ideal-typical – nonetheless it is an important one in the Trinidad-derived carnival; adherents to either position will argue at length about the worth of a particular band, even though in a sense they are arguing about two different approaches to masquerade. Some designers of carnival bands have attempted to articulate both emphases (Koningsbruggen 1997). Those who make serious mas often accuse makers of pretty mas of being commercial sell-outs. The dichotomy also manifests itself in the music of carnival, as a distinction between 'serious' calypso, with social commentary in the lyrics, as against 'wining', 'party' or 'jump' Soca – high-tempo dance calypso. As shown by Rohlehr (1990), the debate over these emphases goes back to the nineteenth century for calypso in Trinidad. The two emphases exist in a structural relationship with each other – the one is meaningful to the extent that it can be shown to contrast with the other (Alleyne 1998b).

By making 'radical mas', by emphasizing the serious side of mas over the pretty side, Peoples' War critiques what they see as a secular tendency toward commercialism and empty frivolity in the carnival. Michael himself feels so strongly about making serious mas that he on several occasions told me he was prepared to withdraw altogether from carnival activities if the event became fully commercialized. Serious mas could be seen to be oriented toward a transcendent temporal notion in that it tries to say something about the past and to imagine a future; pretty mas can be thought of as transient because it is grounded in the pleasure of the moment, where past and future are less important than the immediate gratification of the revelry. The contrast between transcendence and transience is a motif that runs through the work of the circle and will come up again in later chapters.[26]

Michael's political involvement in the carnival is wider than his role in founding Peoples' War (La Rose 1990). He has built up his own considerable archive of materials on carnival over the years; he travels to the Trinidadian and other overseas carnivals; he is a commentator and analyst on carnival arts (La Rose 2000). In 1989 he was part of a group that started the Association for a Peoples Carnival (APC), which seeks to criticize the existing arrangements of the carnival, to make public participation and that of masqueraders more enjoyable, and to have some of the revenue generated by the event channelled into supporting masquerade bands and steelbands. The APC publishes a regular newsletter. It advocates the preservation of more traditional (i.e. rooted in Trinidadian carnival) aspects of carnival, like steelbands and masquerade bands, in the face of the growing presence of giant concert-type sound stages catering to a taste for forms of popular music like garage and techno which draw a different audience than that for steelbands and masquerade. As Michael sees it, part of the APC struggle is to 'gain a cut of the financial benefits of the inevitable commercialism of carnival, and to strengthen the Carnival cultural elements and to repay those who sacrificed and struggled to establish the carnival' (Personal communication, 28 February, 1998).

Media reports on the Notting Hill Carnival tend to open with a statement of the law-and-order aspect of the event (this has been so for the period 1996 to 2000, during which I followed closely these reports on television and in the broadsheet press). It appears that these media commentators know little, or perhaps care little, that the carnival is a cultural event. It is here that the work of the Association for a Peoples Carnival is significant: by focusing on the creative dimension of carnival, they counter the ill-informed mainstream view of carnival as mainly a problem to be policed.

Summary

The idea of culture as a resource for individual and social transformation is one of the threads that runs through the narrative to this point. Taking culture as resource has meant for the circle that projects would be organized to mobilize people around, for example, carnival masquerade, and simultaneously a political outlook was articulated. It would be wrong to assume more than that this specific politicization of culture was a project of the members of the circle as social actors – whether the other people these actors mobilized in campaigns shared this politics is a question that cannot be settled within the framework of the present work.

A radical democratic politics is another thread running through the work of the circle. Their humanist belief in the personal, social and political value of education and of the creative arts would seem overly optimistic when viewed through the lens of contemporary identity politics. My interlocutors are not concerned with debates around cultural politics and identity in academia, but if we were to set up a dialogue between the circle and famous activist-intellectuals, the best interlocutors from the latter would be C. Wright Mills or Jean-Paul Sartre, for their humanist Marxism. Outside the academy, the circle's stress on empowerment and autonomy strongly suggests Paulo Freire's ideas and practices for a pedagogy of liberation, for a politics of education as empowerment for democratic citizenship (Freire 1985 [1972]). Like C.L.R. James in a recent collection of his views on organization (James and Glaberman 1999), the New Beacon circle see access to education broadly defined as essential for equipping ordinary people to combat injustice and to strive for improvement in their life conditions. Their vision of social transformation is arguably less apocalyptic than James's; the organizations that they set up were certainly longer-lived.

This and the previous chapter have presented a mostly historical narrative of the work of the New Beacon circle. The next chapter will look at the work of the circle from the perspective of some recent sociological theories of social movements and activism.

Notes

1. Liberal and left-wing British teachers, both White and Black, formed a number of organizations to combat racist exclusions around this time. One such was the National Association of Multiracial Education – NAME – and another was Teachers against Racism (Carter 1986).
2. Coard, after some years as an academic, became part of Maurice Bishop's revolutionary government in Grenada, from 1979–1983. Coard was jailed for his part in the assassination of Bishop and others in 1983. He is currently serving out that sentence in Grenada.
3. Supplementary schools remain important for parents of ethnic minority children (Mirza and Reay 2000). A number of local education authorities in London have in recent years taken the existence of supplementary schools into account in their planning and policy development. In June 1997 I met with two administrators of Hackney Education – Gary Burton, introduced to me at New Beacon bookshop, and his boss, Gregg Wildig – to talk about the current state of supplementary schools in Hackney (a borough with one of the highest proportions of ethnic minorities students). Hackney Education saw supplementary schools as an aspect of community-based education, which the authority supported provided such education met certain criteria. I was told that Hackney Education required those supplementary schools which it supported to have substantial links into the national curriculum. The authority also required 'qualified teachers and proper facilities'. Six supplementary schools were funded in 1997 by Hackney Education. I was also told that some supplementary schools were set up according to cultural/religious agendas which sometimes led to conflict with the requirements of the national curriculum. Most served pupils in the area of primary education. The range of facilities and skill available in these schools varied widely.
4. The George Padmore Institute organized in late 2000 a series of three meetings on the supplementary school movement; the sessions were tape-recorded with a view to using the transcripts as documentary material for a planned publication.
5. There were, in mid-2000, plans to restart the school (which is run entirely on voluntary labour, with its expenses met by parental contributions in the form of cash or other items).
6. A number of bulletins reporting on events in Guyana and offering analysis of events, were published by the 'Alliance of the Black Parents Movement, The Black Youth Movement, Race Today Collective and

Bradford Black Collective'. Bulletin no. 3, November 1979, was titled 'Guyana: The Terror and the Time'.

7. Rodney is best known for his Marxist labour history of Guyana (Rodney 1981), and for his work on African underdevelopment (Rodney 1972). Trained as a historian, he worked in Jamaica, Tanzania and Guyana (Rodney 1990 [published posthumously]).

8. This reading of the interconnection of school, police and courts under the umbrella of the state is akin to Althusser's conception of ideological and repressive state apparatuses (Althusser 1984), and the analysis of policing developed by Stuart Hall and others (Hall 1978). Structural Marxism was growing in influence on the left in Britain in the 1970s (Benton 1984). The members of the New Beacon circle, as progressives, have often been engaged with elements of the activist left, even if sometimes the contact was contentious.

9. The personnel of these three organizations were also the core membership of the BPM and BYM.

10. Several members of which were involved in the Mangrove Nine trial in 1971, which came about when nine activists were arrested and charged for assaulting the police. John La Rose, along with the film-makers Franco Rossi and Horace Ove, produced a documentary on the events surrounding the trial, which is seen in Black political circles as a watershed case in the struggles against racist practices of the British police.

11. The bookshop of the Socialist Workers Party – Bookmarks – was situated in 1997 just five minutes' walk from New Beacon in Finsbury Park. On several occasions in New Beacon bookshop I overheard Sarah or Janice direct people to go there for items not held by New Beacon. Bookmarks has been located in Bloomsbury since early 1999.

12. This section is based mainly on interviews I conducted with Michael La Rose in July and August of 1997; he was 41 years old at the time (Alleyne 1998b).

13. There is a small but growing literature on the London Notting Hill Carnival: (Alleyne-Ditmers 1997; Cohen 1993; Pryce 1990; Roussel-Milner 1996).

14. The first book-length study on the London carnival was written by social anthropologist Abner Cohen (1993). I have raised some points of difference with his account elsewhere (Alleyne 1998b). I wish here only to point out that his account is contested by a number of persons in the milieu of which New Beacon is part, notably in one review (Roussel-Milner 1996).

15. To 'lime' is a verb in Trinidadian English which means to spend time in a relaxed manner in the company of others. 'Sparrow' is the sobriquet of Francisco Slinger, one of the longest-established Trinidadian calypso singers. C.L.R. James wrote of Sparrow that he was one of the foremost creative artists in the Caribbean, on a par with Derek Walcott and Aimé Cesaire (James 1980 [1961]).

16. The 'roadmarch' is the most popular calypso of the carnival Monday and Tuesday parade in Trinidad.

17. After a particularly oppressive police presence at the 1976 carnival, so-called 'riots' erupted, in which groups of youths fought running battles with the police. There were numerous calls afterwards for the carnival to be either moved to an enclosed area or banned altogether.

18. This type of event is an illegal party in a house where you paid to get in and where food and drink were sold without a licence.

19. The membership of the Peoples' War Carnival band in 1997 comprised roughly 120 masqueraders, mostly young people, born in Britain of Caribbean or African heritage. The membership comes mainly from the London Boroughs of Camden, Hackney, Haringey, and Islington. In addition to the 120-or-so masqueraders, there are other people associated with the band, mostly adults – parents of many of the young masqueraders.

20. A T-shirt band is one where the masqueraders all wear T-shirts with the same or related emblems or designs; it is a relatively cheap and easy way to produce a masquerade band for Carnival.

21. 'Pretty mas' refers to a masquerade which is intended mainly or solely for its visual impact; the notion contrasts with 'serious mas' – a masquerade intended to convey a social or political commentary. The two are not mutually exclusive.

22. The *Time Out* Guide to the 1997 Notting Hill Carnival lists 42 masquerade bands as appearing for that year's parade. Each entry gives the name of the band, its theme for the current year, a list of the sections, the name of the band leader, the number of players, and a short paragraph of commentary. The comment for Peoples' War reads: 'A less political theme than usual, the band this year celebrates musical styles from the African diaspora' (page 67).

23. 'Victory at Cuito Cuanavale' refers to a battle in Angola in 1985, where a combined Cuban/Angolan force defeated the South African Defence Force. 'Jean and Dinah' is the title of a calypso roadmarch hit by the calypso singer whose sobriquet is 'The Mighty Sparrow'.

24. From Barbados, Antigua, Grenada, St Kitts, Dominica, St Lucia, St Vincent and Guyana.

25. Michael, on reading an early draft of this chapter, suggested that 'reality' could be a synonym for 'serious', and 'fantasy' for 'pretty' (Personal communication, 28 February 1998).
26. I borrow the terms from Miller, who developed them as part of his work on dualism in Trinidad (Miller 1994).

–3–

Activist Work and the Workings of Activism

Introduction

Organization of people, ideas and other resources is at the core of activism, whatever the ideological persuasion of the activists concerned. The New Beacon circle have in the course of more than three decades of cultural and political activist work developed analyses of the environment in which they operate, and skills in imagining, sustaining and manipulating inform-ation and networks which connect people and resources.

We may think of a symbolic economy or, more specifically, of symbolic work when assessing the praxis of activists. The creation and manipulation of symbolic resources underlay the bookselling, publishing and related activities of the circle, as we have seen. Much of their political and educational work involved the contestation of a political symbolism of race and class hierachy and exclusion.

I will employ the notion of *cognitive praxis* (Eyerman and Jamison 1991) to capture a range of issues to do with the world view of the circle and their approaches to technical and political organisation in their work. I will consider their work in terms of strategic use of various forms of capital in economic, social and cultural manifestations (Bourdieu 1986b).

In 1996 I became involved in a project to organize an archive at the George Padmore Institute. I end this chapter with a short ethnographic account of my involvement in that project, which continued to the time of writing. That account shows how the various elements of cognitive praxis and multiform capital were combined in a single project, which was itself a synthesis of the work of the circle, in that it set out to gather, preserve and eventually make available to interested parties the consid-erable quantity of documentation and other material accumulated over more than three decades of activist work. In the summary to the chapter I will present a graphical representation of how I have modelled the work of the circle.

Social Movement Activism as Cognitive Praxis

Eyerman and Jamison (1991: 94) write: 'We conceive of social move-ments primarily as processes through which meaning is constituted'. They begin with problematic social situations, wherein agents conceive and try to realize various projects. They cite C. W. Mill's *Sociological Imagination* (Mills 1959) as a textual forebear for their own work (1991: 56), which is the main reason why I find their ideas commensurate with my project, concerned as I am to render an agent-centred account. Basing their scheme on a historically-grounded adaptation of Habermas's (1972) transcendental knowledge interests, Eyerman and Jamison set up three dimensions to cognitive praxis (1991, chapter 3, esp. 68–9): a cosmo-logical dimension, a technological dimension, and an organizational dimension. I will outline each of these briefly.

The *cosmological dimension* pertains to the world view of the social movement activists in question – their sense of what is wrong with the present reality, who are the actors and interests with whom they are in alliance and to whom they are opposed, and what kind of world they wish to bring into being. Unlike Habermas's transcendental emancipatory interests, the cosmological dimension is historically grounded, and may thus be found represented in specific texts and speeches of the social-movement activists in question. From the pamphlets and printed journals of the early abolitionists, the Chartists or the more recent printed and televized campaign material of the Christian Right in the USA, to the Internet announcement to the world of the 1994 Zapatista uprising in Chiapas, Mexico, the cosmological dimension of the social movement is presented.

The second aspect of cognitive praxis is the *technological dimension*, which refers to specific issues of technique and technology employed and challenged by the activists in whom we are interested, again found in specific texts and contexts. The technological dimension has taken on great importance in contemporary social movements, as their actors have had to come to terms with the fact of late modern societies being decisively shaped by the manipulation of symbols, in what Castells (1996) refers to as the network society. Network society is characterized by long-distance trade in goods and services, transnational financial flows, communication media of global reach; all these are underlain by a complex structure of information technology – computers, telecommunications and multi-media. The ability to use these new technologies effectively is important for activists wanting to constitute, expand and sustain their projects; these new technologies are 'force multipliers' for the collective generation of knowledge in which all activists must engage in order to pursue goals for social change.

Communication technology has always been important to social movements. We must be careful to leave aside the contemporary association of this technology only with microelectronics. The development of printing technology and the spread of print literacy were both vital in constituting a context in which ordinary people could organize and pursue contentious politics against powerful entrenched interests; it is in this context that social movements enter history. The information-technology revolution is merely the latest instance of the communication revolution which is one of the defining characteristics of modernity itself, but it nonetheless offers greatly enhanced possibilities for politics of all types. In the 1980s, the personal computer brought a new dimension to the work of activists. The management of information resources such as campaign and membership lists could be automated. Desktop publishing meant that small collectives or even individuals could produce sophisticated document-ation and outreach material. Relatively cheap user-friendly camcorders and desktop video editing and production have brought greater image-manipulation power into the hands of small groups and even individuals. An important element of autonomy was introduced to the work of activism, in that activists had greater control over the production of their documentation and outreach materials. Jim Murray, a self-described cultural activist and director of the New York-based C.L.R. James Institute (to which I was attached as a researcher in 1994–1995), recalls the positive impact of desktop publishing on his own work, enabling him to produce the interdisciplinary activist journal *Cultural Correspondence* (Murray 1999). Murray recounts (personal correspondence) the early days of personal computers and desktop publishing, when these technologies meant that activists could do their work more effectively and in a more democratic fashion: decisions about the content of documents could be discussed, reviewed and changed at the last minute, just before going to press, because the requirement to have work sent to professional typesetters was eliminated. A greater variety of viewpoints could be incorporated into a document without significant cost.

The Internet, though overblown by its cheerleaders, who see only its growth in the most privileged parts of the world system, offers a whole new order of magnitude for producing and disseminating knowledge. Social-movement activists have not been slow in exploiting it (Walch 1998), though we must always be mindful of the hype surrounding 'cybersociety', and would do well to remember that ordinary people do use the Internet to get on with ordinary projects in everyday local settings

(Miller and Slater 2000). The New Beacon circle have adopted some of these new technologies and at the time of writing in mid-2001 were involved in a project to take their work onto the Internet, as we shall see shortly.

The third aspect of cognitive praxis is the *organizational dimension*, pertaining to the relations and forms within which cognitive praxis unfolds. Important here are questions of organizational form, lines of leadership, decision-making, conceptions of democracy within the movement. The question of democracy and how it might be conceived and activated has been central to both older and newer social movements; indeed, it could be argued that social movements have been created by people who felt that either they themselves, or persons on whose behalf they felt moved to organize, were being excluded from full participation in society. More bluntly, women, wage labourers, gay people, people of colour among others, have time and again organized social movements to combat structures and practices which barred them from the rights of citizenship. They moved to democratize the societies in which they lived.

In addition to drawing on these ideas of cognitive praxis, I want to look at the resource underpinning of the circle's work, not primarily in the strictest sense of material resources, but in terms of multiform capital – social and cultural.[1] Social capital consists of interlocking memberships of the persons engaged in the activist project. Who the activist is as a person is an important factor conditioning the outcome of projects. At the most basic level, fundamental social-structural characteristics such as class, gender, ethnicity, and sexual orientation can both enable and constrain the work of an activist. On the one hand, identity may be the pivotal dimension as when women engage in feminist politics; on the other, that very identity may work to constrain the individual's access to important social networks, as when Black people find themselves barred from important memberships and resources in the public sphere due to racism. Sometimes the signification of one's identity as socially excluded may be one of the most important symbolic resources in activism lending affective strength and a sense of solidarity; under other circumstances a dissident activist from a socially dominant group may turn his or her identity – as a university- educated White male, for example – to advantage in gaining access to resources which might then be used to make attempts to subvert the sources of that very privilege. Of course activists from relatively powerful social positions may engage in activism in support of rather than against that power.

Access to economic capital in the form of money and property is obviously vital to the activist project. Where such capital is sourced is crucial: where activists must depend on public resources for funding their work, they become vulnerable to changes in the political order, as when many multicultural initiatives foundered with the demise of the Greater London Council after the Conservatives under Margaret Thatcher abolished that body. Similarly, dependence on corporate funding is clearly risky for activists: while some businesses now see fit to fund certain green initiatives, their support is dependent on such initiatives not going so far as to link capitalism causally to environmental degradation. In similar vein, corporate support of the National Organization of Women and of the National Association for the Advancement of Colored People in the USA has made many feminists and Black activists wary of if not openly hostile to both these organizations. State and corporate funding often come at the risk of co-optation. In order to maintain their autonomy, activist projects generally must have access to economic capital with no strings or weak strings attached. Ideally, they should generate economic resources from within their movement or from sympathetic sources. This last point is central to the strategy of the more radical wings of the anti-globalization movements (Starr 2000).

The major theorists of the new social movements agree that such movements are centrally concerned with struggles over meaning (Castells 1997; Melucci 1996; Touraine 2000). Given this, it is clearly important that activists have command over the appropriate cultural capital, in the form of formal and informal education and training, and information in whatever medium – printed or electronic – and access to appropriate media for research and dissemination. The environmental movement is an excellent example: due to the complex cutting-edge nature of the knowledge involved in, for example, nuclear power production or genetically modified food production, green activists engaged in struggle against these must have access to advanced training and informational resources in order to assess and challenge the state and industrial interests in these fields (Diani 1995; Berglund 1998). Such knowledge cannot be acquired quickly or easily. Contemporary environmental activist projects, in order to be effective, must have among their membership experts in various fields of engineering and life and natural sciences. And given the increasing impact of information technology, it is also desirable to have at the project's disposal specialists in computers, multimedia and networking technology, in addition to people with more traditional skills in public speaking and producing and distributing printed documentation. The struggle to keep up with new information technologies, in order to match their (often better-resourced) opponents, is one of the greatest challenges to activists everywhere.

My adaptation of Bourdieu's (1986b) notions of multiform capital serves to illustrate the enabling aspects of activism. Social capital (memberships and connections) interacts with economic capital (money and property); these both interact with cultural capital. Cognitive praxis – cosmology and organizational strategy – is enabled by and in turn impacts on multiform capital. Cognitive praxis is aimed at bringing about transformations of dominant discourses and practices to which activists see themselves as opposed. They aim to transform these dominant discourses and practices by bringing to bear on them different meanings, different practices and different social relations. In this chapter, I will use these ideas to discuss the work of the New Beacon circle. The following three sections develop the cosmological, the technological and the organizational dimensions of cognitive praxis.

An Activist Cosmology

The Black Parents Movement (BPM) held a conference on 27–28 October 1979. Present were parents, teachers, and students. The core members of the circle were present. A number of documents came out of this conference, the most important of which was published as a four-page pamphlet, *Independent Parent Power, Independent Student Power: The Key to Change in Education and Schooling* (Black Parents Movement 1980). This document lays out the social analysis of the BPM, and outlines a strategy for making interventions into the education system in Britain. The BPM saw the relations between parents, teachers and students as follows:

1. Parents and students, unlike teachers and ancillary workers, are generally either unorganised or badly organised to protect or advance their own independent interests in schools or with education authorities. This is particularly true of black and white working class parents.
2. Teachers and education authorities have been *against* the idea that parents and students should actively influence what happens in schools or with the education authority.
3. Certainly, teachers will appeal to parents to help fight against the cuts; but naturally the main concern of teachers will be to protect their own jobs and working conditions.

The BPM then offer a radical analysis of schooling:

> The B.P.M. *sees schooling as the preparation and selection of workers for the labour market.* Some for better-paid factory jobs, some for professional

or middle-class jobs, others for the low-paid jobs or unemployment. The exam system is the means by which this selection is made (emphasis in original).

In this document we have the outlines of the cosmological dimension of cognitive praxis that I discussed in the preceding sections. Conflict of interest is seen as inherent to the social environment in which the school is set. The bureaucratic requirements of school management are seen to conflict sometimes with the needs of students and parents. There is an explicit criticism of instrumentalist practice in the differentiation made between education and schooling, in the title of the document and in the main text. The BPM's vision of education is as a process including but not limited to schooling as preparation for the labour market. The circle have sought to realize this holistic perspective on education in the issues which were added to the standard curriculum at the George Padmore Supplementary School: non-European history, a cultural overview of the Caribbean, Latin America, Africa and Asia, including music and cuisine.

The social reality represented in the document is one structured by social class and race, with complex relationships between the two dimensions. There is always the potential for conflict:

> The interests of parents and school teachers will not always be the same. Indeed, they are often in conflict. The same is true of teachers and school ancillary workers. *What will unite sections of all these groups will be their radical or revolutionary outlook and interest.*
>
> Equally low-paid working-class parents may see the schooling system differently from the highly-paid working parents or professional middle-class parents. At the same time, although black and white working-class parents and their children may share many of the same problems with the schooling system, black parents and school students have experienced the additional problem of racism.

What the BPM authors appear to be doing in this document is bringing their radical critique of race and class hierarchy in the wider society to bear on the specific field of education. They reject the liberal constructions of the classroom as a neutral space, of the assumed commonality of interests of parents and teachers. Where the liberal would see a partnership of parent and teacher working toward fitting the student out for productive citizenship, the BPM's analysis brings social conflict into the heart of education, pointing to the class and culture gap between typically middle-class teachers on the one hand and working-class parents and ancillary workers on the other; the gap is further widened when race becomes a factor. Unsurprisingly, the BPM's position is that a 'radical or revolutionary outlook' is needed to unite the conflicting interests. The BPM's radical critique of schooling under liberal capitalism is akin to analyses that are established in socialist humanist studies of education (Freire 1985 [1972]; Illich 1971).[2]

Out of the BPM's social analysis comes a strategic position from which to effect change in education:

> The B.P.M. also realises that radical or revolutionary teachers will always be in a minority in the system. They may be able to mobilise majority support around the struggles for wages and salaries, but they will not be able to do so on the question of the structure and authority of the education and schooling system.
>
> On the other hand the working-class parent and the working-class student is the effective majority in the school system. But their potential can only be realised if they are organised independently as parents, independently as students, and around their interests.
>
> The parent is outside the authority of the school and education authority and can mobilise political support against the system.
>
> In the course of mobilising this support it will be necessary to wage struggles against those measures employed to divide the parent from her/his own child, the student, for example in the interview with the head about complaints against the child. The child who is the parents' only informant is excluded from the interview and is only brought in afterwards to be given a good talking over by the head with the support of the parent. Situations such as these, and other situations with the police and social workers, will have to be confronted and dealt with . . .
>
> So the B.P.M. regards the alliance between parents and students as vital and fundamental to the waging of our struggles (Black Parents Movement 1980).

The transformative strategy is built around class-consciousness, consciousness of how race affects class action and perception, emphasis on the subjectivity of the student, emphasis on autonomous power of parents and students vis-à-vis the school and educational authorities. The outlines of a political world-view reveal themselves: a class-structured society, in which education is a site of conflict, exacerbated by the problems of racist exclusion. Inter-generational tension is also highlighted as a potential source of conflict, at the same time that alliances of parents and teachers are seen as necessary to finding solutions. In sum, the cosmology as represented in these documents is that of a humanist outlook which takes a view of education as broader than the strict confines of the classroom and the specific relationship of teacher-pupil.

Another important part of the cosmology of social-movement activists is the definition of who is the enemy, of who is the Other against whom they struggle. In the case of the New Beacon circle, the chief enemies are race- or class-stratified institutions and ideas. In this regard, the circle lay out in detail their own political world-view and related strategy as different from those of what they term the 'white left' – especially the British Communist Party and the Socialist Workers Party. In a 1991 'Forum Statement'[3] the following was written:

> The blacks, and in particular the organisations that later made up the Alliance, pioneered the theory/attitude that saw the lumpen proletariat/unemployeds/ semi-employeds as key groups in the making of any radical change . . . whoever was attacked by the police, courts, schools, etc., it was important to take up that struggle . . .

Then the contrast is made with the 'white left':

> This analysis and attitude was markedly different from that of the white radical left who did not support the struggles of the white working class against the police. For them these were lumpens, trouble makers and not to be bothered with. This is the heart of the weakness of the revolutionary movement in the UK, that they do not get involved in struggles on the ground.

The 1991 'Forum Statement' summed up their ideological position thus:

1. UK is a country of nationalities and ethnic groups[4]
2. Class struggle exists within each nationality and ethnic group. These were two critical points that had to be argued for in the 1970s and 1980s. Questions that arose on the basis of this analysis include:
   (a) The question of revolutionary national struggles and how they relate to working-class struggles
   (b) The possibility of forming alliances across race and ethnicity and based on class interests
   (c) The necessity for black people to organise in independent autonomous groups – autonomy of political self-expression will lead to explosion of influence (CLR) [i.e. C.L.R. James]
   (d) Internationalism – we have to make links with struggles taking place in the countries from which we came.
   (e) International cultural links developed naturally through the work of New Beacon and Bogle-L'Ouverture
   (f) For democracy and democratic peoples power. Against the conception of the Stalinist state.

What we have in this statement is an articulation of a socialist world-view which, while having much in common with established perspectives on the British Left, adds an awareness of race and ethnic issues as complicating class position. This is a modification of the classical line on class which gained in popularity on the left from the 1960s onwards, but in the case of the circle, their connection of race and class has a longer genealogy, going back to earlier anti-colonial struggles which the circle articulate through their bookselling, publishing and educational activities, and an internationalist and inclusive outlook which they sought to concretize in projects such as the Caribbean Artists Movement. The race-class perspective is one which can be traced back to the writing and work of figures such as C.L.R. James (who is referred to in the Forum Statement) and George Padmore (who is perhaps the most important symbolic figure for the circle, as we shall see shortly). We see as well in the statement a claim to relative autonomy for Black politics within broader struggles for social change. Moreover, the distancing from the Stalinist legacy is to be expected from activists who consider themselves broadly on the left yet autonomous and concerned with grass-roots organizing. There is also in this statement an articulation of the importance of culture for radical politics and social transformation: a recurrent theme which may be traced back through their earlier work.

New Beacon on the Net

After almost two years of wrangling, in early 2001 the corporate giants of the music industry won in court against Napster.com, the online 'free' music distributor. The era of 'free' music in cyberspace was effectively over. Despite claims about its revolutionary status, the Napster phenomenon was little more than privileged teenagers playing at being rebellious, with nothing like the fully thought-through ideological challenge to market relations and capitalist notions of intellectual property rights which has been developed by the open software movement.[5] The political naivety of the Napsterites is evidenced by the ease with which the likes of Sony and EMI were able to force Napster.com, MP3.com and others to become more conventional – i.e. commercial – music distributors.

While the Internet has not had as severe an impact on copyright struggles in the book business as it has had on the music industry, there is still tremendous excitement as well as more than a little unease among publishers and booksellers as to how these new technologies will affect them. All of the stakeholders in the book trade are excited by the prospect of the Internet enabling new channels of distribution and even a new medium in the form of e-books (which can be downloaded and read on a computer). Experience has differed on both sides of the Atlantic. In the

USA, where online bookselling took off first, the newcomer *Amazon.com* came to dominate the industry, forcing established operators such as Barnes and Noble to scramble to catch up. Because developments in the UK and the rest of the EU lagged two or three years behind those in the US, the established large publishers and booksellers saw what had happened in the US and had time to prepare for the onslaught of e-commerce. While Amazon's UK operation is one of the big players it does not dominate the UK online book trade as it does in the US. WH Smith and Waterstones have been able to protect their share of the lucrative UK book market by diversifying into online bookselling, as has Germany's Bertelsmann with *Bol.com*. There has been considerable consolidation in UK bookselling and publishing since the 1980s, and while a special-interest bookseller like New Beacon has an assured niche market (allied to the long history of specialist bookselling in the UK), they have had to keep abreast of these developments.

Transformation brought on by new technology in bookselling and publishing does not begin with the Internet. Desktop publishing in the 1980s gave a greater degree of autonomy to small publishers and booksellers. Roxy Harris, a core member of the circle, explained that his development of skills in desktop publishing in the late 1980s enabled the economical production of a number of publications, and also provided greater control over the production process (personal communication with author). The advent of the personal computer in that decade meant that accounting and inventory control became less labour-intensive and often more accurate. New Beacon Books, in the persons of Sarah White and Janice Durham, has invested considerable time in investigating and trialling software packages to help manage the operation. White found that in the mid- to late 1980s when New Beacon first decided to get a computer system, the available software packages were all geared towards stock control, while New Beacon's major concern was to be able to produce catalogues with item descriptions, organized according to categories. This requirement reflects the bookshop's origins as a book supply service and its continued substantial mail order business. They started with a simple off-the-shelf database system in late 1986 which produced monthly catalogues and managed book-descriptions, but did not process invoices or orders, nor did it have purchase and sales ledgers. The lack of accounting modules led to their acquiring, in 1989, a PC-based Pegasus accounting system, on which invoices were entered up manually, and purchases and sales ledgers were available. New Beacon discovered Aries – a specialist developer of bookshop and publishing management software – at the London Book Fair in 1994; they soon after started using the Aries integrated bookshop system, with accounting inventory and catalogue management in one package; they have remained with Aries since.

The use of Information Technology (IT) by New Beacon Books exemplifies a small business employing new technology in order to work more efficiently and to increase productivity, getting closer to the nirvana of business consultants and computer salespeople. The resources which they have invested in various systems over the last decade are seen to be sound investments that make it possible for the shop to be operated by two persons, and sometimes by one. What must be borne in mind is that walk-in sales are only one part of the work; processing and shipping orders are at the core of their business.

My own experience as a commercial computer programmer suggests that the bookshop, with two almost full-time and one part-time staff, is able to handle in-store sales from a stock of around 18,000 titles, a monthly list of eight to ten pages, numerous purchases and orders, shipping, etc. because they have appropriated the new technology effectively. The two full-time operators – Sarah White and Janice Durham – both possess a high degree of technical competence and are able to make quite clear requests of their IT system supplier in terms of what they want to accomplish in-house. Both have transferable IT skills acquired using their computerized sales and inventory system.

New Beacon Books set up a website in 1994 (www.newbeacon-books. com); this site is, however, no longer (June 2001) in operation. Based on a Paris web server, it was mainly a web presence, describing the shop and giving some indication of its range of stock and selected descriptions. It was the first stage of website evolution in online commerce, where an organization simply announces its presence on the Net and lists its activities, products and/or services. The first New Beacon website was not interactive, did not facilitate online searches of the bookshop's catalogue and did not have online transaction processing. Persons visiting this site could contact the shop by email; these emails were relayed from the Paris-based web administrator back to the shop's London site.

Sarah White felt that this arrangement, while useful for getting on the web initially, was not satisfactory, given advances in online retailing. She wanted to make New Beacon's full catalogue available online, allowing searches by site visitors, and ideally, the real-time processing of credit card orders. A redesigned web site with a link to the back-office (IT jargon for the shop's computerized catalogue) was needed, according to her. I offered my knowledge of IT and the Internet, and White and I proceeded to hold a number of discussions on this issue, including a visit to the office of Aries, the bookshop's software system supplier, at Cheltenham, in May 2000. In August 2000 Sarah White and John La Rose took a decision to implement a full e-commerce site hosted through Aries, with a new World Wide Web Address. This decision was made at a point where Sarah had in a sense 'normalized' e-commerce to her management of the bookshop. She talked of the proposed website as another branch of the bookshop, with the advantage of low overheads as it would not require a human operator. New Beacon's management have no expectations for exponential growth due to their website; for them it is a form of advertising in a new medium, as well as an extension of their mail-order business, with the possibility of reaching new customers. When compared to the hype over e-commerce (cooled somewhat by the decline in the technology sector in 2001) in specialist magazines such as *Wired* or *Internet*, New Beacon's steady-as-she-goes e-commerce policy seems sensible. It is in keeping with their overall strategy of confining their activities to projects which they can pursue with their own resources, and at a pace that they can control.

Autonomous People's Power

We turn now to consider the organizational dimension of cognitive praxis, by examining a general statement of strategy produced by the circle, followed by close reading of a narrative on how the circle mobilized for courtroom cases. Engagement with popular culture and politics from the perspective of the majority of people is an important element in the way the circle articulate their own praxis. On the one hand, they see themselves as offering some degree of leadership in cultural and political activities; but on the other, they insist that space must be allowed for the free expression of the needs of the mass of people in whose struggles the circle engage. This is obviously a difficult path to tread.

A 1991 'Forum Statement' (see note 3) contains an explicit account of organizational strategy for the Black Parents Movement and Alliance:

1. Organisational method: BPM/Alliance stages of action:
   (a) Start from where people are
   (b) Link individual acts of oppression with the system
   (c) Link people's ideological development with individual acts of oppression
   (d) Don't try to impose leftwing ideology on people who know their own oppression
2. Primacy of accurate honest information as the basis for political action
3. Build wide basis of support. Political action not seen as a method of recruiting members. The idea was to struggle with people in their own

interests . . . people who went through that experience could then take on
their own battles in the future . . .

4. Belief in autonomous action/organisation . . . right of youth to organise
themselves . . . for an alliance of youth and parents but not for . . . youth
to be controlled by . . . parents
5. Discipline of leading members speaking on behalf of organisation
6. Need for intellectual autonomy of members, supporters and allies
7. Need for regular meetings even when there is no campaign or particular
action on . . .
8. Financial autonomy.

This document sets out as a basic principle the necessity of starting from
ordinary people's life situations. This is a position often articulated by
activist groups of all ideological persuasions. On the left its grass-roots
outlook has emerged from the New Left struggles against the large
bureaucracies of labour and social democratic parties and trade unions.
The more radical wings of the women's and black liberation movements
in Western democracies were also characterized by a rejection of top-
down politics. Some activist tendencies indeed emerge out of this very
critique, which became central to their politics – consider, for example,
the 'workerist' rejection of vanguardism developed by CLR James and
colleagues in the *Facing Reality* tendency (James and Glaberman 1999),
and also the anarchist-inspired rejection of bureaucratic and indeed most
forms of organization in the globalized movements against capitalism
(Starr 2000). How successful these critical tendencies were in building
alternative democratic structures is a complex issue and is central to analyses
of new social movements, but is outside the scope of this book.

In the 'Forum Statement' there is articulated a tactic of grounding
consciousness-raising in people's own experience. In point 3 we see the
most distinctive aspect of their strategy: political action is seen as aimed
to empower people to engage in their own battles. There is an explicit
rejection of the recruitment of a mass membership. This style of politics
is characteristic of many new social movements and is what often sets
them apart from the mass-membership organizations of the established
labour movement. We can see the various elements of this strategy at
work more closely in the following narrative of organizing for court cases:
inclusiveness, starting from people's life situation and seeking to equip
people to engage in their own struggles.

The Black Parents Movement saw themselves as offering political
direction to legal defence campaigns. The political direction offered is
one that is premised on a need to work within the existing legal system.
This choice was significant because many young Blacks, and their parents,

had come to believe by the late 1960s that they could not expect justice from the British state authorities. Against a growing tendency to mobilize resistance against heavy-handed policing and biased court decisions in militant terms, the BPM aimed to work within the existing legal frame-work. The BPM sought to draw in the widest possible public participation in each case, as well as taking steps to bring the cases to a public beyond that which was able to join in demonstrations and appear in court. The insistence of the Black Parents Movement on working closely with the legal counsel and even giving direction is an indication of their unwillingness to cede direction of the defence campaign to expertise that was constituted outside of their own political framework. Several members of BPM had had some legal training themselves. Their approach was predicated on direct intervention into the legal process based on their own legal knowledge.

John La Rose accounts in part for the methodology of the BPM by drawing upon his own experience as a labour organizer and activist in Trinidad in the 1940s and 1950s, from which he has drawn insights into the play of power in the courtroom:

> For example, the next step is when you go to court, and everybody is in court to put pressure on the court, because the court is predisposed to believe the police. I had seen that to my shock and horror in Trinidad . . . in my only case in Trinidad, about [being charged for] obstruction that I told you about. These were not contested cases, they were police cases. [La Rose laughs.] [The policeman would say] 'yes sir, I met this man, he was drunk, and so and so, he did so and so'; 'what you have to say?' [the magistrate to the accused person] they [the accused] would be cowed by the very tone of the magistrate; 'sir . . . I didn't . . .' [the accused]; 'Come on now, speak the truth!' [the magistrate]. [Loud laughter from both La Rose and myself.] The police already told him the story, and that is the story, you get it?

> *Brian Alleyne*: yes

> Then he [the magistrate] would turn back to the police and say: 'now let me get the true story' [laughter again] . . .

> *Brian Alleyne*: The true story being the story from the policeman . . .

> That's right. I saw that . . . that is why the working-class people behind the bridge[6] would say 'cite me and relate me',[7] this was no theoretical thing: cite me and relate me came out of practical experience of court from types behind the bridge who had no lawyer. Whatever the police

had brought you there for . . . to equalize your situation you had to manufacture a case in the same way the police would manufacture a case in court. So cite me and relate me means that you will tell me what you want me to say and I will go as a witness for you to answer the police-manufactured case in the court. That was for me a great eye-opener. I had read *State and Revolution* by then already, but Lenin never mentions anything like that in the book . . .

The notion of 'cite me and relate me' points to a critical assessment of the power dynamics of the courtroom. Colonial Trinidadian policemen and courtrooms were in fact severely biased against defendants from lower socio-economic classes (Trotman 1986).

There is evidence that police and courts in Britain also were often disposed to assume the guilt of young Black defendants (Hall 1978).[8] The BPM developed an elaborate critique of the working of the police and court system for Black defendants, one which allowed for defendants being located anywhere on a continuum from innocence to guilt, all the while assuming that the courts would presume the guilt of the Black defendant:

Some of the people we were being asked to defend were prostitutes, had been thieves, engaged in burglaries and so on, but we would still defend them once we were convinced that they had not done what the police were accusing them of doing. The police would go into court and lie and the magistrate would – our then slogan was: the 'magistrates courts', we used to say this frequently all over the country – 'the magistrates courts are a rubber stamp for the police'. One of the things we learnt was the extent to which in police training the way they are taught to appear in court is a fundamental part of their training . . . When you have cases like the ones we weren't involved with, the [police would say that the accused] man was lying and getting hysterical in the court, [there] is no way of countering that [i.e. the police presentation]. Because they [the police] would say: 'sir, the man behaved hysterically'. They called all West Indian behaviour all the time hysterical, so they had to use force to control it, right? Now very frequently the behaviour of these people in court, unprepared people, was very often like that, because they were so worked up by the way the police were lying about what had happened that they couldn't contain themselves. Now we would warn our defendants, and witnesses: listen, you have prepared to go to court and you're better prepared than you would have been had you not contacted us, you have seen the solicitor, you've seen the barristers, they have the best [sic] information than most barristers and solicitors, because a barrister's case is what has been passed to him, he is briefed by the solicitor; we have acted as your solicitor . . . we have done pre-solicitor's work for you and then gone with you to the solicitor to make sure that he (the solicitor) in questioning you understands your case, and then that brief is passed on to the barrister. Now we're in the court. A court case is not what happened, but what is said in court – that is what a court case is; you think in a court case it is about what has happened, but let me just tell you, it is not about what happened . . .

The separation in this preceding passage of what is said in the court from what 'happened' is the logical consequence of the preceding critique of the reliability of police evidence. It opens up to contestation a space generally seen as secure and objective in bourgeois legal discourse and resonates well with various critiques of the notion of linguistic neutrality in police and courtroom procedure (Boyle 1994). One important doctrine of English courtroom procedure is that the jury decides on the 'facts' of the case while the judge decides on the 'law' (in the case of high courts, at least; in the lower courts the magistrate decides on both). The application of this doctrine proved highly problematic for Black defendants in English courts during the period of the 1960s to 1980s, which La Rose is discussing. The general climate of racial tension and mistrust meant that many Black defendants believed that the 'facts' of their case were likely to be read differently by majority White juries on the one hand, and Black ones on the other, with the former tending to assume their guilt. Many Black defendants did not consider majority White juries to be a collection of their 'peers'.[9] In contrast, the members of the circle who were most closely involved in court cases apparently did not share this concern over racist dynamics in the courtroom: 'I can't remember us worrying much about the composition of juries. I can't remember us discussing it' (Roxy Harris, personal communication).

La Rose brings to his account a reading of the class complexity of the Black 'community' in Britain. In so doing he sets off his position as middle-class activist from that of the mostly working-class people in whose legal defence the BPM got involved:

We had to make our young members aware – like Michael [La Rose, son of John La Rose] and so – of how this so-called lumpenproletariat behaves. For example it would often happen that they [young people accused of crimes] are macho people, you know that thing about Judge Dredd? A thousand years? But, when the police would catch them, they would begin to sing, on their comrades, their friends, each man for himself. It was not the solidarity of working-class organized struggle; it was the temporary solidarity of action, of plan, and if you're caught you're on your own, and you would do whatever you can to get out of it, at whoever's expense. So you would very frequently find that if it was more than one [accused of an offence], they'd sung on one another . . . and the police knew how to get that [the accused to 'sing' on one another] because they would say: 'well OK if you don't talk – there was what you call verbals – if you don't talk you'd spend the night here'. So [the police would] verbal [the accused] and then they would write down what they said, and then they would write a statement and then they would get them to sign it. So once [the police] came with that [statement] it made the case much more difficult, so we'd tell [those arrested]: 'don't sign nutten [sic], don't sign, say you want to see your lawyer, if you could stand the pressure', because they'd be under pressure from the police, in the station, so we tell them: 'don't sign nothing' [sic], that was our demotic language with them – don't sign nothing because once you sign there is nothing we can do beyond saying that you signed under pressure . . .

In the opening lines of the immediately preceding passage, La Rose is critical of the behaviour of the 'lumpen' element. His value orientation is toward 'organization' and 'solidarity', which are characteristic of the type of working-class struggle he approves. This may be read as a simple class prejudice. I suggest instead that we consider him taking a *political-strategic* position against individualistic responses to problems faced by working-class Black people in Britain, especially a disproportionate propensity to fall into the hands of the police. His preference for organized struggle over the temporary solidarity of plan is an indication of his trans-cendent orientation toward politics, which is in conflict with what he sees as the transient outlook of the 'lumpen element'. The transcendent orient-ation permeates La Rose's self-representation as an activist, as I will discuss in Chapter 4.

The tension between, on the one hand, La Rose's unambiguous adop-tion of a leadership role in these accounts and, on the other hand, the BPM's inclusive mode of campaigning, is a specific instance of the more general question of the relationship between leaders and other membership in activist groupings. The BPM themselves would sometimes come into contact, and even conflict, with the police during a court case. Here again they developed a methodology, according to La Rose:

We would try to get maximum attendance in court, so that the court would know that this man is not there by himself, fighting this case by himself. Not only that, we had pickets outside . . . Now very frequently when we had these demonstrations, we would not announce that we were having a demonstration, we would just go with the demonstration; in those days there was no law to prevent you from doing that, now there is a law; in those days anybody could hold a demonstration . . .

Brian Alleyne: Without special permission?

No special permission. And we would come with a car with the posters, and ten people outside the car right away. And then the police would come up and ask: who is in charge? the usual business, because that was the one they wanted to arrest or to provoke or something; we understood police behaviour, we were really expert at understanding police behaviour. And we would say: nobody is in charge, what do you want to ask, you can ask any one of us; but they would know of course, they would work out who is in charge, but we were not going to give them any assistance . . . That is the methodology and how you approach these matters. And you campaign politically around it. And that is now so common.

Many Asian and White working-class youth were finding themselves on the wrong side of 'SUS' as well. The BPM was not the only organization involved in legal defence of young people. Organizations of the established left, as well as some set up by other Black and ethnic minority groups, got involved in defence campaigns. The BPM frequently worked in conjunction with some of these, but at times differences came up over questions of ideology, strategy and tactics, as La Rose explains:

But what you find is that most of the organizations which took up these cases subsequently would not understand the politics. They would superficially carry out the elements of practice – for example, we would do nothing without consulting the families, because as we said it was their case, but they [the subsequent organizations] are so accustomed to directing the working class – whether the SWP [Socialist Workers Party] or the Communist Party, whichever party it is, or other organizations they'd formed – they would be so accustomed to directing the working class, they would want to lead it in the way that they were accustomed to, which of course did not carry the same political meaning or the same political expression as what we had been doing. . . .

While La Rose's account here is undoubtedly a partisan one, he seems clear on what he sees as the differences in praxis between the BPM and the SWP or CP: it did not follow from their being working-class, that the defendants and their relatives in these cases would take easily to following the line of seasoned left-wing militancy. More than many other activists in the area of anti-racist politics, La Rose says he was aware of the tensions between Blacks and Whites on the left, and so insisted on relatively autonomous organization, for some struggles, from the established British left-wing parties, though he was not averse to working with them in certain situations. La Rose's critique of vanguardist approaches to activist organization came up frequently in our conversations.

Building and Managing the Information Resource

The struggle over meaning is crucial to social-movement activism. In the discussion of their cognitive praxis so far, I have sought to elaborate a world-view and an organizational strategy for the New Beacon circle. In the remainder of the chapter I want to look at the creation and management of information itself as another side to cognitive praxis. One aspect to building and handling the circle's information resource is the countering of dominant meanings and reinscription of meaning from an alternative standpoint. Another is the practical organization of their informational resources. A third is their articulating and deployment of political symbols and icons. All of these relate to the management of cultural and symbolic capital. We may name this activity collectively as symbolic labour.

Meaning and Counter-Meaning

The assertion that Britain was a multi-ethnic and multicultural nation long before the arrival, in significant numbers, of Black and Asian settlers is an unambiguous reversal of the conservative and nativist notion of Britain as a homogenous White, predominantly Anglo-Saxon nation. Representations of Britain as a conglomerate of different 'nations' are long established, but these nations were traditionally confined to the Welsh, English, Scots and Irish (Crick 1995). The assertion in the 1970s that working-class parents and students should be equal partners in educational decision-making was radical and ran against the established notions of teaching and managerial expertise that then held sway in British education. The assertion that British police were sometimes biased, racist and corrupt is a bold challenge to the notion of the efficiency and fairness of the British Bobby (Hunte 1986 [1966]); though the impartial Bobby is admittedly a view held more by the middle than urban working classes (Hobbs 1988). To assert that African or Caribbean literature was as worthy of serious critical attention as mainstream English and other Western European literature was to challenge the dominant idea of the superiority of the Western literary canon of great works. This multicultural approach to literary culture, in pursuing which the circle were innovators in Britain, remains still highly contested, as do all of the above counter-meanings.

Notwithstanding the radical revisionism of their counter-meanings, it is in their overall *positive* weaving of webs of meaning, in their constitution of an alternative symbolic universe of Black and third-world literature, arts and social transformation, that we may most clearly see cultural activism at work as a symbolic activity.

The use of the images and life narratives of exemplary individuals is a feature of many social movements, old and new. The Zapatistas use the name of Emilio Zapata as a rallying figure. Ernesto 'Che' Guevara's image was an icon for the 1968 student rebellions and for numerous protest movements since. Bob Marley's image and music are important symbolic resources for a range of movements and individuals that resist bourgeois society worldwide. Of course, Guevara's and Marley's images have also been drawn into the circuits of global consumer culture because their very iconic status guarantees recognition. For many involved in women's liberation in the 1960s and 1970s Simone de Beauvoir was an icon (Okely 1986). This list could be easily extended; the point is that icons are often as important in a social movement as ideas. In their ethnographic work on local branches of the Italian Communist Party (PCI) both Kertzer (1996) and Shore (1990) point to the importance of symbols in articulating the identities of Communists. The singing of *Bandiera Rossa* (Red Flag) and the *Internazionale*, and the addressing of one another by *compagna/compagno* ('comrade') were all important markers of communist identity in Italy. Another important symbol was the figure of the 'founding father' of Italian Communism – Antonio Gramsci. The evocation of Gramsci's name and image served two important purposes: first, as mentioned above, he was the founder of the PCI and therefore the 'common ancestor' of all Italian communists; secondly, with the party's increasing distance, from the 1960s, from both the Stalinist legacy and Moscow's direction, the ability to evoke the figure of an Italian Communist militant intellectual of world renown was important in the indigenization of Italian Communism.

The New Beacon circle has its own icons and ancestors. Chief among them is George Padmore (1903–1959). Padmore was born Malcolm Nurse in Trinidad. He migrated to the United States in his early twenties and there became involved in radical student politics (Hooker 1967). Through his work with the Communist Party of the USA, he came to the notice of the Communist Party of the Soviet Union. He eventually broke with Moscow over their colonial policy – they had made a *volta faccia* on the colonial question as part of establishing détente with the West – but he remained a Marxist anti-imperialist and internationalist (Padmore 1955). Padmore articulated demands on behalf of colonial people from a humanist and universalist standpoint, one opposed to ethnic/racial nationalism. Like C.L.R. James with whom he organized the International African Service Bureau in London in 1936, Padmore was critical of Marcus Garvey's Black nationalism. Padmore's ideas and life's work – socialist, internationalist, anti-racist, humanist and universalist – are an important part of the overreaching ideational and symbolic framework for the New Beacon circle. New Beacon Books published the proceedings of the 1945 Pan-African Congress (Manchester), which was organized by Padmore (Adi and Sherwood 1995).

Over the more than four years I have known John La Rose, I have heard him make public speeches on literally dozens of occasions, to small groups at the bookshop and to larger audiences elsewhere. He always takes the opportunity to say a few words about the life and work of George Padmore. Padmore's internationalist, socialist and anti-colonialist outlook are publicly evoked by John La Rose as a model of activist praxis. Padmore's name is borrowed for the Institute in which La Rose, White and their closest associates have placed their hopes and efforts for the continuation of much of their activist work. In 1999 the circle obtained photographs of Padmore from Ghana; a special event was held to show them and John La Rose set out to have the photographs framed and displayed at the Stroud Green Road premises.

There are other important figures. Often mentioned in events constituted by the circle is Claudia Jones, for her contributions to the early struggles of Caribbean migrants in Britain and her role in initiating what is now the Notting Hill Carnival. While C.L.R. James's work is important in the circle, he appears to offer to them more in the realm of ideas than models for activism. Still, John La Rose does not miss the opportunity to talk publicly about the common Trinidadian origins of Padmore and James; in this there is a hint of patriotic pride, which should not be overestimated, given that it is James's and Padmore's *internationalism* that is almost always alluded to. In public speeches, La Rose often places these two in a context of important Caribbean figures who struggled against colonialism, such as Frantz Fanon, Aimé Césaire, Marcus Garvey, Walter Rodney and Fidel Castro.

Action: The George Padmore Institute

The George Padmore Institute will be a library, and education and research centre incorporating archives of major institutions in recent British society and history – the black education movement, the Caribbean Artists movement, the New Cross Massacre Campaign, the International Book Fair of Radical Black and Third World Books, to name just a few (from: 'George Padmore Institute Building Fund', Flyer, no date).

A major fund-raising thrust for the George Padmore Institute (GPI) and New Beacon Educational Trust[10] began in November 1993. According to the 1994–1995 Annual Report of the GPI, the organization decided to celebrate the fiftieth anniversary of the 5th Pan-African Congress (Manchester, 1945) by a series of lectures and forums. By the end of 1995, a sum of £8500.00 had been raised and used to carry out major structural strengthening work on the three upper floors of the building occupied by New Beacon Books. By mid-1996, a seminar room, toilets, and mini-kitchen had been completed. A large room on the second floor had been set aside to house the GPI archive (see Appendix Two), and plans were afoot to obtain a computer system and to create a computerized catalogue of the documents. It was at this point that I began working closely with John La Rose. I volunteered my services to assist with the computerization exercise, feeling confident in doing so because I had had nearly a decade of working with computers.

By January 1997, the facilities were ready to host the first 'Life Experience with Britain' series of public talks (the subject of Chapter 5), which ran from January to July. On 23 January, I attended a meeting of the Library and Archive sub-committee. The persons present were John La Rose, Sarah White, Gus John (a long-time member of the circle, then working as an educational consultant in Manchester), and Garry Morris (an archivist and outreach worker at the Liverpool Maritime Museum, and associated with several New Beacon circle projects since the 1980s). The main topic was the setting up of the GPI library. John and Sarah began by giving a tour of the facility – seven rooms of varying size over three floors. Impressive renovation work had been done, the details of which they explained. Impressive too were the plans for setting up the library and a computer facility. The meeting decided that priority should be given to locating all relevant documents, some of which were at homes of various members of the circle, and then to begin to take inventory of these materials. I intervened at this point with a suggestion that a simplified computer index could be made of the documents as a first stage, with a more sophisticated system for retrieval by members of the public implemented at a later stage. This was agreed. John La Rose and Gus John promised to make up a directory of where all the relevant materials were located, Sarah to look into furnishing and finishing the room in which the archive would be stored and to identify a suitable shelving system. Garry Morris promised to look into document preservation.

Based on my previous experience I recommended that a software package be used for creating an index which would allow the index format to be changed and also for the whole database to be exported to another package if future needs change. This was agreed. The other members of the archive committee were insistent that the original *political* nature of the material must be preserved. As it turned out, accepted archival practice advised that the provenance of materials be preserved (as opposed to a library, where books would be physically arranged according to a pre-given indexing schema – Dewey Decimal, British Library, Library of Congress – without regard to how, when and with what other materials a book was obtained). The reverse holds true for archives: the indexing scheme must, as far as possible, come out of the way in which the archive was physically put together by its original creators. This is what archivists call the principle of provenance. Sarah explained to me that this principle would mean, in the circle's case, that the political nature of their archives must be preserved, as the provenance of the materials lay in past political activity. This in turn meant that materials must be kept together according to the campaign with which they were originally connected.

The archive committee came up with the following scheme for organizing the materials (Figure 3.1): on the first level was the particular campaign or organization, e.g. New Cross Massacre, Black Parents Movement, etc.; at the next level down were events within campaigns or projects – meetings, court cases, demonstrations; at the third level were types of material – transcripts, notes, minutes, posters, photographs.

The virtue of this schema is that one can tell from a glance at the highest level which were the organizations and campaigns in which the circle have been involved, and successively work down to greater levels of detail. This indexing scheme constitutes in its full form a kind of information map of the work of the circle.[11]

By September 1997 a computer system had been obtained and installed, and I proceeded to design a simple database for indexing the documents in the archive. In early 1998 Sarah White and Janice Durham began working part-time at indexing documents. In 1999 the archive project picked up speed, with proper archive materials obtained, and training laid on for the GPI volunteers. On the one hand, the GPI archive project was able to benefit from the expertise of specialists from the London Metropolitan Archives and the Liverpool Museum, who made on-site advisory visits. On the other hand, professional archivists were sometimes wary of what may have seemed to them to be a DIY archiving project. Activists'

Level 1

New Cross Massacre   Black Parents Movement   International Book Fair

Level 2

Meetings Court Cases   Marches

                     Meetings, Demonstrations

                                  Workshops, Performances

Level 3

Transcripts, Memos

               Minutes, Posters, Flyers   Photos, videotapes

Figure 3.1 Scheme for organizing the GPI archive

and professional archivists' views on organizing an archive differed, as we were to learn.

The archive committee took a consistent line that their aim was to go for skills transfer and periodic consultancy. But this aim seemed at times to conflict with expertise of professional archivists, or so it seemed to Sarah White and myself as we attended seminars and got to meet members of the profession. Help with preserving documents and training GPI volunteers in conservation was obtained through the personal network of one of the trustees. Some archivists offered their expertise, provided the GPI project was done in a 'professional manner', which I took to mean having a trained archivist on hand at the GPI to ensure that standards of cataloguing and storage were adhered to. This seemed somewhat in conflict with other professional advice we received about arranging the archive, which suggested that there was no fixed schema for organizing archives, and that the norm for small archives was in fact variation. I took the insistence on having expert input by most archivists whom we consulted to be an instance of a professional group guarding their expert knowledge, and resisting its objectification and reconstitution by enthusiastic amateurs.

Sarah White eventually met one professional archivist, in early 2000, who was willing to do an initial survey on a contract basis and who pointed the GPI to short-term training programmes in archiving techniques, which is what the committee had been after for some time. This was a significant breakthrough. In early 2000 a volunteer started coming in one day a week to clean and file papers, working with Janice Durham and Claire Shepherd. During the months she was attached to the project a great deal of progress was made in terms of preserving and filing documents. She died in June 2000 after a sudden illness.

By early 2000, our discussions had resulted in the following staged plan for getting the George Padmore Institute onto the Internet.

1. Launch of Web Site

This initial phase would see a website developed which would present:

- an overview of the GPI, its history and the people behind it
- telephone, postal and email contact details, i.e. information needed to contact the institute for personal visits by appointment or to request documents to be copied and sent out by post; information on use of materials like copyright and a schedule of document delivery charges
- a summary of the GPI's holdings and resources; at this stage, users of the website will be able to look at several pages which list the nature and scope of the institute's holdings
- announcements of upcoming events at the institute
- A key feature at this stage would be to have the GPI website linked through the Internet to UK and international universities and colleges, and other institutions which would find its work useful; this would be done initially through strategic gateways, e.g. The UK Social Science Gateway, The Institute of Commonwealth Studies (London) website, the main Internet search engines like Altavista and Yahoo

2. Making a searchable database available to Web Users

Then next stage will see users of the GPI-website being able to search an online catalogue of the institute's holdings. The search results will be automatically compiled on the GPI's computer and then forwarded to the GPI staff, who would then either make the requested information ready for consultation in person at the Institute, or would prepare photocopied material for despatch by post.

3. Documents available for reading and controlled download over the Internet

This stage would see selected documents being scanned and converted to electronically readable format, then stored on the GPI's computer database. At this stage, the GPI will make a subset of its holdings available for use in the public domain in electronic form.

At this point there would also be electronically formatted documents available to callers in person at the GPI, who could access these materials through an on-site computer terminal. The security and preservation of documentation would be greatly enhanced by scanning, as the originals would then be stored free from any handling. Obviously, not all of the GPI's holdings could be scanned, nor might this be desirable, but rare items in particular would suggest themselves for scanning (from a report prepared by Brian Alleyne for the GPI, 11 April 2000).

Over the more than three-year period from 1997 to early 2001, a computer system and software were obtained for the circle's archive project; an internet connection was set up, volunteers were trained by myself in the use of Windows 95 software, and a plan for making information available over the Internet was discussed and finalized. Since Christmas 2000 a small team comprising Sarah White, Remi Harris (daughter of core circle-member Roxy Harris) and myself have been working on building the GPI's website. The work has gone slowly because we were all learning the intricacies of Web development. Plans are for a launch of the website in September 2001. What this account of my own involvement with the GPI archive project shows is the way in which my interlocutors make a gradual series of steps toward a goal. Indeed, a slogan of the circle is that they are 'slow builders and consolidators' – this can be said in a sense to be one of their guiding principles.

Summary

It is important to realize that the projects discussed in this and the previous two chapters did not take place in a strict sequence. There was considerable overlap in terms of time and personnel (see the illustration in Appendix III). A number of projects took place simultaneously: the Book Fairs were active at the same time as other campaigns involving its three founders: committees against repression in Kenya and Guyana, alliances with Nigerian activists. The New Beacon bookshop and publishing house had to be run during all of this. The sheer intensity of activity is an important feature of the work of the circle. It indicates the commitment that would have been required of the people involved, as well as resource strains which meant that some projects had to be wound down.

The activism of the New Beacon circle involves accumulating and managing various forms of social, economic, cultural and symbolic capital, which enables and is impacted upon by what I see as their cognitive praxis. I illustrate this in Figure 3.2.

My adaptation of Bourdieu's (1986b) notions of multiform capital serves to illustrate the enabling aspects of the work of the circle. Their social capital (memberships and connections) interacts with their economic capital (money and property); these both interact with cultural capital in the form of literature, personal narratives and education. The circle's cognitive praxis – their cosmology and organizational strategy – is enabled by and in turn impacts on their multiform capital. Their cognitive praxis is aimed at bringing about transformations of dominant discourses and practices of racism, national chauvinism and social exclusion in British society. In their symbolic labour of generating meanings and counter-meanings they aim to transform these dominant discourses and practices by bringing to bear on them different meanings, different practices and different social relations.

I stress that the members of the circle possess considerable symbolic capital in the sense that much of their social and cultural is socially recognized and legitimized by the very dominant discourses and practices which they seek to transform. I must stress also that this implies that in their own social persons and wider social relations, the members of the circle may achieve positive social recognition *without* a cognitive praxis aimed to bring about social transformations. They *choose* to act, to be activists; that choice is *not* explicable solely in terms of the structural relations among dominant discourse and practice, multiform capital and cognitive praxis as I have illustrated these here. It is through their narration of their own and use of other people's personal narratives that we gain some clue as to what motivates them to engage in activism. This takes us to the second part of the book, where the focus will be placed in the next two chapters on personal narratives.

Notes

1. The approach to thinking activism in terms of resources which I am using here is not derived from the well-known school of resource mobilization theory (Eyerman and Jamison 1991: 23–7); my aims are more modest. I restrict myself to borrowing Bourdieu's (1986b) concept of capital as multiform and capable of being converted from one form to another.

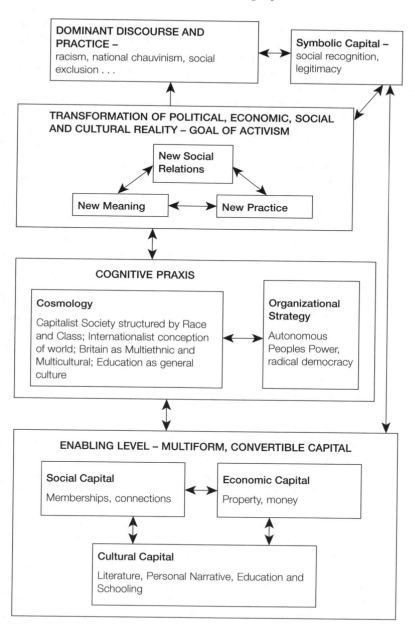

Figure 3.2 Relationship between Cognitive Praxis and Multiform Capital

2. The name and ideas of Paulo Freire came up in interviews and at discussions at which I was present. Apart from Coard's (1971) study, in the 1970s activist journals such as *Race Today* and *Black Liberator* published pieces on race and class conflict in the classroom context (for example Cambridge 1971; Dhondy 1978; Leon 1971).

3. I will quote extensively from the 'Forum Statement' because it resulted from wide discussion in a number of meetings (the minutes of which I have read), and because it results from the circle reflecting, in 1991, on more than two decades of activism. The forum was the body which took over the running of the International Book Fair after the withdrawal of the inputs of the *Race Today* Collective and Bogle L'Ouverture Books. The New Beacon circle – core members and close associates – were the majority of the members of the forum. The statement came out of meetings held earlier in 1991. According to 'Notes of Forum meeting held on Sunday 10th November 1991', the agenda for that day was 'Forum Statement', and 'European Action/Germany'. Present were: Gus John, Sarah White, John La Rose, Roxy Harris, Michael la Rose, Eleanora Henry, Irma La Rose, Leroy Coley, Barbara Duncan, Garry Morris, Suresh Grover. Apologies: Ian Macdonald, Linton Kwesi Johnson, Akua Rugg, Pat Harris, Ali Hussein, Dave Feickert, Clem John.

4. A frequently articulated position, it is always elaborated by members of the circle to stress that these nationalities and ethnicities include Saxons, Celts, Scottish, Irish and Welsh. The arrival of Africans, Asians and Caribbeans is seen as adding to what was already a complex ethnic reality.

5. The comparisons of Napster's model of facilitating free music to the Open Software model are ill-informed: while they provided outlets for new artists who wished to circumvent the existing channels of music distribution, a large part of the activity of Napster and its ilk was in effect facilitating the illegal copying of music; unsurprisingly, this brought them to the attention of those responsible for policing copyright. By contrast, the focus of the free software movement (free as in free speech, rather than free beer) is on producing computer software which people may use, distribute and modify without charge. One would in any event be excused some scepticism towards students at elite private US universities claiming that they were resisting corporate culture by downloading music from Napster. Unlike 'free' music, free computer software allows an autonomous revenue stream: end-user support. Some companies in the open software field make a considerable living by charging for support rather than selling their software

initially. Crucially, the open software movement is not built on copying and redistributing commercial software products. Many green and left-wing activists have chosen to use open software in support of their campaigning work because it moves outside the capitalist circuits of commercial software. For a full discussion of the open software phenomenon see Moody (2001).

6. 'Behind the bridge' is the folk term for the eastern part of Port of Spain: known to middle-class Trinidadians as an 'immigrant' quarter (where persons from the less developed economies of the eastern Caribbean moved in large numbers in the hope of finding work) and a place where 'respectable' people should not go. This is the part of the city where some popular oppositional cultural forms such as the steel band had their origin (Steumfle 1997).

7. Trinidadian colloquial term connoting a 'manufactured' alibi.

8. Mistrust of the police by many British Blacks continues. In April 1998 a special inquiry was held into the death of Black teenager Stephen Lawrence, who was allegedly stabbed to death by a gang of White youths in 1994. Campaigners insist that the attack was racially motivated, and more seriously, they accuse the police of racism in their handling of the case. While the case is widely seen to have opened up a much needed debate on institutional racism, as of June 2001 no progress had been made toward finding those responsible for the killing.

9. Courtrooms are no more immune to the power effects of race, class and gender than any other social setting; indeed, critics suggest that such social differentiations may be heightened in the courtroom setting (Allen 1987; Ireland and Laleng 1997, esp. chapter 4).

10. The New Beacon Educational Trust is a registered charity set up in 1991. According to its Prospectus, its aim is to 'advance the public in matters relating to the political, social and cultural history of persons in the United Kingdom of Caribbean, African and Asian descent'. To achieve these objectives it plans to 'establish and develop a library and resource centre; provide facilities for study and research and publish results of such research where possible; provide facilities for study and practice of cultural forms including dance, theatre, music, poetry and drama'. The 'George Padmore Institute is the name of the Trust's library, educational resource and research centre'.

11. At the time of writing in June 2001 it is the basis of an interim computerized index of over 1200 items. In May 2001 a decision was taken to invest in a specialist archival software package, as part of a wider project to seek funding for the next three to five years' operations of the GPI archive.

−4−

Slow Builder and Consolidator: A Life History of John La Rose

The pleasure and paradox of my own exile is that I belong wherever I am.

George Lamming, *The Pleasures of Exile*

Unlike Fukuyama I think that history, the story, has no end and that man is lasting and enduring. Home, then, is a kind of solid moving foothold, in the imagination, in the dream, in the uneasy voyage of hope, in the uncertain complexity of fulfilment. There is no fixity nor can there be any.

John La Rose, 'Everchanging Immanence of Culture'

Introduction

I first met John La Rose in Trinidad in July 1994, at the first Assembly of Caribbean Peoples, which brought together trade unions, NGOs and activist groups from the Spanish-, English-, French- and Dutch-speaking Caribbean. The assembly was organized in part by the Oilfields Workers Trade Union of Trinidad (OWTU); I was a volunteer worker for the event. I knew that La Rose had republished C.L.R. James's novel *Minty Alley* in 1969, and that he had founded a radical bookshop in London. I told La Rose of my interest in James and of my intention to research James's life and work. La Rose was encouraging; we chatted for twenty minutes or so, while hundreds of people swirled around us in one of the halls of the convention centre. We parted. I promised to keep in touch and to visit his bookshop when next I was in London. At the time I was on the way to starting graduate school in New York. By July of 1996, I had left the USA for the UK, to become a research student in social anthropology at the University of Cambridge. I had begun fieldwork in London, then conceived around researching life histories of migrant writers. La Rose agreed to begin a series of life-history interviews with me. These continued for more than a year. Since 1999 I have been in regular contact with La Rose. Our conversations continue.

On numerous occasions since we first began to work together La Rose said to me and to others in my presence that he was averse to giving interviews about himself, his associates and his associates' backgrounds. He pointed out to me though, that he has given 'lots of other general interviews on radio, in newspapers, journals and on television'. He said as well that he had agreed to work with me mainly because I had come recommended by his close friend Susan Craig – who had taught me sociology when I was an undergraduate in Trinidad in 1989–1991. Craig had stayed at the London home of La Rose and his partner Sarah White in the late 1960s, when she was engaged in fieldwork for a thesis on the Black Power movement in Britain. It was Craig who had first brought La Rose and his associates to my attention.

In our early meetings, La Rose asked many questions about my own background: who my parents were, where I went to school, what were my political and intellectual interests. He seemed to attach some significance to my having attended the same boys' grammar school that he had himself attended four decades earlier. We had established some commonality of interest fairly early in our meetings. When I told La Rose that my parents had been keenly interested in the 1950s nationalist movement in Trinidad, taking part in a numerous rallies and attending the famous public lectures on colonial history given by Eric Williams, and that my father had been a working-class autodidact who had educated himself about political theory and history, La Rose responded, 'of course, I know that type of person well'. He asked probing questions about history, politics and literature in our early conversations. Sometimes I could answer straightforwardly, other times not. I believe I was assessed by La Rose who early in our meetings decided that I was a suitable person with whom to share his life story. I believe too that our having met at the Assembly of Caribbean Peoples, and my having been a volunteer for one of the trade union organizers – the Oilfields Workers Trade Union, for whom La Rose is European representative – contributed favourably toward my gaining access to La Rose and his associates.

Where La Rose was situated in his own life cycle impacted on our interaction as well. When we began to work together in July 1996 he would have been 68, and had been through more than one serious heart attack and coronary by-pass surgery. He had by then retired from much of his public work. He thought carefully of the numerous requests for interviews he received, refusing most of them. I believe that I began to work with him at period in his own life when he found himself in circumstances that led him to reflect on his life and work.

Slow Builder and Consolidator

What did we want from these conversations, John La Rose and myself? For my part, I was a doctoral student in social anthropology and La Rose was an expert informant on the milieu in which I was interested; or rather, I came to realize that he had long experience as an activist, and in the course of our early conversations I redefined my research project from a study of C.L.R. James to a study of La Rose and his closest associates. There was the question of convenience and access: he was willing to be interviewed, made the time and provided a comfortable setting in his home. Then there was affinity: we got on well from our first meeting. What did he want and get from our meetings? I can only sketch an answer negatively. What he did *not* need was someone to tell his story to the world. That should be obvious given the projects I discussed in the preceding chapters. Unlike some of my more politically engaged colleagues in that first fieldwork period of 1996–1998, I did not see myself as giving a voice to the oppressed. I was certainly not 'studying down'. Moreover, I was not trying to write a celebratory, feel-good account of Black politics; indeed, one of the reasons I wanted to work with La Rose after I had had my first insights into his milieu, was what I perceived as his profound distance from racial-nationalist politics. (I had been drawn to C.L.R. James's life and work for the same reason.) At the same time, I was not 'studying up' in the sense of trying to penetrate a powerful and elite milieu as a relatively powerless outsider. Perhaps *studying across* would be the best notion. Reflecting on the four years in which I have known La Rose and White, the notion of research as dialogue seems most apt to capture the process out of which this book emerged. La Rose was older and vastly more experienced politically than I was. He was no stranger to the sphere of intellectual activity, though he made a distinction between himself as a politically engaged intellectual on the one hand and on the other academics, whom he saw as using social reality to generate ideas, as opposed to his own activity of bringing ideas to bear on projects of social transformation. For these reasons I was spared the young (usually Western or Western-educated) anthropologist's fear, or perhaps vanity, of occupying a forbiddingly-privileged standpoint vis-à-vis his or her interlocutors.

The above notwithstanding, I was not the sorcerer's apprentice. It would be fruitless to speculate as to how my relationship to La Rose might have been shaped if I had come to him as a trainee activist, rather than as a research student. Throughout my early (i.e. in 1996/1997) conversations with La Rose, I represented myself as no more than a graduate student with an interest in cultural activism and social movements. I must admit however, that in the course of the last few years I have indeed come to learn something of the workings of activism, but I have learnt as a scribe rather than as a practitioner-to-be.

A Portrait of the Young Activist

John La Rose was born in Trinidad in 1927 to a Creole[1] middle class family; he now lives in North London. My purpose here is to construct interpretively his life history; in order to do this it is necessary, though not sufficient, to understand the social and cultural context in which a subject of biography – La Rose in this case – lived, and to seek insight into how that context was experienced by the subject. For John La Rose's life history, it is necessary to come to grips with the social and cultural history of the society out of which he came: for his formative and early adult years that context is Trinidad in the early decades of the twentieth century; for his middle to later years the context is Britain. This spatial and temporal delineation of the context for La Rose's life story is not an arbitrary choice: it comes out of our encounter, wherein I as interviewer was cued into the space-time contexts of the life story by the articulation of times and places which La Rose in telling his life story used as organizing points and signposts.

The Social Structure of Colonial Trinidad

At the turn of the twentieth century in Trinidad there was a close correlation between 'race' – marked off by skin colour – and social class: while the middle and upper classes were occupied by a cross-section of persons, but with Whites disproportionately present, the lower strata were overwhelmingly peopled by those of African or South Asian descent. A decisive form of segmentation, as distinct from stratification, in colonial Trinidad had to do with that between African and East Indian-descended elements. This segmentation has led some to describe the society, as others in the Caribbean, as plural (Smith 1965). Others have referred to it as a Creole stratified society characterized by a three-way struggle between White, 'interracial' or 'mixed', and Black (Braithwaite 1975). Some have argued that the three-way struggle was fundamentally a class struggle even if understood by the participants through an ideological lens which focused on race and colour, while others have posited a scenario of co-determined class and race/colour stratification (Brereton 1979; Ramdin 1982). The consensus in the literature on Trinidad's social structure in the early twentieth century is that it was a Creole stratified society with colour and social class highly correlated.

The chief route to social mobility for non-European-descent persons in twentieth-century colonial Trinidad was secondary education followed by some kind of career in the civil service, commerce or, if they managed to acquire higher education, the professions (Campbell 1986). Few coloureds and virtually no Blacks had access to the capital required to enter commerce on any but a small scale, and the doors of polite colonial Trinidadian society were barred to shopkeepers and tradesmen. By dint of grinding study, a young lower-class Black or Asian boy (for the avenues at the time were open mainly to males) could win a scholarship to one of the island's secondary schools where for a five-to-seven-year period the youngster would be exposed to a British-style grammar school education which would fit him out to take up a clerical position in the colonial civil service. Or if he were very 'bright', he might win one of two or three Island Scholarships and then proceed to England to study at university for a profession (Williams 1969).

The colour-coded class struggle of colonial Trinidad manifested itself in the sphere of culture as struggle over signification of Black and coloured identities. In parallel, the struggle of Asian-descent persons to claim cultural space was gathering momentum. Struggles over ethnic identity are inscribed in the writings of the free coloureds of the early nineteenth century (Campbell 1992), of the progressive Black humanist John Jacob Thomas (1969 [1889]) in the latter part of that century, and of the *Beacon* circle of the 1920s (Sander 1988). These writings are literary artefacts of cultural struggle. Another line through which these cultural struggles may be traced is the history of the Carnival (Cowley 1996). For much of the island's post-Columbian history, whatever cultural production there was in the public sphere was based in unimaginative imitation of the mores of European, especially French and British, 'high' culture. While the *Beacon* circle constituted the first serious intellectual challenge to the Eurocentricism of the educated strata in Trinidad, they were themselves from those very strata and inherited from them much of their general cultural orientation. Theirs was a gradualist critique of colonial society, not a revolutionary challenge. Nonetheless, by the 1930s strong currents of class struggle, anti-racist struggle, and anti-colonialism were impacting on the social formation of colonial Trinidad.

La Rose's early life

Arima – the small town in Northern Trinidad where La Rose was born and raised – holds an important place in his life story. He and his friends were proud of their orderly little town:

> We were Arima nationalists, we loved Arima, there was no place like Arima! The Dial [a clock-tower] was the symbol of Arima, the heart, we're talking about old Arima. A town of about three thousand people. And our families, especially my family, were very much founders of that kind of place.

The centre of the town was the 'Savannah' a large grassy area enclosing a horse-racing track and cricket and football pitches. People of all classes would stroll around the savannah on an evening. Arima is a place to which La Rose returns often in his personal narrative. Connected to it are childhood memories as well as his first social awareness. It was a microcosm of Trinidad society in the early decades of the twentieth century: there was a White elite, a coloured middle class, and a Black and Asian lower class. Arima has a long tradition of Black self-assertion, in a space where Whites were dominant, but not to the extent as in the capital.

In a memoir published in 1973, La Rose inscribed his memories of the social structure of Arima. The Whites are at the apex, with a tight hold on the institutions of civil society:

> They formed their own society together with the doctor and the engineer whose official quarters were next to their homes. The doctor and the engineer were white throughout my early years. Though the engineer changed more often than the doctor, his replacement was always another white man wearing shorts and Baden Powell stockings. As I approached my teens, the doctors became brown and black and Indian and splintered their earlier idyll. Though the white people were few, they were reinforced from other parts of the town by the de Verteuils, the police inspector, the Anglican minister and the Catholic priest (La Rose 1973: 50).

Across the Savannah from the homes of the Whites the Black poor lived:

> Where the beaten, foot-made, water-made paths led to Cocorite and Malabar and where it led to 'Over the Line', the train line . . . The roads were dirt. The houses sat squat on the ground covered with thatch. The structures were made of tapia.[2] Only a few box bungalow houses prevailed. One wonders what tradition of consciousness was at work. How had discontinuity devoured imagination and memory. Here the Middle Passage landed its indigestible cargo (La Rose 1973).

In the same memoir La Rose alludes to a distancing of his coloured middle-class milieu from that of the Black peasantry:

> [And] Victoria was a queen, one of whom we regularly asked God to save. And she, with William Wilberforce, ranked high in our esteem, because 'Queen

Victoria and Wilberforce *freed the slaves*'. These words were axiom and proverb. They detached us from the source and wellspring of an ancient affliction which lay at the root of our trying ambiguity. No one claimed ancestry from enslaved Africans. Not then, in Arima (La Rose 1973).

La Rose's ethnic self-representation is heterogeneous: one component is European, derived from the Spanish and French cocoa planters who formed the elite of Trinidad in the eighteenth century; another is native American; a third source is African. By the time of writing his memoir, La Rose had clearly come to his own understanding of the internalized conflict over the African elements in his coloured/Creole identity. Yet there remains some trace of the objectification and distancing of the African, as indicated by the last-but-one sentence in the quoted passage above: 'no one' can be read as 'no one from the coloured middle class'.[3] La Rose's family were from that coloured middle class; they owned estates and some had acquired professional education. The young La Rose, by virtue of this, had access to the upper strata and spaces of Arima society. At school and at play he mingled with the Whites and others of his own background, and those few Blacks and Indians who had made it over the educational hurdle. His own curiosity led him to 'cross the line' into the milieu of the Black and Indian lower class.

The world over the line, the world of the other, was also the world of the East Indian-descent peasantry:

I had known 'Over the Line' before I set foot in its particular geography. It had come to my mother's house with milk cans, borne on orhnis, patiently ladling its measure of milk for pouatique. Offering cucumber, eddoes, tomatoes, chives, watercress as bargains. Its style of dress particular, its style of speech nasal with Hindi. Ankles and wrists hugging thick silver bracelets, tight. Sometimes nose pieces were gold. Skirts billowed and fell to the ankle like the Virgin Mary's . . . Yacub, my good school friend, took me there. It was different. I felt comfortable and warm. This was the world of grass-knife and the animals, the trace, the smell of cowdung; houses built of earth remained intimate with the ground; not paint but white mud; the colour held fast. Clusters of long thin beflagged bamboo gollettes stood guard outside houses; prints of the monkey god and the lota; the Hindu temple and Muslim mosque where Mr Aziz said prayers, on the hour, facing Mecca. Food was eaten by hand; dhal and roti tasted nice. Elders, not so trusting as we, smelled treachery (La Rose 1973).

The inscribed exoticism of the 'nasal speech', the jewellery, the unfamiliar houses and food, indicates the cultural divide perceived by La Rose to separate himself from the world of Yacub. The only indication that the encounter was problematic for East Indians is the reference to the 'treachery' smelled by the mistrustful elders. The Creole/Indian divide, and the problems attendant upon attempts by Trinidadians to bridge it, is a recurrent figure in the imaginative literature of Trinidad. In Sam Selvon's novel, *A Brighter Sun* (Selvon 1952), the proletarian Black couple, Joe and Rita, encounter problems in coping with the home life of Tiger and Urmilla, the Indian teenage couple with whom they become friends; chief among the misunderstandings are those over food and the arrangement of living space. In Earl Lovelace's *The Dragon Can't Dance* (Lovelace 1981), Pariag, a man of Indian descent, comes into value-conflict with the Blacks on the 'Hill', who interpret his small entrepreneurship as intended to mark himself off as somehow better than they.

La Rose recalls of his mother: 'My mother was a Roman Catholic and taught at the RC school. She taught all that generation of Arimans who became famous, at the Arima girls' RC school'. Being a schoolteacher had a special meaning in Trinidad in the early decades of the twentieth century: virtue, public respectability and a salary.

> [Arima] was a cocoa place, cocoa was king as they said in those days, and so we [La Rose's family] would have come over from Venezuela in some earlier period, and would have been involved in cocoa. So there is a Venezuelan-Trinidadian connection. Arima is a Spanish-speaking part of Trinidad to a certain extent, and also a Carib part of the country.[4] And [F.E.M.] Hosein and my father were connected with the Caribs. You've heard of the Santa Rosa festival? each year at the festival they [the Caribs] used to put bamboo things in front of my father's house; when I was growing up they always had it, and also in front of F.E.M. Hosein's house. Both of them must have done some special things for the Caribs, and this was their way of honouring them. It continued to be done for quite some time until my eldest sister told them: listen, we the children have not done anything for the Caribs, our father did, and there is no reason you should continue putting it for us.

La Rose recalls his father as playing an important role in Arima:

> He had been trained as a teacher, but he had a bad temper, he couldn't deal with those kids . . . so he never went along with teaching. Though in my family there are teachers, but he never went along with that. He went into business, and he also went into law, because land meant law; and he opened up a small law office in Arima and he had people working with him . . .

> *Brian Alleyne*: As a solicitor?

No. He was not a solicitor, he was a businessman who had to deal with the law because land law was important to him. And all the Arimans were interested in land, all these people were involved in land. My father had estates at that stage, [though later] he lost his money with the collapse of the cocoa and so on. But he was part of that Arima. So he would have helped a lot of people who would come to him and his solicitor and barrister.

La Rose received his secondary education at Roman Catholic St Mary's College, becoming a boarder in Port of Spain and travelling back to Arima on weekends. St Mary's was one of two elite secondary schools in Trinidad that were modelled on the English public school, and established in the mid-nineteenth century. The other elite school was Queen's Royal College, set up by the colonial authorities along more secular lines. Both St Mary's College and Queens' Royal College pursued the same syllabus, leading to the external examinations of the Oxford and Cambridge secondary and higher school certificates, which were roughly equivalent to O levels and A levels. C.L.R. James wrote of his time at QRC in the second decade of the twentieth century:

> I spent eight years in its classrooms. I studied Latin with Virgil, Caesar and Horace, and wrote Latin verses. I studied Greek with Euripides and Thucydides. I did elementary and applied mathematics, French and French literature, English and English literature, English history, ancient and modern European history. I took certain examinations which were useful for getting jobs. I was fortunate enough to go back to the same school for some years as a teacher and so saw the system from within. As schools go, it was a very good school, though it would have been more suitable to Portsmouth than to Port of Spain (James 1963: 37).

La Rose pursued a similar course of study. Early in our meetings, on learning that I had myself attended St Mary's College, he commented:

> My education at St Mary's gave me an assurance in dealing with people and situations that was useful here in England. I would meet grammar-school-educated people, and I felt completely at ease in their company. Sometimes I would have to tell them about the kind of schools we had in Trinidad.

On leaving school, La Rose was a secondary schoolteacher for a time at the same St Mary's College. Later on, he became a business executive, all the while establishing and deepening links with the 'radical political, cultural and trade union movement'. We get some clue as to why La Rose should have tried to combine a respectable career as a (quintessential bourgeois) business executive with trade-union politics if we consider his account of his earliest political activity:

> I became interested, as a youngster, in something called the Phoenix Literary and Debating Society [PLDS] in Arima – there were many literary and debating societies at a stage in the development of our culture and civilization . . . And like a Phoenix it would die and subsequently be revived. So when I was a youngster, we revived [it] . . . We revived the PLDS and then we took part in the Arima elections, we fought under the CIO – the Citizen's Improvement Organization. When we formed the CIO, we were two young boys whom Arimans admired, and we were continuing the spirit of Arima as we saw it. And therefore we thought we should enter local politics, and we studied the constitution of the Arima Borough Council, which was a Charter granted by Queen Victoria in 1889 . . . We formed the CIO to take part in the elections, and unbelievably we won the elections. I amaze myself even thinking about it. I was about eighteen at the time, and Nello[5] was just over twenty-one.

Having won, Nello duly took a seat on the Municipal council. The success in that election was an 'epiphanic'[6] moment for La Rose, one which made the possibility of taking part in political activity become a reality. La Rose accounts in part for his early interest in social issues by pointing to his 'social Catholicism':

> we had this history of social Catholicism; I was very much a social Catholic, besides being a religious Catholic, in the sense that I wanted to be a missionary in Africa . . . [we had] a strong element of Roman Catholicism dedicated to spiritual as opposed to material culture. I'd seen people making money who were very dishonest, and corrupt, and that was one way of making money, but there was no reason why they should be respected because of that.

At this stage in his development – mid- to late-teenage years – La Rose was being exposed to ideas of social responsibility that were egalitarian and at the same time permeated by paternalism – as exemplified in the wish to be a missionary in Africa. This wish was planted and nurtured by La Rose's schooling at St Mary's College, where he was encouraged by the teacher-priests to contemplate whether he had a 'vocation'. La Rose points out that while recognizing himself as a Black person at this time, it was not common for someone of his class background to identify closely with Africa: 'I was aware of Africa but felt very little connection to it – it was a place where I wanted to go as a missionary.'

Tensions developed between his Catholic upbringing and his growing knowledge of socialist and anti-colonialist ideas. Even a 'social' Catholicism was not able to accommodate La Rose's attempts to reconcile his own comfortable home life with the poverty that was also part of Arima. Engagement with socialist ideas would propel him into another phase in his development. La Rose locates a pivotal point in his engagement with socialism around his friend Neville Giuseppi's lending him a book by James Maxton on the life of Lenin (Maxton 1932): 'this book opened my eyes to a new conception of politics, to a new conception of the world, which was not grounded in a kind of liberal colonial politics'. At the same time he and a number of close associates were reading what was available on the history of Trinidad and the Caribbean. Of particular importance was the work of J.J. Thomas (the nineteenth-century Trinidadian intellectual whose work was republished by New Beacon as I discussed in Chapter 1):

> We studied Thomas, *The Theory and Practice of Creole Grammar*, particularly. We who were interested in the pre-English-speaking folklore of Trinidad, had to study Thomas, as a figure who made this enormous contribution in the field of Creole linguistics.

The interest in Creole linguistics and folklore did not mean that 'high' culture was neglected. La Rose studied the piano for a short time. He recalls attending classical music recitals at the British Council in Port of Spain, in the company of his then partner, who was training to become a concert pianist. In talking about the importance of culture for his lifetime of political work, La Rose stresses that for him, distinctions between high and popular culture are of no significance. This emphasis is in keeping with his conception of culture as knowledge and skill which generally serve democratic ends in that they enable people to make sense of their lives through the exercise of creativity – a humanistic perspective which was characteristic of the Caribbean Artists Movement and which underpinned the International Book Fairs.

La Rose at this time – the early to mid-1950s – was an active participant in several study groups on local history, Marxism, and literature. La Rose knew of the earlier impact of the *Beacon* circle, and of the first works of C.L.R. James and Eric Williams, works that were rethinking colonial history and were becoming more widely known, in particular *Capitalism and Slavery* (Williams 1964) and *The Black Jacobins* (James 1980 [1938]). La Rose recalls: 'We were trying to fill a gap in our history for the period between 1838, when slavery was abolished, and the 1930s labour unrest and reforms. The early writing of Arthur Lewis[7] and Eric Williams began to fill that gap. We read avidly'. The inter-war decades in Trinidad saw many persons questioning both the failings of capitalism and the colonial order (Ramdin 1982; Singh 1994). The Trinidad Working Men's Association, which dates from the 1890s, became radicalized under the new leadership of Captain Andrew Cipriani[8] after the First World War, and became the Trinidad Labour Party. La Rose points out (conversation with author) that 'further radicalization occurred from the newly emerging trade union and cultural activism'. The Negro Welfare Cultural and Social Association (NWCSA) was articulating a radical programme (Reddock 1994). The Black nationalism of Marcus Garvey was making large numbers of converts. La Rose remembers that that period of ferment in the 1930s loomed large in his consciousness as a young person. The memory is not of his own direct experience of the unrest: born in 1927, he was too young to have been an active participant; he was informed by older people in the circles where he moved as a young adult, and who had participated in the 1930s agitation and shared their memories with him. La Rose remembers Jim Barette[9] to have been a remarkable oral historian of that period and someone from whom he learnt a great deal about Trinidadian labour history.

La Rose frequently pairs the terms 'political' and 'cultural' in his personal narrative. He often said to me: 'I came to politics through culture'. He was involved, with his 'close friend and comrade' Lennox Pierre (a solicitor, folklorist and musician) in attempts to organize the Trinidad steel bands into more cohesive units, and away from a self-destructive trend towards fighting against one another instead of against the colonial authorities and their local class allies who sought to limit their cultural expression. Then as now, the steel band was a musical expression of the Black Trinidadian working class, born in the slum yards of east Port of Spain (Steumfle 1997). La Rose was one of a number of progressives (Belgrave 1993) who sought to bring an informed left praxis to these ghetto musicians and their rebel music, to 'win them over to a new political and cultural position by acknowledging their musical genius, by promoting conciliation between rival bands and by opposing their suppression by the colonial authorities'. La Rose, Pierre and others sought to forge stronger links between the pan-players and the trade-union movement. La Rose had as well had early contact with the Carnival in Trinidad but there was some tension between his family's Catholicism and the carnival revelry, even though a paternal aunt and uncle were practising carnivalists:

Though we came from a very strong Catholic family, my uncle from Arima and my aunt – they played mas'. I would run away to play in the night, on carnival night in Arima – we played mas at night . . . so I used to jump up like everybody did, but my father and mother were both . . . my mother was very Catholic, was very religious and so on, so she wasn't part of carnival. But my aunt and uncle on my father's side, they were part of that.

In 1948 the Marxist study group of which he was a member joined with the Negro Welfare Cultural and Social Association – no longer as powerful as it had been in the 1930s – to form the Workers Freedom Movement – an organization dedicated to struggle for an improved standard of living for the working class. Trinidad saw a ferment against the colonial order in the 1930s and again in the 1940s, as the colony was buffeted by the waves of international capitalist restructuring. This period saw the development of an organized and articulate movement for independence from Britain. La Rose became involved in this movement, as an activist in the West Indian Independence Party – formed in 1952 – which agitated for a federal self-governing Anglo-Caribbean, and for a democratic socialist society (Kambon 1988; Ramdin 1982). He paid a heavy price for his involvement in socialist politics. After a 1953 trip to Eastern Europe as a delegate to the World Federation of Trade Unions Congress, he found himself blacklisted as a dangerous subversive when back in Trinidad: the cold war played itself out in the tiny English colony of Trinidad, as it did on the wider world stage. That 1953 trip was to prove another important turning point in La Rose's life story. After travelling throughout Eastern Europe, he and Lennox Pierre, radical lawyer and 'comrade', came in La Rose's words 'to realize that what we were seeing was not socialism' (personal communication). This realization spurred him to rethink the socialist project and to develop an 'autonomous socialism', a conception of which has stayed with him throughout his life. After 1953 La Rose found himself unemployable, and moved to Venezuela, where he had family and other connections, and where he worked as a schoolteacher and continued his political, cultural and trade-union activities.

The life experiences and world-view that La Rose sees himself as having brought with him to Britain are encapsulated by his assertion, frequently made in various different contexts, that

I was not formed here in Britain, I was formed in the Caribbean, especially in Trinidad, an industrial society. Because of the complex little society that it was I had learnt much about the world by growing up there. We had the whole world there: Africa, Asia, Europe, the Americas; peasants, workers, and industry. It was all there.

La Rose uses his memories of Trinidad as a lens on the world; in narrating his life story he is in ongoing engagement with his memories of its social and cultural history. His imagination of Trinidad is a dialogical one: his past there (and in Venezuela and the wider Caribbean) speaks to his present in Britain. His reading of its history is often employed in constructing his transformative vision of society. The Trinidadian part of his life story is used to figure a process of personal development that is richer and more complex than many people he encountered in Britain realized; 'they did not know who we were' is a frequent assertion of his, hinting that he sees himself (and his associates) as possessing capacities not recognized in the British context.

By 1961 La Rose like many West Indians had decided to move to Britain, he told me, in order to acquire professional training – in the law, in his case – in the hope that he could return to Trinidad and work as an attorney for the labour movement. In a 1983 interview La Rose was asked 'how would you sum up your experience in the UK?', to which he replied:

> I did not intend to stay [in the UK] more than three years. I intended to study law. I broke with it almost in the first year of my being there. It's an illusion which I broke with – that you could study law and return to work in the Caribbean (La Rose 1985b: 27).

La Rose elaborated on this conversation with me: 'I intended to return anyway but stayed when my family relationship broke down' (he and Irma separated not long after the move to Britain). In making this move, he compares himself to George Padmore and C.L.R. James, both of whom chose the life of the activist over a more conventional course of higher education followed by a profession.

As we saw in Chapter One, La Rose, Edward Brathwaite and Andrew Salkey decided to start a forum for the meeting of Caribbean-descent writers, artists and students in Britain – the Caribbean Artists Movement. In 1966, together with his partner Sarah White, La Rose founded the New Beacon publishing house and later book supply service. La Rose recalls:

> There was a need to produce work that would validate the culture and history of blacks, as a counter to structural racism in Britain . . . You should not depend on an establishment with which you are at times in conflict for the validation of your culture and history. We had learnt that in Trinidad,

we had learnt that by studying Thomas. You had to have the means of intellectual production under your own control. And that meant publishing and distribution. We knew we had to get into that.

They were wary of incurring debt, so for the first years the publishing house and book service remained small. La Rose also recalls that the models for their operation were the minimalist practice of the Viet Cong, 'who were able to defeat the greatest military power on earth on a bowl of rice a day'; 'the small Indian and Chinese shopkeepers with their shop in the front and their dwelling places behind the shop until their businesses grew'; and the Syrian and Lebanese traders of his childhood in Trinidad, who traversed the island with suitcases full of goods for sale, slowly accumulating capital until they could open a fixed business place.

> Our guiding principle was to use what you have; too often in Trinidad I had seen blacks enter business on a large scale, borrowing money and setting up an elaborate small business. Where are those businesses now? Many went under, they borrowed money from the banks and were not able to service their loans. From early on Sarah and I decided that we were not going to do that. We would build up the publishing house and bookshop from our own resources, at a rate that we could control. We were not going to let anyone else control our development.

Having sketched a developmental narrative of La Rose's early life, I want to turn now to examine the theoretically oriented strands in his thinking. I conceive this as a mapping exercise, in which I try to render the lines which stabilize La Rose's self-representation as an activist, being quite aware that any such stability is always no more than temporary, for as the life changes so too does the life story. The map which I am drawing here is, then, one of terrain which is, in La Rose's own words, ever-changing, but which I conceive to be fixed in the context of the dialogue out of which this account emerged.

Portrait of the Older Activist

This chapter is mainly about one person's life and ideas, seen through that person's self-representation. I am not concerned to assess the truth of that life or the validity of the ideas; rather I want to ask: why represent oneself in this way and why give emphasis to these ideas? This not a question which lends itself to a direct answer, but is amenable to an oblique probing. We must engage in some reverse engineering. In *The Idea of History,* Collingwood (1994 [1946]) suggested that we ask of the ideas, practices and institutions we study historically the following: to what question is this object an answer? In this way we may avoid (*unreflexively*, I would argue, though Collingwood does not use the term) mapping our own concerns onto historical objects. I have drawn upon Collingwood's historiographical approach to pose the following questions to La Rose's personal narrative: to what kind of question or concern could this personal narrative be an answer? And after Sartre (1963: 141–3) I also ask: what kind of person can the subject be in order to produce the work before us, so to objectify him or herself in this text? In order to begin answering these questions I want to turn to La Rose's ideas, to the 'superstructure' of his activist self-representation.

Autonomous socialism

A key element of La Rose's self-representation is that of autonomous socialism. In positioning himself within the broad expanse of socialist politics he is marking off a space within a complex and charged political field. What kind of socialist he is not is key here: he is not Trostkyist; he is not an academic Marxist nor a reductionist Marxist. All these negative positions were elaborated by him in our conversations. He represents himself as firmly non-aligned. We saw earlier that his 1953 trip to Eastern Europe led him to conclude that the system that obtained there was not the socialism to which he understood himself to subscribe; but just what kind of socialism does he subscribe to? He insists that his understanding of Marxism was grounded mainly in his own life experience:

> There weren't many Marxist books in Trinidad at the time [when La Rose was in his late teens to early twenties], there was *Wage Labour and Capital*, a little pamphlet; *Capital* we never saw, all those major Marxist texts which were subsequently [published] by Penguin, that was nowhere available.
> Anyway, as I kept saying to people when I read those books, this is not a bible, this Marx book *Capital*, all of it, is not a bible. I know it's not a bible, because [people] who never heard of it are themselves revolting, and working out theories of how to revolt and succeed, and succeeding. Nothing to do with Marx . . . He himself says this. And he is not saying that people who read his books must be Marxists, it is exactly not that, it was the very opposite . . . My own experience had taught me all the things, had taught us, how to analyse those things without being burdened by the book of Marx; . . . so there were no revolutions before Marx? why were there revolutions before Marx? how come these revolutions succeeded, what made them succeed? the human capacity for invention

and organization has to be clearly understood – it has nothing to do with Marx.

In discussing La Rose's socialist autonomy an obvious figure of comparison is the most famous Caribbean-heritage Marxist – C.L.R. James. La Rose explains that while he was formed in the same social context as James, his approach to socialism was more grounded in actual struggles, as against that of James whom La Rose views as 'a brilliant social critic and an exceptional literary, cultural and historical figure but a not-very-successful politician who failed to engage successfully with popular struggles'. La Rose is also careful to distance himself from Trotskyism:

> . . . [B]ut we valued Marx, we valued Lenin, we valued Stalin; we valued what they had been able to achieve, which made our situation easier to achieve. We understood that, so that's why we found the Trotskyists a bit tiresome, because they had no power to hold back imperialism; I mean they were complaining about what was going on in the Soviet Union, but they had no power to deal with, to counter the imperialist thrust, and therefore there was no way that anybody could benefit from their position simply because they had no power to exercise it, and when they came close, like the POUM in Spain, they blew it; when they came [close] in Peru and places like this they blew it, so it meant that it was unworkable. On the other hand the communists had seized power, they were well organized, and they could deal with the United States and confront it to the extent where Bandung was possible, Communist China was possible and so on, so we couldn't, anyway, we found that tiresome; we knew all that Marx had said about the transformation of society; that came out of our own experience . . .

A key to decoding La Rose's autonomous standpoint is to be found in the last of his words quoted above. His socialist vision of transformation comes out his own experience of life under colonialism, as a trade unionist and as someone who believes in the classical humanist notion of culture as a force for personal and social change. We cannot judge this assertion empirically; it is more useful to understand it as marking out a space in left-wing political thought.

Socialist autonomy is articulated by La Rose in a different register from that of the visceral anti-Stalinism which is typical of Trotskyism and many culturally oriented leftists, including C.L.R. James. In our conversations La Rose frequently expressed open admiration for the achievements of the Soviet Union in bringing Russian society into the modern era. He spoke approvingly of the many achievements of Soviet science and technology, about which he knew a great deal from his own reading, and partly from exchanges with Sarah White (who had written her doctoral dissertation on Russian science history); also because he had read *Soviet Weekly* regularly in Trinidad in the 1950s and he had first learnt of the automated factory from that journal. Among the numerous books in their shared home are many on Russian history and science, and on Soviet-era society and politics. Sometimes in the course of conversation he would fetch one of these books in order to read me a passage. He has had a life-long interest in the social implications of science and technology, and has generated from this interest ideas that are incorporated into his transformative vision of society.

While La Rose is very much Old Left in his admiration for Soviet development and its positive contribution to the world anti-imperialist movement, he asserts that Gorbachev's reforms were essential and that the USSR had to change. We did not speak much about Yeltsin. Old Leftism notwithstanding, there are elements of social democracy in his conception of socialism:

> . . . [B]ecause we have to be in a revolutionary situation, it doesn't mean that we don't recognize that this is a situation where you can only get reforms or hold back the tide of exploitation; that is what the Labour party does, it's a dike, that's what the trade unions are, they are dikes; when they burst through that dike, we are in trouble. They offer us some protection, and we can move forward from there. That's what reform movements are like. The only reason they become revolutionary is when the reform is so mass-oriented and so broadly-based that they see for themselves that they want more and they can't get anymore except through revolution . . . it means you are trying to change the whole basis of the society – it doesn't mean you're going to win, because I know you can lose – but even so it becomes a revolutionary struggle, attempting to make fundamental change. But the reform is important, and we are part of the reform movement; we are part of the Labour Party and Trade Unions reform movement, that's what the society can tolerate at this historical moment and point in time . . .

This is an unambiguous statement of a problem which confronts many on the left: should their support be given to reformist parties? That question is particularly acute in the contemporary British context where New Labour's reformist credentials are brought into question by the party's apparent shift to the centre. La Rose's answer to the question would probably be yes. He would agree, I think, with *Guardian* columnist Polly Toynbee, who on the eve of the June 2001 British general election, allowed that there was much justified left-liberal discontent with Tony Blair's New Labour government, yet called on discontented progressives to support New Labour's programme of social reform which had had some positive results (Toynbee 2001).

Transformation of work

La Rose's interests in politics and culture come together in his vision of the current horizons for social transformation of society:

> The reordering of the world economy, now constantly taking place, on the basis of the new technologies and the phenomenal increase in productivity which they have brought with them, present us with possibilities for 'a shorter working day, a shorter working life, and more time for rest, recreation and cultural creativity' in whatever way this is accomplished and geared to the realities of particular economies and societies. We can have either that or the continual growth of an international crisis of the underclass, with its expectations and life experience, the descent into the drug economy with its various consequences; and the emergence of what has been called in Europe, especially during the recent French general elections, the world of 'social exclusion' (La Rose 1996).

In the same article La Rose goes on:

> Looking back at the agora in ancient Greece, we see the outlines of this process. The Greek *skole* or leisure, from which words like scholar and scholarship originate, allowed for time, for discussion, for debate and interaction, which underlined the development of philosophy, drama and democracy. It was the rigour of slave labour which made all this leisure possible.
>   In the Caribbean the unemployed, in their enforced leisure created Calypso, the famous mass popular Carnival and Steelband. It was the unemployed from Behind the Bridge in Port of Spain, Trinidad, who created the language, the music, the dance, the instruments, the organisations, which gave birth and originality to these institutions. They were like any other artist – with time for withdrawal into intense moments of creativity, working for hours and hours at their artform and producing brilliant episodes of invention.

In his ideas on the shorter working week, La Rose is broadly on the same territory as several well-known writers (Gorz 1999; Rifkin 2000). Moreover, there is provocative resonance between La Rose's ideas on ordinary peoples' autonomy and those of writers on the 'autonomist' wing of Marxism who have raised the possibility of the socially excluded turning the new technologies to their own ends (Negri 1989; Witherford 1994).

These authors see the development of information technology tending toward the subversion of wage labour, because increasingly less labour time is needed to produce the material necessities of life. Information-rich networks with flat profiles, reduced hierarchy and the possibility of decentralized productive activity, could mean that capital's hold would be loosened, at least in the 'post-industrial' societies of the north. In keeping with his emphasis on the importance of culture for social change, La Rose sees that an important effect of the shorter working week would be human life enhanced through greater possibilities for learning and creative activity. This is at least as important for him as the weakening of capital's hold on labour; indeed he sees the greater space for cultural activity opened by the new technologies as pointing towards a short-circuiting of capital-labour struggles in that people could come to invest less of themselves in seeking and holding wage labour. The Caribbean unemployed to whom La Rose refers in the passage quoted above are usually seen by policy-makers in that region as a problem that can only be solved by expanding wage labour; in contrast, La Rose, like Gorz (1999), conceives work as far more than wage labour, and so credits the Trinidadian urban working classes with creativity born out of their 'enforced leisure'.

The shorter working week, allowing time for creativity and leisure, is one of the issues to which John La Rose returned most in his personal narrative. For him it defines the current possibilities for social transformation. This conception incorporates several key strands in his life history: his exposure to the popular culture of Trinidad; his days as a labour organizer, and later as a publisher and activist. He maintains a keen interest in these issues. On our first meeting after he and Sarah White had been on holiday in France during summer 1997, La Rose showed to me a large pile of newspaper and magazine clippings on the debate over the 35-hour work week, which he had collected while in France (he is fluent in French); backing this up were several book-length studies. 'You must read these', he said, 'this is the most pressing social and economic issue right now, and it is going to define the future of Europe'.

Vindication

While La Rose occupied a relatively privileged position in Trinidadian society, being coloured and middle-class, he nonetheless came to contest being a colonial subject. In Britain, he contested the construction of Black migrants as colonial/ex-colonial, and as black-therefore-lesser in White supremacist discourse. His life history highlights numerous projects in which he was engaged that set out to vindicate the history and culture of the Caribbean, of Africa and of Asia in the face of Eurocentric discourse. His personal narrative inscribes many instances where he asserts that the culture and intellectual history of colonial Trinidad were in no way backward compared to that of Europe. His activism and publishing and bookselling sought to make cultural products from outside Europe more widely available in Britain, so that socially subordinate persons there – often but never exclusively people of colour – could build up a store of cultural capital and with it their self-assurance in the face of various classist and racist exclusions they experienced in Britain. His vindication is not merely individualist (though he frequently asserts his own command of canonical European cultural capital): he stresses group rather than individual vindication. His self-representation is not so much about his being an exceptional individual but that he was able to accomplish exceptional things by helping to forge and by being part of a community of interest, the right kind of cohort.

The narrative of vindication is a recurrent form not only in La Rose's life story, but it is widespread in the personal narratives of West Indian migrants to Britain.[10] The recurrent narrative of vindication varies with the gender of the subject, and also with 'race' and age. The way in which La Rose deploys the vindication sub-narrative is strongly affected by his racial positioning in Britain and by his socialist self-identity: he is moved to vindicate the working class and people of colour chiefly, in the face of racist and classist discourse and practice. Ageism and sexism are not his chief concerns.

Leadership but not vanguardism

La Rose is critical of the way established left-wing parties in Britain sought to direct anti-racist campaigns. He is critical of 'vanguardist' approaches to leadership. Yet, he sees himself as occupying a leadership position in these campaigns. The seeming contradiction is partly explicable if we consider La Rose's leadership as issue-based and tactical. He emphasized to me that he and his colleagues would 'walk away' at the end of a campaign. He stresses that, unlike several other radical and Black groups, he and his associates were not interested in building up a mass membership:

> If [the people we had helped to defend in court cases] wished to be committed to us, we would then consider if we want them to be members, but they weren't automatically, because we weren't looking for members, we had our own membership, and it was a selected membership, it wasn't a mass membership,

and we didn't intend to build it into a mass membership. We were very clear about that.

One could read a hint of elitism here, but I would argue instead that La Rose conceives of himself and colleagues as engaged in a project larger and more long-term than the legal defence campaigns. He conceives of projects such as New Beacon bookshop and the George Padmore Institute as transcending the immediacy of struggles such as clashes between Black youth and the police. He asserted, in an address at a fund-raising luncheon in December 1996: 'we are working toward building a better Britain'. La Rose's self-representation incorporates a value orientation toward the long- term, toward consolidation, toward proceeding in an orderly fashion. He differentiates his own praxis from a transient response to the issues of the moment.

How can socialist leadership be constituted without it evolving into vanguardism, into the politics of an enlightened minority organizing and directing the political action of a comparatively 'ignorant' majority? A commitment to grass-roots democracy by leftist activists is not enough, for if it were then this question would not remain one of the most vexing ones for left-wing politics. French activist-sociologist André Gorz, in responding to an interviewer's question about his (Gorz's) relationship to the philosophy and politics of Jean-Paul Sartre, replies:

> [I share a desire] with Sartre to be unorthodox, disrespectful of established standards and involved through my writings in the main conflicts of my time – not simply as a supporter of this or that side, but in a way that would help raise people's consciousness of the meaning of what was at stake (Bowring 2000: 186).

This conception of the intellectual-activist contributing to the general cause of consciousness-raising resonates strongly with La Rose's ideas on leadership. Consider that the Black Parents Movement played a leading role in various campaigns but at the same time did not seek to build up a power base through mass membership; this might lead us to allow that there is some substance to La Rose's claims around non-vanguardist leadership. How does he pull off the trick? Or does he? The leadership of the New Beacon circle is best understood in terms of coming up with an agenda and mobilizing[11] to raise debate around that agenda as, for example, was the case with the international book fairs, where the organizers raised the question of how to build up a transnational network of radical Black and third-world creative intellectuals and artists and communities that would support their work. That question-raising and promotion of debate could be conceived as intellectual leadership. If there is substance to the non-vanguardist claim to leadership it would lie at least in this: having raised the issue and organized debates around it, the next vanguardist step would be to build up a mass followership and seek to mobilize that followership toward clearly stated political ends. That is exactly what did *not* happen with the Book Fairs. A problem is raised when one comes to measure leadership in terms of consciousness-raising: how do you know to what extent, if at all, consciousness was raised? With the classic vanguardist leadership one could gauge effect at least in terms of a growing membership. Instead, we have the George Padmore Institute, aimed to engage in the long-term project of raising consciousness, and doing so without the security of a mass base. The kind of existential choice raised above by Gorz would seem to be vital for making sense of a project such as the Padmore Institute. Perhaps some idea of the aesthetic avant-garde is better suited than the Leninist vanguard would be to represent the standpoint of La Rose and his associates on leadership. It would have to be, though, a *politically engaged* avant-garde, one with a self-conscious cultural politics.

Transcendence and universalism: mediating tension in the self-representation

La Rose's self-representation in his life story is complex. He was socially coloured and middle-class in Trinidad, is socially Black in Britain, and is anti-racist in outlook. He denies Black nationalist essentialism while employing Black as a strategic essentialism, as an organizing political label when he judged the circumstances to warrant such. He is a self-proclaimed autonomous socialist, with respect for the achievements of the former USSR, while also expressing appreciation of the realism of New Labour. Near the end of my initial fieldwork period, in July 1997, he showed me a Labour party membership card: after three and a half decades involved in progressive politics in Britain, he had joined the Labour Party.

La Rose repeatedly asserts that his early education in mass politics was largely based on his exposure to the working class of Port of Spain: 'behind the bridge' (a reference to East Port of Spain, overwhelmingly Black and working-class) is an important symbol of Black working-class life and struggle for La Rose, and an important part of his political imaginary. In an article on 'The changing language of Riots in Britain' he wrote:

The language of the riot is not polite. It is rude, vituperative, brutal and explosive. Language and action fuse into a violent response to the everyday brutalisation from the police, from fascists and racist attackers, the social security, the racist employer, from the casually racist citizen, to all of which the rioter is responding. Action by the rioters and low intensity counteraction by the state then become a public drama (La Rose 1986).

In contrast to this Bakhtinesque rendering (Bakhtin 1984 [1965]) of the mass-in-movement, he states that he is opposed in principle to 'loud' and 'hysterical' styles of discourse. One afternoon we are watching a televised broadcast of a post-election (i.e. after May 1997) Labour Party conference. A young Black man has the podium; La Rose commends the 'calm and measured' style of this man's delivery, saying:

A mistake that many black militants made in the early days here was always to use a loud and aggressive style. That is necessary sometimes, but the British generally do not like that style. They prefer a controlled and measured delivery. I prefer the controlled delivery as well.

Here, as so often in the life stories he told me, La Rose articulates a value preference for the 'respectable'. Yet, in his engagement with the cultural and political expression of the socially excluded, in Trinidad or Britain, La Rose takes on an opposed value orientation. Peter Wilson (1973) has suggested that the contrast between reputation and respectability was characteristic of Creole Caribbean societies. These were seen by Wilson as two philosophical principles that order social life: 'the structure of Caribbean social life is, then, the dialectical relation between the two principles' (1973: 9). Without committing myself to Wilson's thesis in a strong version,[12] I would argue that La Rose's life stories can be read as representing his own working through these two principles. His political activity was in one sense contradictory to his middle-class – respectable – upbringing in colonial Trinidad; at the same time the realization of radical politics in his case meant that he got involved in the social and cultural life of the Trinidadian working classes and unemployed, the people 'behind the bridge' for whom Wilson's principle of reputation was dominant over respectability. It is through imagining and working toward a radical democratic politics that La Rose, in his self-representation and his political work, is able to go (or attempt to go) beyond the opposition between himself as a middle-class activist and the working-class milieu into which he projects his cultural politics.

La Rose, like C.L.R. James, is of the 'old school' (James 1963) in addition to being a radical; though not as much a 'Victorian with the rebel seed' as George Lamming described James, La Rose is, as James was, a person at the cultural crossroads of Euro-America, Africa and Asia. His identity is an intentional hybridity – a wilful transgression of ethnic, national and class barriers – with all the possibilities and strains which such entails. Potential tension between varied and even contradictory social positionings is mediated in La Rose's self-representation by a humanist, transcendent and universalist narrative of social transformation. The struggles over workers' rights, against colonialism, against racism and arbitrary police oppression, are transient way stations on the journey to a better society, one characterized by what La Rose terms 'democratic and autonomous peoples' power'. The struggle to achieve democratic and autonomous peoples' power is conceived by him in universalist terms – it cuts across national, racial, class and gender lines. This struggle is seen by La Rose as transcending, ultimately, the day-to-day conflicts in which people are everywhere involved. He acknowledges a necessity to engage in immediate issues and conflicts, but tries to keep in sight a long-term vision of a transformed society. I will offer no judgement as to whether La Rose has 'succeeded' in making these integrations and connections. What is central to what I wish to do here is that he thinks it *politically* important that culture ought to be conceived in hybrid and transformative terms. In assigning that political importance to cultural-crossing, and even cultural transcendence, La Rose is articulating a socialist humanism.

Something of a map lies before us now, but much remains to be filled in. The cartographic exercise will yield further results if we widen our focus. John La Rose's personal narrative relates dialogically to other narratives from the milieu of the Creole Caribbean intelligentsia, the milieu from which La Rose, as C.L.R. James, emerged.

Puritans and Rebels: Life Stories of the Creole Colonial Intelligentsia

> Two people lived in me: one, the rebel against all
> family and school discipline and order; the other, a
> Puritan who would have cut off a finger sooner than
> do anything contrary to the ethics of the game.
>
> C.L.R. James, *Beyond a Boundary*

From the range of personal narratives written from colonial Trinidad and the wider Anglo-Caribbean,[12] I will concentrate on those of Eric Williams and CLR James, two representatives of what I term the Creole intelligentsia. (I will make brief reference to other life stories from that milieu.)

These two individuals were the products of the acculturation process set in train by the British colonial rulers to create a local non-White elite who could eventually take over when the British handed these colonies over to self-rule. As with many top-down cultural (or better, acculturating) projects, this process did not always work as expected. The personal narratives of James, Williams and others from their context set John La Rose's life history into a background. Their stories do not directly give shape to his narrative; rather, he is in ongoing engagement with the cultural history which formed these other narratives.

Schooling and scholarship occupy a large space in the personal narratives of the Creole intelligentsia, and we saw this in La Rose's narrative as well. For the few colonial West Indian Blacks who managed to get there, grammar school was apparently a safe haven from the stresses of living as a Black person in White-dominated colonial society. C.L.R. James (1963) describes his time at Queens Royal College in Trinidad in the second decade of the twentieth century as 'idyllic'; he wrote: 'The race question did not have to be agitated. It was there. But in our little Eden it never troubled us' (p. 39). School was a place where the colonial racial playing field was levelled, or at least tilted less steeply away from them; as such they attach positive memories to a time and place in their lives when and where they could achieve a measure of vindication.

School and sport played the major role in James's teenage years; both were virtually of the same character as those offered to elite public and grammar school students in England of the early decades of the twentieth century. At Queen's Royal College (QRC), James would have been tutored by graduates of elite English institutions: Eton, Harrow, Oxford and Cambridge. At QRC James played a lot of cricket and was also an all-round athlete; he set a national youth high jump record which stood for more than three decades. He absorbed the public school ethos of honour, teamwork and bearing stress and defeat without complaint. He seems to have started out well academically, but soon went off on a tangent. He read voraciously, but what interested him most was European literature and history. According to him, QRC had an excellent library, the legacy of the generations of Oxford- and Cambridge-trained schoolmasters who had passed through the institution and left their books behind. Seven years of reading in that library would prove critical to his later development: he grounded himself thoroughly in the canon of 'Western Civilisation' (Worcester 1996).

In spite of his early indoctrination into social propriety, as a young man James seemed to find the colonial lower-middle-class milieu into which he was born and raised to be mainly dull and overly concerned with imitating the mores of the British middle class as he had come to learn of these through his reading. He led a double life as a senior student. Having become impassioned with sports and games, he neglected his schoolwork, though not his self-directed reading; he resorted at times to lying and devious manoeuvring so that just one more game could be played. But, on the playing field the public school code held (1963: 34).

James writes that he had an agenda that was different from that of his parents and schoolteachers; he wanted to write books, despite his not knowing anyone who actually earned his or her living as a writer. His father, schoolmaster and highly regarded coach of future scholars, was understandably disappointed that his own son in whom he had placed the highest hopes seemed destined not to win an Island Scholarship but rather to become a brilliant tearaway (1963: 35–8). The young James in *Boundary a Boundary* is a rebel and romantic in the making; not for him the dusty corridors of the colonial civil service nor the staid propriety of a profession in law or medicine.

In his early fiction, written in the 1920s in Trinidad (James 1971 [1936]), James implicitly criticized the superficial view of the plebeians that was held by the educated middle and upper classes. In his autobiography he narrates his young self as looking below the seemingly chaotic surface of lower-class life and finding there richness and vitality. This early social vision was inspired, he claims, by his readings of Fielding, Thackeray and Dickens – writers who brought the picaresque character to prominence in English literature. Here we see striking similarities with La Rose's life stories: the tension between propriety and autonomy, and consciousness-raising through exposure to working-class life.

Eric Williams (1911–1981) was like James a prize-winning student at Queen's Royal College in Trinidad. As a bright primary-school student, Williams was of course coached for secondary school. He won one of the coveted government scholarships to Queen's Royal College (QRC). There he was for a time taught by C.L.R. James, himself a product of the colonial educational course of hurdles, as we saw earlier. Williams was recognized scholastically and wore the school colours in cricket and football. When Williams won his Island Scholarship, he departed from the norm in that he opted to read history at Oxford University rather than take the route of medicine or law. In 1932, when he boarded the ship which would take him to England, Williams was already a seasoned warrior of the scholarship wars. He had by then internalized a fiercely competitive ethic in an environment where a few colonials had already proven themselves the equals, in scholarship, of the British (Williams 1969).[14]

The authors of these life stories[15] appear to have embraced a liberal humanism, and then come to see a tension between the universalist values expressed in that humanism and the realities of racial and class domination in a British colony. In their accounts, this realization spurs them to question colonialism and racial stratification, and to engage in nationalist politics to varying degrees. For this reason I term them members of a Creole intelligentsia.

George Padmore makes an interesting contrast to James and Williams. He was a childhood friend of C.L.R. James; he attended St Mary's College for a time. Unlike the others, Padmore proceeded to the United States for further education. Padmore did not write an autobiography. One of the founders of the modern Pan-African movement, he worked both officially and underground as a labour organizer. He was a journalist for many years, but he did not write his memoirs. It would be fruitless to speculate on why, except to note that his years as an anti-racist activist in Jim Crow America (which led to his assuming the new name of George Padmore) and then as a clandestine organizer for the Comintern, were understandably not conducive to writing a personal narrative.

Padmore's biographer notes that Padmore came to resent the racial glass ceiling of 1920s Trinidad. After finishing school, he worked as a reporter for a local newspaper, where he ran afoul of the English editor, described by Padmore as 'one of the most arrogant agents of British Imperialism I have ever encountered' (Hooker 1967: 3). Unlike James and Williams, Padmore never returned to Trinidad, not even for a visit. Hooker describes Padmore's life as one characterized by constant movement, intensive writing, organizing and, after his break with the Comintern, always on the social fringes and financially insecure. The Trinidadian Creole intellectuals I discussed above were peripatetic, but Padmore was again unique in that he was foremost an activist. This last is one of the most important aspects of Padmore as a model for the praxis of the New Beacon circle.

The biographical narratives I discussed here are inter-textual and dialogical. John La Rose's own life history is part of that dialogue. This is so for a number of reasons. The authors all came out of the same social milieu and social stratum. Several recurrent themes in the self-representations of the Creole intelligentsia are deployed by La Rose in his own personal narrative. All strove to achieve vindication as a response to the racial stratification of colonial Trinidad. Scholarship became important in their lives, both as a means to self-development and as a means to social transformation towards more just societies. A dominant cultural factor in their formative environments was a strong ambition to achieve self-realization through acquiring an English-style grammar school education. In doing well in the brutal scholarship wars, these men gained considerable social prestige, becoming almost folk-heroes – understandable when one considers that scholarly prowess was virtually the only way people in their social position could achieve upward social mobility. Here John La Rose differs in one important respect: unlike the other men discussed here, he was born into a middle-class family and, as such, social mobility through scholarly success would have been objectively less important to him; a grammar-school education would have been assumed in his family circumstances.

For women contemporaries of these men the situation was quite different. Even the severely restricted path of the Island Scholarship was unavailable to Trinidadian women until after the Second World War. Olga Comma Maynard, born in 1898 (Maynard 1992), a friend of C.L.R. James, became a primary-school teacher through the route of apprenticeship in a school of which her father was principal. Though from the same upwardly mobile class circumstances as James or Williams, there was virtually no possibility for her to pursue further education, as the colonial government did not fund such training for women at the time. A dominant gender ideology also served to construct 'respectable' – established or *nouveau* middle-class – women as housewives, and to discourage intellectual and indeed any career pursuits on their part: this ideology was largely irrelevant for lower-class women (Brereton 1998). Maynard recounts having to suspend her teaching career in order to raise her children: in the early decades of the twentieth century, female civil servants were required to resign their posts on marriage and, implicitly, on becoming pregnant (Reddock 1994).

In La Rose's as in these other narratives, we may discern the outlines of a model of the self, or indeed several models, by which I mean structured ways of representing the self. The models of the self which may be read in the personal narratives discussed in this chapter are formed out of a colonial upbringing and education. The non-White person is situated in a milieu where there is a broad consensus on the value of European – British specifically – middle- and upper-class culture. For many non-Whites in these societies, there was a complex, attenuated link with anything that could be described as an indigenous culture. Because there was in a sense no pre-colonial source from which to build an anti-colonial consciousness, the Creole intelligentsia constructed resistance to colonialism by employing Western liberal humanism. In contrast to Cabral's (1973) call to return to the cultural source of the colonized people for resources with which to resist colonialism, or Gandhi's imagined pre- and anti-modern community (Fox 1989; Gandhi 1983), this Creole intelligentsia – exemplified for Trinidad by early nineteenth-century humanist Jean-Baptiste Philippe (1996 [1826]), J.J. Thomas, James and the 1920s *Beacon* circle, and Eric Williams – drew upon the social and cultural capital available to educated non-Whites, and turned these to counter-hegemonic ends. They made of their Eurocentric education a platform from which to assert a vindicated Creole anti-colonial self.

The Black or coloured Creole person in Trinidad (and the wider colonial Caribbean) could employ several strategies to constitute vind-icated selves. Assimilation was the earliest. As with Philippe (1996 [1826]) and the 'free Coloureds', one tried to imagine the self in the cultural works and social relations of the hegemonic European stratum, tried to inhabit this world as if Blackness were irrelevant, to deny otherness, to 'turn white or disappear' as Fanon (1967a) put it. Ultimately or eventually persons pursuing this strategy would find themselves rejected by the Whites at the apex of the social structure. This strategy had obvious limitations, and was decisively abandoned by the social realism of the *Beacon* literary circle of 1920s Trinidad, when lower-class Black and Asian people were first figured as subjects in Anglo-Caribbean literature (Sander 1988). This was one point when a Creole intelligentsia could most clearly be seen to have emerged in Trinidad.

One of the more radical strategies of vindicating the self was to subject the social structure and ideology of colonial society to an immanent critique; to point out discrepancies between the liberal ideology of the British dominant culture and the social exclusionist practices of colonial Trinidad. One demanded fair treatment under the existing rules of the game, whether in cricket or in life generally. This is the model of the self that shapes La Rose's account of his early life in Trinidad. Or one could simply leave the colonial territory to pursue anti-colonial politics on a larger stage, as did George Padmore. Yet another strategy of vindication was to seek to affirm the worth of being Black as did John Jacob Thomas (1969 [1889]). Yet another strategy was to invoke the praxis of Marxism or that of social democracy and adapt it to anti-colonial politics, as did some of the early Trinidadian labour movements and nationalist political parties (Ramdin 1982).

A sometimes contradictory experience of modernity in a colonial variant comprised the dominant formative influence in the personal narratives of John La Rose and the others discussed in this chapter. Their subjects were represented as either drawn toward the libertarian or radical strands in modernity or as employing modern ideas of the self and citizenship in radical ways. This is partly explicable by these subjects' contradictory social positions: Black or coloured in racist society, colonials in a subject society schooled in a humanist tradition based on the idea of human equality; well-educated men chafing at the strictures imposed on either themselves or others around them by a patriarchal and racist society which nullified the potential advantages of their gender because of their subordinate racial personhood. Their radicalization was an unintended consequence of their social and cultural formation for a colonial elite.[16]

Summary

Researchers committed to the humanistic model of research that makes use of the personal narrative have had to consider the question of generalization from the individual life story. Angrosino notes: 'An autobiography is . . . a record of individuality, and often the bias that stands behind the production of the text is one that exaggerates the individuality even further . . . Autobiographies, then, illuminate diversity, not generality' (Angrosino 1989: 8).

On the one hand, we may argue that the individual whose life history is under consideration is somehow a typical case of some broader social category and/or some social setting. The establishment of typicality requires us, in a sense, to work in reverse, in that we must already be in possession of considerable knowledge of the category or milieu of which our individual case is held to be typical. We would thus hold out an individual case as an example for illustrative purposes. For Angrosino, however, the personal narrative may not be best suited to illuminating the typical, due to in-built individualist bias. On the other hand, we may argue of our individual life history that it is relevant precisely due to its unique characteristics, its atypicality: this is where Angrosino sees the bias of autobiographical accounts as tending. This second approach to the personal narrative is influenced by Kant's notion of the individual as an end in him- or herself, and by Sartre's call for the human sciences to treat the individual as a universal singular.

These two approaches to justifying the value of the life history need not be mutually exclusive, if we take the *aims* of a person in narrating his or her life history into account: persons may wish to set themselves apart, but they may also wish to show how they fit into some category or milieu. In the same account, the subject may shift from one pole to another. We can see evidence of both these tendencies in La Rose's life history. He constitutes himself both as a unique individual and as part of social milieus. In recounting their lives it may be the case that people are not overly bothered by the perennial social scientific problem of navigating between agency and structure. If there is a 'truth' in La Rose's life history it is not that he was either typical or atypical, but that he employed elements from remembered social situations in conjunction with his own drive to realize his projects, and that these are seen by him to have come together in given social relations. While I have set his life history into a broader context, it is of sociological value as a humanist document in its own right (Plummer 2001). The 'truth' of his life history is to be found in the space where autobiography meets history. That is the space I have tried to map here.

Notes

1. 'Creole' has a number of connotations: it can refer to persons of mixed European and African descent (also known as 'coloured' in the colonial Anglo-Caribbean); it can refer to Spanish- or French-descent persons born in the Americas; in Trinidad it can mean anyone of non-Asian, but especially of African descent. I use the term regarding La Rose in the first sense.
2. 'Tapia' refers to a material and a construction technique for small dwellings. Of Amerindian origin, it consists in building with mud reinforced by straw fibres; the structure is roofed with thatch.
3. On reading an early draft of this chapter, La Rose told me 'it was not just the middle-class blacks who did not talk of African ancestry – with few exceptions, working-class blacks did not either.'
4. Though disappearing, there are still a few members of that Spanish-speaking minority (Moodie-Kublalsingh 1994). 'Carib' in Trinidad refers to the descendants of the original Amerindian inhabitants. The general perception of most Trinidadians is that no 'true' Caribs exist after centuries of intermixture in a small island. Nonetheless, those who consider themselves to be Carib elect a Queen to a life-term. They take part in the annual Santa Rosa festival and have had themselves recognized as a group of indigenous people by the United Nations.
5. Nello Lambert, a friend of La Rose since early childhood. La Rose recalls of Lambert that he 'had been a bright Maths student, also at St Mary's College, and was expected to win an island scholarship'.
6. The epiphany is an episode narrated by the subject as a decisive turning-point in the life history (Denzin 1989).
7. St Lucian-born economist and Nobel Laureate. A pioneering thinker in the field of development economics, his work helped to shape the

development policies of several newly-independent Caribbean nation states in the 1960s and early 1970s (Lewis 1977 [1939]).

8. Arthur Andrew Cipriani, of Corsican descent, became after the First World War, a labour leader in Trinidad. As a commanding officer of the West India Regiment during the war, he became popular with Black West Indian troops for demanding that they be treated fairly. Though progressive, he was not able to keep abreast of the demands for social change in Trinidad in the 1930s, and came to be seen by radicals as an impediment to progress.

9. Jim Barrette and Christina King were key activists of the NWCSA of which Elma François, a Black working class woman, was ideological leader. In her history of women and labour in Trinidad and Tobago, Reddock writes of the NWCSA that it 'was a Marxist-Leninist-oriented nationalist organization strongly influenced by the Comintern position on "The Negro Question", with a predominantly working-class membership, a large number of whom were women' (Reddock 1994: 108–9).

10. See Beaton 1986; Gilroy 1976; Phillips and Phillips 1999. Though her narrative also allows vindication a large space, Beryl Gilroy's (1976) account of her work as a Black teacher brings a different gender perspective to the fore. For personal narratives of other Black female settlers in Britain see Webster (1998).

11. I am grateful to Jim Murray for this idea, which emerged out of his attempts to engage with my work on the New Beacon circle in terms of his own history as a cultural activist going back to the 1960s US counterculture (Murray 1999).

12. For a critique of Wilson see Besson (1992).

13. For example Bridges 1980; Besson and Besson 1989; Clarke 1980; Gomes 1974; Lamming 1992 [1960]; Maynard 1992; Solomon 1981; Williams 1969.

14. Commenting on the educational environment of colonial Trinidad, Oxaal writes: 'Also of the greatest importance in accounting for the high level of competitive scholarship in Trinidad was the fact that the colony's secondary schools were the first colonial institutions to participate in the external examinations of Oxford and Cambridge' (Oxaal 1968: 62). According to Campbell (1996), the 'cult of the Island Scholar' was more highly developed in Trinidad than elsewhere in the colonial West Indies; the competition between Anglo-secular Queens' Royal College and French Creole Catholic St Mary's College represented broader social and economic conflict between the two opposed cultural factions of the White ruling class of colonial Trinidad.

15. William Besson was another contemporary of C.L.R. James. In keeping with the pattern we have seen, Besson's school days at QRC are portrayed as a haven from racial tension (Besson and Besson 1989). He later went on to win an island scholarship which allowed him to study medicine in Edinburgh. Also like James, Besson devotes a chapter of his life history to his school days; the chapter is entitled 'School Days with C.L.R. James: Trinidad, 1912–1921'.

Patrick Solomon, a contemporary of Eric Williams, trained as a doctor and pursued a second career as a diplomat in the service of newly independent Trinidad. Predictably, Solomon opens his account of school life with examinations, in which he soon demonstrates his prowess (Solomon 1981: 5). At ten he was 'considered fit for the special or Exhibition class' – the penultimate year of elementary school. In his second year in the exhibition class he was joined by 'an undersized youngster' by the name of Eric Williams. When in that year Solomon passed his Exhibition and was placed first in the whole country, he wrote: 'Eric Williams did not succeed on that occasion but the next year he knocked spots off everyone else.'

16. The themes I discussed here are found in the personal narratives produced by Black intellectuals and activists in other parts of the Atlantic world system (Mostern 1999).

$-5-$

'Life Experience with Britain'

Introduction

In this chapter I draw on my own attendance at two series of talks held in 1997 and 1999 at the George Padmore Institute (GPI), entitled 'Life Experience with Britain – Lectures and Conversations', in which various prominent Black figures narrate aspects of their life stories. I discuss these talks as events; I then consider the personal narratives presented as 'documents of interaction' (Angrosino 1989), looking at them as narratives grounded in the circumstances of their telling. The events in the 'Life Experience with Britain' series followed a common format. Flyers were sent out to all the people on the GPI mailing list. The venue – a fair-sized room on the floor immediately above New Beacon Bookshop – could accommodate at most sixty persons, so people were asked to book their places in advance. A contribution of £2.00 was collected from those attending. There were seven talks in both series; I attended six in 1997 and five in 1999. The talks were all either fully attended or with just ten or so seats free from a capacity of around sixty. In terms of attendance, then, the series was a success. For each speaker, a short biography of about 500 words was produced and distributed by the GPI.

The atmosphere of the talks was lively. Many in the audience were in a sense already converts to the purpose of the series, probably due to many having been involved in the same terrain of cultural activism as the New Beacon circle. Persons who were featured speakers at one talk were in the audience at many of the others. Many, but not all, of the people present seemed to know one another, in some cases quite well; about a third of the regular attendance were persons I had seen at a December 1996 fund-raising event where the talks were launched. The attendance pointed to the existence of groupings beyond my interlocutors, comprising people who were interested in the kind of political and cultural activism dealt with by the speakers in the series. The stated intention of the GPI board was that each series should be published.[1]

The first series of talks ran over a seven-month period from January to July 1997, with one each month. I attended all save the second, which took place in February. The second series ran from January to July 1999, also with one talk each month; of these I attended all save the second and sixth. The speakers and their topics are as follows.

For the first series, in 1997, Pearl Connor-Mogotsi, Trinidad-born, and 'best known for her pioneering and campaigning work in the areas of arts, particularly theatre',[2] spoke on 20 January. Her talk dealt mainly with the history over the last four decades of establishing Black people in the performing arts in Britain and the role she played in these processes. Garth Crooks, British-born to Jamaican parents, 'leading British foot-baller – and now football TV commentator, radio journalist, newspaper columnist and writer', spoke on 18 February about 'the experience of being black and prominent both as a footballer and as a member of various professional sports organisations'. Linton Kwesi Johnson, Jamaican-born, 'internationally acclaimed dub poet', spoke on 17 March about 'his first moves into poetry, public performance and music'. Courtenay Griffiths, Jamaican-born, a 'leading lawyer' (now, but not then, a QC), spoke on 14 April on 'the interaction and dynamic between the experiences of his youth and his development into becoming a young professional barrister'. Michael La Rose, Trinidad-born, 'co-ordinator of the Peoples War Carnival Band, chairperson of the Association for a Peoples Carnival, one time vice-chair of the Carnival Development Committee', spoke on 12 May about 'the rise of the sound system in popular culture and social life'. Alex Pascall, Grenada-born, 'broadcaster, journalist, drummer, carnival and folklore specialist' spoke on 16 June about 'the historic BBC Radio London programme 'Black Londoners' for which he was the presenter and co-producer'. The last speaker in the first series was Tobago-born[3] Colin Prescod, who spoke on 'becoming an academic sociologist and social analyst'.

For the second series in 1999, Dennis Bovell, born in Barbados, 'accomplished musician, sound engineer, composer, band leader and producer, Britain's reggae maestro', spoke on 25 January about his career as a musician and producer. Althea McNish, born in Trinidad, 'leading textile designer and artist', spoke on 22 February about her artistic development. On 15 March, Grenadian-born Gus John (a core member of the circle and a George Padmore Institute trustee), professor of education and ordained minister, spoke about his varied career in education administration, research, youth work and activism. Reverend Wilfred Wood, Bishop of Croydon, Barbados-born, spoke on 19 April about his vocation in the Anglican Church and allied community development work.

Aggrey Burke, Jamaican-born and like Gus John a GPI trustee, 'consultant psychiatrist and a pioneer in his field in Britain', spoke on 17 May. Yvonne Brewster, Jamaican-born 'actress and theatre director, founder of the Talawa Theatre Company', spoke on 14 June about her work in the theatre in Britain and Jamaica. Alexis Rennie, Grenada-born, was the last speaker, on 12 July; 'civil engineer and building contractor', he spoke about his experience in the construction industry as a salaried professional and as an entrepreneur.

The speakers were all Black persons, all save Crooks born outside Britain but who had spent most of their lives in Britain. There were three women and eleven men. One speaker was born in Britain, four were born in Jamaica, four in Trinidad and Tobago, two in Barbados, and three in Grenada. All were at the time of making their presentations intellectuals broadly defined: Prescod, Pascall and Crooks in journalism; Brewster in theatre, Connor-Mogotsi retired from the theatre but writing a biographical study of her South African husband; Johnson a writer and performer; Bovell a producer and recording artist; McNish an artist and designer; Burke a psychiatrist; John a minster and education consultant; Griffiths a barrister; Rennie a civil engineer; Wood an Anglican bishop. All to varying degrees have come to public prominence in Britain. All have had involvement to varying degrees in political struggles involving Black people in Britain. Virtually all have had long involvement with cultural production (if we count professional sport as a form of cultural production, so as to include Crooks; it might be harder so to treat engineering). Most of these speakers are or have been cultural activists as I conceptualized the term in this book's introduction: they work or have worked in the area of cultural production – journalism/media, theatre, poetry, visual arts, further education – and they have sought to bring to their work a radical consciousness grounded in an attachment to equality and social justice.

Narratives from the 'Heroic Generation'

Roots and Origins

In late modern societies, having a life implies having a life story, which is the account we render to others by way of explaining who we are (Giddens 1991: 53–4; Linde 1993). As all narratives the life story has a beginning. In the stories people tell about their own and their immediate family's origins, we find important indicators of the structures and processes which are incorporated and constituted in making up the subject's self-representation. In this section I will look at how roots and origins were presented by speakers in the GPI life experience series.[4]

Pearl Connor-Mogotsi: I was born into a very large cosmopolitan family in Trinidad, and my father, Alfred Nuñez, he was a headmaster in Arouca, and my mother Georgiana Nuñez, was a teacher also, before they moved to Diego Martin in north Trinidad. Father to take up a post as ward officer of the district, mother as registrar of births and deaths as well as running the post office . . . My mother was a white woman with red hair, but she had some Carib blood in her; in Trinidad she was considered white. Father was a Portuguese of African origin; his mother was the daughter of a freed slave, she had been educated by the family with whom her father worked and made certain that all her children were educated. Father's two sisters also became teachers . . . Father's blackness was never a problem, it was more a matter of class. There was a great mixture of colours in my family, some black like ebony, others white with curly locks, some red and orangey [sic] like me[5] with bushy hair like fibre, yet there was never any difference between us. Father was very proud that he was the grandson of a freed slave, but in my family there were not many like that.

Colin Prescod: My ancestral roots were somewhere in West Africa, and which were part of my life through the presence of Obeah and Shango, Shango ceremonies which happened in my yard, I remember the drums, I remember the fire, I remember the spitting of rum from the mouth, I remember people catching the spirit[6] . . . My cultural underpinning as a citizen of Trinidad-Tobago, was a mix of cultural inventiveness from Africa, Asia – India in particular – and from European influence.

Courtenay Griffiths: Our roots are [very deep] in the Jamaican working class – my father was a carpenter, a cabinetmaker; on many occasions he had to leave my mother with this large family to go to work . . . it was during the Second World War, he was working on the rebuilding of the Panama Canal and moved to the US, that was the way of life during that period – mass unemployment and underdevelopment . . . [his father left when Courtenay was ten weeks old] . . . I never saw him to recognize him until I arrived off the boat train from Calais, at Charing Cross in 1959, having just completed a three-week sea crossing.

Michael La Rose: I came to Britain as a little six-year-old from Venezuela, a South American country, with the Caribbean just coming off the tip of it. And there we had colour TV . . . skyscrapers . . . big cities. So when I came to England, I did not come as a 'country bookie'[7] as someone who didn't know anything. I saw England as a very green, a very dull place, a lot of soot in the air and a lot of people wearing grey suits and brown suits . . . the same kind of clothes . . . the houses all looked the same, there were no skyscrapers, there were just little houses, so I thought this was a country of little people as there were just these little houses everywhere. That is what I thought from the train.

Aggrey Burke: We started off in a little village on the edge of St Ann where Garvey was born and I have very few memories of that period, except that my godmother lived nearby and though she now has a stroke she still ranges as one of the three or four people of greatest importance to me. There were these proud, middle-class black people in the villages in Jamaica and only recently I have come to have some understanding about how I might have been part of this business, that is the Jamaican, and Caribbean and African experience.

Gus John: We belonged to a family that was quite unusual in some respects – my maternal grandmother was a member of a large Louison family and my brother has constructed a very elaborate family tree . . . among the Louisons there were those that were poor, there were those who were middle-class and the relatively rich. My grandmother was a very humble hard-working soul . . . I'm told that she was a pillar of the village and did a lot of things in terms of getting women of the village organized marketing produce and those sort of things.

Burke's and Prescod's emphasis on having been raised in organic folk culture was quite pronounced; John and Connor-Mogotsi to a lesser degree. On the evidence of the overall narratives presented by these people, I would argue that no simple traditionalist harking-back-to-the-good-old-days is involved: the importance of the folk backgrounds seems to be to establish the difference between where these people see themselves as having been born and where they are now – Britain.

The evocation of an African-derived folk culture is significant for some Caribbean-heritage persons in Britain. In the GPI series it was an indicator of how the racialized dimensions of the self are constructed. The context for this construction in the cases of Connor-Mogotsi and Prescod is their remembered construction of class-colour stratification of the colonial Caribbean, from which their narratives of roots are spoken. For persons of colour in the colonial West Indies the issue of African ancestry was a complex one, with the general tendency of those who understood themselves to have such roots being to downplay them or to be ambivalent about them (Nettleford 1992). There were exceptions, exemplified by the assertion in the mid-nineteenth century of Black humanity's worth by J.J. Thomas (1969 [1889]); but generally African ancestry was not something one boasted of.[8] Taking him as the paradigm case of the Black Caribbean-heritage intellectual-activist, several commentators have pointed to C.L.R. James's seeming ambivalence over his African ancestry, for which they usually cite passages from *Beyond a Boundary* (James 1963) in evidence; they have concluded that James, like many middle-class Black West Indians, was caught in the double consciousness of being both a modern and a Black subject, because the discourses of the former generally exclude the latter (Buhle 1989; Tiffin 1995; Worcester 1996). Such a notion of ambivalence of Black identity resonates well with Connor-Mogotsi's assertion:

> [Our parents] did not want us to mix with the villagers in Congo village, which was a short distance away from our home – because she said we would talk Congo; at that time I did not even know that the Congo was a country.[9] Mind you, nothing at all about Africa ever came into our home, because under colonialism Africa was backward. Father was upwardly mobile and did not want us to speak badly, we had to speak the King's English, hence we were deprived of the little patois. He imported sheet music from England and had us singing . . . English ditties around the piano, especially on Sundays.

The social formation and ideological climate had changed considerably by the 1960s, which saw Black Power enter public discourse and political practice throughout the Atlantic world.[10] For the generation who came to consciousness in that era, the notions of 'Black power' and 'Black is beautiful' had gone some way towards deconstructing the embarrassment or ambivalence over African roots that was part of the life-world of earlier generations of Black people. Nowadays it is not only militant Black nationalists who assert their African roots. This is the outcome of Black Power struggles throughout the Atlantic world, allied to though sometimes in competition with affirmative struggles by other non-White groups. The post-1960s political/cultural climate, wherein difference is promoted and celebrated by many academic, media and other cultural discourses in the Atlantic world, is one which has been supportive of discourses of Black roots and identity; ideas and symbols of roots and identity as markers of difference have been central to post-1960s cultural politics. We may usefully contrast the way Connor-Mogotsi talks about the issue of African roots in her narrative,[11] to Colin Prescod's bold assertion of West African ancestry; the difference is accounted for partly by the difference in age: he is in his forties while she is three decades older. Unlike Pascall or Connor-Mogotsi, the relatively younger speakers – Prescod, Johnson,

Griffiths and Michael La Rose – locate their coming to a radical political awareness in a 1960s period of upheaval and related Black assertiveness.

The class origins of each speaker were variously stated in each narrative. Griffiths spoke of his family's roots in the Jamaican working class; he and his seven siblings were raised in West Kingston; he remembers his father frequently being away from home in search of work. Gus John too remembers a father who migrated for work, to Aruba in his case. Johnson noted that his mother was a domestic worker, and his father did odd jobs. Prescod's family are described by him as an important Tobago family, who had formerly owned a lot of land, but had seen their circumstances deteriorate because the land was not sufficiently productive; he said that he believed that the uncle he lived with as a child was severe on him about schoolwork and conduct because that uncle had 'failed' to increase his inheritance. Prescod stated that his father was from Grenada and his grandmother from Panama, emphasizing his pan-Caribbean family tree. Michael La Rose took a deconstructive tone in talking about his origins, overturning the usual centre-periphery paradigm by juxtaposing modern Venezuela with its skyscrapers to the little English houses he first saw from the train. The effect of this rhetorical tactic is to establish that his own links to modernity in its urban manifestation predated his arrival in Britain.

Childhood and Early Schooling

Courtenay Griffiths: The kind of school I went to was [one] where [you were told] . . . not that you were going to be a production worker; you were told that you were going to be one of the power brokers in this society; and I see that difference between myself and some of my black colleagues at the bar today: that in certain situations, they lack the confidence which comes from that kind of educational background.

Pearl Connor-Mogotsi: I received my secondary education in St Joseph's Convent in Port of Spain, run by nuns, from Ireland I believe, although I was not a Catholic myself. I was immediately aware of the different [evaluation by teachers] of the students in my class: the French Creoles and the light-skinned ones, and the blondes and the golden-haired girls were put in the front of my class; and all the black children were at the back. But the Indians were even behind us [laughter], because they were coolies; the black children often forgot that they had been called niggers in the recent past – but such is the nature of racism. At that time I could not understand what was going on around me, and I was in revolt, I was driving all the black children and Indians to the courtyard, to protest, and

I could not understand why they were being treated differently; I used to visit their homes and enjoy their way of life. Trinidad Indians and Negroes suffered a lot of discrimination because of colour; I was soon aware of the colour bar. The Chinese were more elitist; they kept apart because they passed as white and dealt in business, keeping to their own exclusive clubs – that is Trinidad for you.

Linton Kwesi Johnson: It was in the panthers [i.e. the British Black Panther Party] that I discovered literature; there were certain books we studied chapter and verse – *Capitalism and Slavery*; *Black Reconstruction* and *Wretched of the Earth*.[12]

Colin Prescod: I thought I would begin by telling you how, as a boy, I came routinely first, or rather top of the class . . . when I was in primary school in Tobago, just before I came to England; I remember at the age of nine or ten . . . every Friday, every end-of-term test, every end-of-year test, I had to be first in my class or I got licks[13] . . .

Michael La Rose: I remember in school [In Britain] . . . I told my teacher I wanted to do eight O Levels. He said, 'O Levels, to do what?' I said, 'Well to do A Levels and go to University.' He said, 'No, no, no you're aiming much too high. You should try to get on a course and be a mechanic.' I said, 'Why should I be a mechanic? Going to university is no big thing. My cousins in Trinidad were lawyers and doctors and they went to university . . .'

Alexis Rennie: Anyway I, like my older brother Neville, attending the Presentation Boys College in St George's for my secondary education. I have actually much fonder memories of the days of my primary education than those in Presentation College. I think mainly because it was obvious, though not an official policy, that the white Grenadian students and those of mulatto origin were treated more compassionately and caringly by the all-white Irish brothers who were the main teachers and who controlled the college.

For Connor-Mogotsi, Rennie, Griffiths and Kwesi Johnson there is a close association between their memories of school and their becoming aware of racial and class differentiation. Connor-Mogotsi drew on her memory of high school to render an ironic picture of the colour, race and class structure of colonial Trinidad. Kwesi Johnson said he first became aware of White racism in his first days in high school in Britain, shortly after his arrival from Jamaica. Kwesi Johnson appeared to have largely negative memories of his high school period. While in elementary school in Jamaica, he remembers, 'I was considered very bright as a child'. After moving to an English comprehensive school, he found himself 'with 95% of all the other black kids' in the C stream, eventually working into the B stream. At 14 years of age he expressed a desire to be an accountant, to which his White teacher's reply was: 'Accountant! A big strong lad like you! We need lads like you. Do you realize you have to serve a five years articleship . . . and anyway, you people are always complaining about the police. Have you ever considered joining the police?' Kwesi Johnson recalls that there were two or three teachers he had respect for. (Implicitly, the one who recommended he look into joining the police was not one of these.) He got involved with the Black Panther youth movement as a teenager, and he attributes a great part of his education to that. Michael La Rose narrated a similar story of low teacher expectations when he was in a British high school.

In contrast, Griffiths, Brewster, and Prescod recall being encouraged to do well in high school. Griffiths, who attended an English public (i.e. elite private) school, narrates his high school years as making available to him a good education and the right kind of cultural capital. Prescod remembers that he was a founder pupil of one of the first major comprehensive schools in London – Holland Park – with 2500 pupils and 'just a few blacks'. He remembers having to fight Teddy boys, saying 'it doesn't hang heavy with me'. He was encouraged to work by teachers, he did well academically, attributing this in part to his home discipline and to momentum built up from the licks he got from his uncle.

Kwesi Johnson remembers enjoying being the 'man of the yard', growing up in Jamaica after his parents had separated. He recalled: 'I got my folk culture from my grandmother, the Bible was the only book in the house . . . My granny told us duppy [ghost] stories at night'.

There was an idyllic side to Connor-Mogotsi's childhood memories:

> There was no electricity in Diego Martin at that time: we used gas, candles and large pitch-oil lamps for light. When we were left to go to sleep at night we thought we could hear all the old frightening folklore characters coming to play, we would jump up and scream and howl in fear; we had that kind of life: a lovely, magical, folklore-based existence.

Griffiths, while recalling there was some racial harassment, relates this as part of a narrative in which he was able to confront harassment:

> [O]f course there was a disability in being the only child of African origin in that school from 11 and a half years to 18 and a half; for example when I was in first year, there was a group of boys in the third year that gave me a hard time, . . . but what they did not know was that I had

older brothers[14] so one day we waylaid them outside the school and gave them a serious kicking [more laughter from audience]; thereafter I never had a problem in school at all; I became a firm favourite [with teachers and fellow pupils]. That taught me a lesson: when dealing with racism and racists at that time one has to be up front and if need be to be prepared to go to the step of adopting violence.

Fights in school, some of which were remembered as racist encounters, were part of the narratives of Prescod and Michael La Rose as well, but not that of Connor-Mogotsi.

Political Engagement

People tend to narrate the factors which influenced them to become involved in activism in terms of events, people, organizations or cultural products such as books or music (Andrews 1991; Johnson 1996). Some events are sign-posted as being pivotal in directing the subject toward an activist standpoint; such pivotal events in the personal narrative are referred to as epiphanies by Denzin (1989). The epiphany occurs in those problematic interactions/situations where the subject confronts and experiences a crisis. The epiphany is a point where the relations between the individual and the social context is brought into dramatic relief. The epiphany for Denzin should be interpreted as a social crisis of the individual: 'Troubles are always biographical. Public issues are always historical and structural. Biography and history thus join in the inter-pretive process' (Denzin 1989: 18). Some of the speakers in the GPI series narrated their coming to political awareness in terms that are arguably akin to epiphanies, while others talked of a more gradual process of politicization. All of these persons are quite reflective on their political development, and appear to have theorized the process to a considerable degree. These reflective (even reflexive) and theorized accounts feed back into a discursive environment – the talks themselves, the networks of which New Beacon is part – where others engage in similar reflection and theorizing.[15]

Colin Prescod: [In the 1960s] I built my political praxis, in support of, or on the margins of, the rise of radical Black Power politics in Britain, and a connected Pan-Africanism . . . I have to say that I recall, I feel that there was this very conscious politics at this time amongst black people, and one that was possibly suspicious of me with my openly white wife . . . I say this not because I felt it was a big deal, but I heard it, I felt it at the time, it was real, I could understand how it was, I'm not making a fuss

– 154 –

about it now, I did not make a fuss about it then . . . so there was a sense in which I did not push myself into the politics of the time . . . I was there, . . . and this was something which affected how I entered the politics.

Pearl Connor-Mogotsi: Now Beryl McBurnie – the Carmen Miranda of the West Indies – was most famous for having established the Little Carib Theatre, and projecting the culture and arts of Trinidad and Tobago – the dance . . . she was my role model and one of the greatest influences of my life. Her associates were Jack Kelshall and Lennox Pierre. There was also Wilson Minshall – father of Peter of carnival fame – and Colin Laird,[16] who both gave Beryl much-needed support; and ever since Jack founded the Trinidad and Tobago Youth Movement and held a conference on Caribbean federation in 1947, which I participated in. Afterwards I travelled to other islands to establish a federal youth movement . . . In that same year I travelled up the islands by schooner; I mean, which was very revolutionary for that time, my father let his daughter go on a schooner – a boat with only men on it.

For Prescod, his activism and his university training are intertwined, perhaps not surprising in the narrative of someone who describes himself as a 'sociological activist'. In 1964–67, after high school, he was at the University of Hull, reading sociology, after deciding that economics was not for him. After that he proceeded to the University of Essex for a Masters degree with the intention of continuing on to a PhD, but stopped off because he 'was suspect of doing academics when things were taking place in the street'.[17] He said: 'Black Power came to Britain in the 1960s'. Prescod's activism seemed to have been closely tied into intellectual pursuits, as evidenced in this self-critical account. (In the mid-1970s he joined the *Black Liberator* Collective.)

We were Marxist Leninists, we published a Marxist-Leninist journal, we were also people involved in the politics of defending black people under attack . . . publishing a journal was a good way to communicate our analysis of the situation to people. It was a very stylish, good-looking publication, expensive to publish . . . we sold the journal all over London, mainly to black people . . . it was a journal, unfortunately, that used words and analysis that were so high that at one point we had to have a glossary . . . we stopped, and why we probably could not go on beyond the 1970s is that even with a glossary, some of the people selling it would have needed glossaries to understand our glossaries . . . [Loud laughter from the audience] . . . still, the BL [Black Liberator] collective made a lot of things happen.

Pearl Connor Mogotsi's narrative has her involved in activism from her teenage years as a founding member of the Trinidad & Tobago Youth Council. She travelled the West Indies talking on a federated West Indies, independent from Britain:

> I went to St Lucia, Castries, and I met Derek Walcott for the first time, and Derek and his friends decided that I must come and talk to them in their school; so, I went to the school. The head of the college was a priest . . . he wanted to know why the boys wanted to hear what I had to say, so I was questioned by him. He said to me what were my motives, and whether I was a communist [laughter from audience]; I told him that I was a nationalist, working for the independence of Trinidad and Tobago and for the Caribbean Federation. I must have [satisfied] him, because he allowed me to address the class. I also visited the French islands of Martinique and Guadeloupe . . .

Linton Kwesi Johnson locates a 1972 encounter with the police as an important event in forming his political consciousness. In December 1972 he was walking through Brixton market when he noticed a scuffle between two White policemen and a Black man. He went to have a closer look, in part he says because the policy of the Black Panthers, of which he was a member, was to get the name and address of any arrested Black youth so that they could inform the person's relatives; he did this and also wrote down the police officers' numbers as he had been trained to do. He recalls then being grabbed by the police and thrown into a van where he was given 'a good kicking'; he was later charged with assault. Within an hour of his arrest there was a demonstration outside Brixton station, he recalls. He was let out on bail after three hours. When his case came up he recalls there was one Black and one Asian man on the jury, 'and if it was not for them I would have been found guilty'. This episode fed into his early work as poet; he says that when he recited verse composed around this incident, people began to take notice of him.

Griffiths points to the time he spent at the Greater London Council (GLC) and then his later work on the Blakelock[18] case as pivotal to forming him as a progressive Black legal advocate. He then worked for some time in Harlem in New York, and credits that period with his realizing that his experiences were common to Black people everywhere. His practice took off after that, he said. His next major turning point was the case over the murder of PC Blakelock; on this case he was junior to noted progressive lawyer Michael Mansfield. He learnt a lot by studying the leading counsel for the defence team at work – a White woman –

who appeared to believe that a good argument was all that was needed for a not-guilty verdict, given the sparse evidence of the prosecution. Griffiths feels that she was unaware of the dynamic of racism that was at work in the courtroom, with a majority White jury and a Black defendant in such a sensitive case. The defendant was found guilty. He surmised from this case that 'we can't entrust our future, we can't entrust our lives to persons who are not committed, who don't appreciate the politics of the situation, [the advocates] have to know how to operate and to defend properly in a case like that'.

For Pascall the mere fact of being Black in Britain heightened his political awareness. When the chance came to broadcast a show for Britain's Caribbean-descent population, he jumped at it, despite poor conditions and unsteady support by the BBC, because it seemed a way to engage issues before a wide audience. Pascall represents his years on the *Black Londoners* programme as exciting but filled with controversy. He portrays himself as a crusading broadcasting figure representing Black people as a group in a hostile media and cultural environment. He says he was quite consciously seeking to combat stereotypes through the use of radio, and trying to politicize the representations of Black people in Britain and abroad.

Michael La Rose's terrain of activism was in the field of popular music and carnival masquerade. His talk in the GPI Life Experience series developed the same themes that were raised in conversations between him and myself. Michael La Rose's narrative developed two lines of resistance: one to racist domination as experienced by Blacks in Britain, another to the hegemony of Jamaican popular cultural forms in the lives of Black youth in 1970s Britain. In his account at the GPI talk the Peoples War Sound System is represented as a project through which Michael and others like-minded sought to make concrete these lines of resistance.

Bishop Wood related an intertwined story of developing his priestly vocation and awareness of social inequality. His initial motivation to move from Barbados to Britain was a concern that the spiritual needs of West Indian migrants were not being fully met in Britain. Soon after arrival in Britain in 1962 he came to see a need for ministering to other needs:

> I became increasingly dissatisfied with a ministry to people's spiritual needs which seemed to ignore their obvious physical needs and raised this with the Vicar. He sympathized with my anxieties but thought that I should first have a proper grounding in the bread-and-butter aspects of parish ministry – supporting people in funerals, weddings, baptisms and illness before tackling social and political action.

Like Wood, Gus John's earliest experiences in Britain are seen through the lens of ecclesiastical work – he was a seminarian during the upheavals of the 1960s and remembers that period as crucial for forming his political outlook. Work with Black migrant communities in Oxford introduced him to the issues of social exclusion and racism in education. In addition to his work around these he recalls:

[T]he one thing that stands out in my mind more than anything else is the work we had to do in relation to immigration maters. Now I'm talking about 1965/1966. We had to form a rota of people who would leave Oxford and drive to Leamington Spa, to Bradford, to Blackburn, to Southall, and find relatives of individuals who were being detained at the Harmondsworth Detention Centre in Heathrow and were likely to be put on a plane the following day if some relative couldn't go there [and vouch for them].

When senior theologians around him discussed how they might engage in social improvement in South Africa, for example, John remembers challenging them for not committing themselves fully to progressives causes. He was not satisfied with their answers. It was decided that he was losing his vocation and steps were taken to help him reorient himself. He went on a country retreat, to no avail. Then, after a period of Jungian counselling, John was judged quite normal and given a dispensation from his vows. He moved to London.[19]

Burke's narrative was highly reflexive – unsurprising in a psychiatrist – with layers of social analysis overlain on his life history. As a student at Birmingham university Burke came into contact with students from the wider Caribbean and Africa. Two key moments in Burke's political memory are the unrest following the expulsion of radical Guyanese historian Walter Rodney from Jamaica in 1968, and the effects of the 1970 Black Power uprising in Trinidad. Burke was in Jamaica and then Trinidad during a period following his initial medical training in Britain when he wanted to work in either Africa or the Caribbean.

Performances of the Self

The Vindicated Self

While it is usually the powerful who write their life stories or have them written by others, it is also the case that autobiography, as other forms of personal narrative, is important in the expressive culture of subordinated social groups – the working class, women in sexist society, migrants, enslaved persons, ethnic minorities. Subordinated people frequently are moved to affirm the self by writing their life stories in the face of domination and marginalization. They speak the truth of their own lives to the power that denies them subjecthood.

Many people, structurally excluded from roles as intellectual, political and social subjects, have been motivated by a 'vindicationist impulse' – where they set out to prove their human subjective worth in the face of exclusionary discourse and practice; vindication of the subordinated persons is achieved by their offering 'testimony' from their own lives, showing in a sense that 'this is what happened to [them] when [they] took on the system, perhaps you can learn something from [their stories]'. Also, because such persons generally functioned outside the establishment, they did not value 'objectivity' as such; to be grounded in spaces of resistance to domination was more important than trying to meet objectivity-criteria of institutions that were not disposed to accept them. In the preface to her autobiography, Angela Davis wrote:

> When I decided to write the book after all, it was because I had come to envision it as a political autobiography that emphasized the people, the events and the forces in my life that propelled me to my present commitment. Such a book might serve a very important and practical purpose. There was the possibility that, having read it, more people would understand why so many of us have no alternative but to offer our lives – our bodies, our knowledge, our will – to the cause of our oppressed people (Davis 1974: xvi).

The narratives presented in the GPI series are those of people who, though they experienced or were at least aware of, class and racial discrimination in their own lives, at the time of relating these accounts were all successful and established in their chosen careers. As such, their personal narratives are those of achievement and thereby vindication of the capabilities of Black and working-class people in the face of racist and classist discourses and practices.

One of the aims of the 'Life Experience With Britain' series, according to John La Rose, was to combat what he saw as a kind of amnesia on the part of mainstream British society, which manifested itself in the forgetting of the contributions made by Black subjects to the well-being of the Empire in colonial times. In the following account, we find Connor-Mogotsi confronting that amnesia:

> George Nuñez [her older brother] was very adventurous, he joined the [Royal] air force and trained as a pilot, he flew a Lancaster bomber, and unfortunately was killed over Essen in forty-three [1943]. There is such

memory about our people and the contributions made from little islands like Trinidad in the Caribbean that we have to remind the people in this country about; that we gave our best, we gave the best that we had, into that kind of struggle, which should be remembered.

Prescod deals with the forgetting of the interwoven history of Black and White in the Empire, by resorting to the discourse of radical sociology:

My life was marked by journeys, and this awareness maybe put me ahead of people whom I eventually came to teach, whose lives were also embarked on journeys . . . I moved from periphery to centre of the world capitalist system, from colonized status to rebel citizen, peasant to proletarian . . . this particular race, class and cultural mix and contradictions set me up with what C.W. Mills called a sociological imagination . . . and a predisposition to sociological activism.

Michael La Rose and Alex Pascall also seemed concerned that the historical record of the impact of Black people on British society should 'be put right':

Alex Pascall: When I hear people today talk about the history [of the London carnival] Mrs Lazlett you did us very well. But Claudia Jones is who did it. And let it not be otherwise written or documented. Let the rest who came around her, many of us, pay tribute as the years go by. Let's put history right.

Michael La Rose asserted that what is now widely celebrated as the club and rave culture of contemporary Britain has got unacknowledged roots in the transformation of late-night entertainment brought by Black Caribbean youth in the 1960s and 1970s:

The social habits of white youth changed. When I used to go out to youth clubs, you would go out at 12 p.m. by bus, and when the clubs closed at 4 a.m., there used to be an army of black youths walking the streets home. They didn't have cars and there were no night buses . . . Today that is completely different. The rave, house and acid scenes see thousands of white youths going out at 2 o'clock in the morning and coming in at 8 o'clock in the morning.

Another aspect of vindication is the attempt to valorize cultural forms which are closely associated with subordinate social groups, and so are themselves devalued. Johnson recalls of his time studying for a degree in sociology that he tried to formulate a 'sociology of reggae music by doing a textual analysis of the lyrics'; he began to think of reggae artists as poets (Johnson 1975). Aggrey Burke devoted part of his presentation to reflecting on the African influences on his own development and wondered what it might offer in terms of a resource for self- and community-development among Black people in Britain. Connor-Mogotsi recalled performing Caribbean folk dances in Britain with her first husband Edric (also from Trinidad):

> Edric had a strong sense of national identity which made him a pioneer of our folk art in Britain. He was constantly promoting our songs, music and folk dances, and we often performed these at social events. We used to dance the bongo, and the doption and so on and I used to dress up in traditional dress, and we used to give the people great thrilling times. He knew all these things but I didn't, because as I told you my father kept us away from all these things, but in two twos Edric got me coached [laughter from listeners]; I was absolutely on the ball, and I learnt all those dances, and I really enjoyed them, you know, I don't know what would have happened if father . . . yes, where was I? . . . so we sang the songs and performed.

We can discern a common structure to narratives of vindication, which held true in the GPI series. The subject comes to a realization that he or she is somehow stigmatized in the wider society – race being the most significant stigma in the narratives discussed here; then through a process of learning and struggle, the subject comes to a critical understanding of how the stigmatization works; the next stage is to become aware of how other people challenged the stigmatization and to emulate or at least to be inspired by their example. This is where the political value of personal narratives becomes apparent; I shall return to this point in the concluding section of the chapter.

A common process articulated in these narratives is that of self- and community-transformation through education. The transformative, consciousness-raising value of education for radicals is explicable in terms of a cultural politics oriented toward the revolutionary end of the conservation-transformation contrast that lends the notion of culture some of its almost paradoxical quality. We saw in the previous chapter that personal narratives by Black male colonial subjects in the Caribbean tended to place great emphasis on the importance of schooling in building a sense of self that could withstand the knocks of racist discourses and practices. This drive to learn holds true for many political-engaged persons.[20]

The Class(ed) Self/The Racialized Self

While in each case discussed in this chapter the self-representation is a racialized Black one, the narrators also represent themselves as positioned in class society. All of these individuals resort to the language of class in their personal narratives, frequently in conjunction with race; in so doing they occupy a distinct place in Black anti-racist discourse and practice. They construct their identities not as solely racialized, nor with race before class, nor class before race, but as constituted out of an interplay of race *and* class. This position says a lot about the kinds of personal and social relations and shared ideological positions which underpin the selection of those who spoke at the GPI series.

Johnson has worked with the New Beacon circle since the late 1960s and he names John La Rose as one of his major influences, along with C.L.R. James (Brasher 1996); James is well known for his insistence on thinking race and class as closely linked; I discussed John La Rose's race-aware conception of socialism in Chapter 4. Prescod is the current chairman of the Institute of Race Relations; he took over the chairmanship when La Rose retired. La Rose, who during his own prior term as IRR chairman (1974–1975), was one of several persons who were instrumental in having the name of the journal changed from *Race* to *Race and Class* so as to broaden its scope (personal communication with John La Rose). Griffiths emphasized the value to him as an advocate of his public school education; for him, that education in conjunction with his Black working-class background equipped him to cross class boundaries in British society, and made him a better criminal lawyer. Connor-Mogotsi is engaged (mid-2001) in finding a publisher for a biographical study that she co-wrote of her second husband, Joe Mogotsi, a member of the Manhattan Brothers – famous for their vocals and song-writing talents in 1950s South Africa, and now trying to recover royalties alleged to have been stolen by their music publisher under apartheid. These connections account in part for their common position of seeing race and class as socially co-determined.

During an exchange in the GPI series, when she was part of the audience at Prescod's talk, Connor-Mogotsi said:

we have to have our own ideas solid before we move out into the world . . . and of course as you know South Africa is the great example, the people who liberated a lot of black Africans were white South African liberals, the blacks didn't have the power, they didn't have machinery, connections with the outside world, and certainly a lot of Jewish people . . . had a lot to do with it . . . so I don't think we should be blinkered at all about our own interest in other people, white, yellow green or pink, Spanish, Portuguese, anything at all.

This was said in response to a speaker who asked whether it made any sense to pursue Black struggle outside of generalized class struggle. I understood Connor-Mogotsi to be referring to Black people when she says 'we' in the passage quoted above. She concedes a universalist case, yet seems to be insisting that there should be a relatively autonomous space for Black struggles. Her concession that many Blacks in South Africa lacked the power and connections needed to react effectively, while many White liberals helped to overthrow apartheid, points to the articulation of an interlocking race- and class-consciousness that is characteristic of the New Beacon circle.

The Self Performed

The personal narrative is more than an 'objective' account of selected life events. The words used in the personal narrative serve functions beyond that of pointing to supposedly real events and people. The 'truth' of the personal narrative is not to be found only in the literal text:

[V]erifiable truth in the autobiography rests not in the historical facts of the life account but in the degree to which the autobiographer's chosen metaphors of self communicate to and link up with his or her intended audience (Angrosino 1989: 9).

Angrosino here reiterates the importance of lending due consideration to the discursive context out of which a personal narrative is written and read.

For the GPI series, the most important aspect of the context out of which the personal narratives was constituted has to do with the people who formed the audience. At the talks I attended there were mostly Blacks, with a minority of Whites and Asians. Males and females seemed evenly distributed; most were adults. John La Rose told me that many of the attendees were persons he had known for a while, or younger relatives or friends of such persons. I discovered, through mingling after the talks, that many were teachers, community activists, people in the arts or media. Many had been involved in the projects and organizations I discussed in earlier chapters. These prior social relations of many members of the audience and the speakers are exemplified by Prescod, who opened his presentation by saying: 'I'm in the position of talking to people who, like John [i.e. John La Rose], know more things about me than I know, and who know more about the kinds of things I am going to talk about than I know'; and by Pascall's opening by paying tribute to John La Rose and to the spirits 'around this house'. I find Connerton enlightening on this issue even though his argument is premised on the speaker-performer being a relative stranger to the audience:

> If we are to play a believable role before an audience of relative strangers we must produce or at least imply a history of ourselves: an informal account which indicates something of our origins and which justifies or perhaps excuses present status and actions in relation to that audience (Connerton 1989: 17).

The requirement to 'play a believable role before an audience' held for the speakers in the GPI talks even though there was some mutual acquaintance and even familiarity at these events. This was so because the requirement of narrating a self-history was the *raison d'être* of these events: the believable role was *explicitly* (rather than *implicitly*) that of a person narrating his or her own life story. In this instance the means – rendering the plausible self-account – was also the end – establishing sympathetic rapport with the audience.

One way to read the GPI series is as an event where the speakers were 'preaching to the converted'. There is evidently some truth to this. But the plans to publish the series do point beyond that audience of familiars, to a wider readership to which New Beacon, as publishers and booksellers, have access. The composition of the audience at the GPI talks has implications for the question of outreach: are the circle's projects reaching as far into Black communities in Britain, and crossing class and culture boundaries, as one of their stated aims? I will discuss that issue more fully in the conclusion to the book. At this point what is most relevant is that this audience composition was important in setting the context in which the narratives were articulated. This is seen most clearly if we move now to consider the presentation of personal narratives as a performance practice.

The speakers in the GPI series drew on shared assumptions of knowledge and value in making their presentations. As men and women of words (Abrahams 1983) – all seasoned public speakers – they depended to a large extent on their verbal skill in engaging the audience. This was done in a mode that was more interactive than the formal delivery of a university lecture. The presentations were often punctuated by the audience laughing or making affirmative sounds. The speakers all played on this audience reaction, secure in the knowledge that a pause on their part would appropriately be filled by laughter from the listeners.[21] There was infrequent – but well-timed – change of register from Received Pronunciation (RP – the English of the Home Counties middle class) English to various West Indian dialect-inflected speech.

Some of the speakers had a distinctive way of dramatizing their presentation. Connor-Mogotsi employed changes of speech rhythm and economical changes of voice tone for irony. Johnson, the seasoned performance poet, gave a subdued delivery, saving his verbal pyrotechnic for the end of his presentation, when he read a poem he wrote in memory of Black German activist May Ayim (who committed suicide in August 1996). When Johnson got to the part where he talked of this woman's thirteen-story death plunge as her 'final stanzas', there was a collective in-drawn breath, followed by total silence.[23] Then we all breathed again. Johnson after all is a pioneer in performance poetry.

Prescod used his whole body in his presentation in conjunction with change of speaking pace and volume. He is quite aware that he is a dramatic, engaging speaker: at one point he tells the audience that a former student had dubbed him as coming from the 'RADA' (Royal Academy of Dramatic Arts) school of sociology – 'a reference to my performing style, I suppose'. Griffiths spoke in RP English, shifting to Jamaican patois on a couple of occasions when quoting persons he knew in inner-city London. All of the speakers employed some Caribbean Creole dialect in some degree during their presentations, to the approval and amusement of the audience.

Several of the presentations could be described as 'multi-media' or 'multi-genre': Prescod, Pascall and Johnson all recited some verse, but it was Michael La Rose who made the most use of another medium, punctuating his presentation with recorded music. He used this music to indicate particular periods and events; for example, ten or fifteen minutes into his talk, he played several recorded pieces (his son Renaldo was operating the tape recorder), introducing them thus: 'Now what I want to do at this point is just play a couple of tunes that give you an indication of feeling of the music at that time. This is especially important for the younger ones here'. He plays three reggae tunes, then says 'I hope that brings back memories for some people and I hope it educates others.'[23] There were four musical intervals in Michael's presentation.

Summary: Personal Narrative as a Cultural and Political Resource

Personal narratives are valuable as a cultural resource because they constitute a stock of social memory. A collection of autobiographical signification is the inscription of the experiences embodied by the narrators. Accounts of what happened to individuals in their own lives, accounts of the development of a local community or an institution, and even complex accounts of the place of a nation in the world are all frequently rendered in narrative form. I concur with Josselson, who writes:

> Narrative is the means by which we, both as participants and as researchers, shape our understandings and make sense of them . . . The truths inherent in personal narrative issue from real positions in the world – the passions, desires, ideas, and conceptual systems that underlie life as lived. People's personal narratives are efforts to grapple with the confusion and complexity of the human condition (Josselson 1995: 32).

In the public telling of their life stories, the people I discussed here are engaged in consolidating and deploying social and cultural capital. They are also engaged in symbolic labour, in constituting new meaning. I use the term *social capital* because in collectively telling their life stories they are maintaining and deepening social connections which have in the past enabled their personal, activist, and professional development, and which may do so in the future. I posit *cultural capital* because, while anyone can tell a life story, it requires verbal, bodily and dramaturgical skill to tell a life story effectively, that is to say, to engage the audience at emotional and intellectual levels, to cause them to make an investment in the narrative event such that they recognize themselves in the teller and in the tale. These life-experience talks were an exercise in consolidating and deploying cultural capital for another reason: the encoded, remembered and even perhaps embodied knowledge which constitutes the life story is a vital resource in maintaining the self, which is among other things a cultural activity. To render to others a convincing account of the self requires the narrator of the self to know what to tell and how to tell it. A life story then is both knowledge in itself and knowledge for itself.

The political effect of personal narratives inheres in their offering concrete, accessible examples of action, of how to organize and conduct various types of life-project. They can offer guidance and suggestion to persons who may not have had the advantage of the schooling necessary to digest abstract theoretical discussions of political theory and tactics. This was one of the ways in which personal narrative was put to use in the GPI series. Personal narratives have been used to counter stereotyping by their representation of lives that run against the grain of the stereotype. Beyond that they can be utilized in both hegemonic and counter-hegemonic constructions, precisely because the significant structures and processes which affect people tend to find their way into their personal narratives, though the refiguration and then reading of the social and cultural in the personal narrative is by no means simple.

As humanistic documents, personal narratives give us partial, mediated access to the inner world of others. While we cannot know what life's vagaries actually mean for another person, we can make informed guesses as to how they construct their symbolic world by engaging with their written and/or spoken self-representations (Crapanzano 1980; Herzfeld 1997). As Crapanzano writes: 'We can know . . . the rhetoric of symbols but we cannot know, except hypothetically, how symbols are experienced' (1980: xi).

In closing the chapter, I return to a problem I have sought to explore throughout this book – that of thinking about 'Black' political and cultural activism in other than ethic-essentialist or bounded-community terms. The persons whose narratives I discussed above see themselves as politically active in the space of Black Britishness, but the representations made in their personal narratives, and the political and cultural aims behind organizing the speaking events and publication of these narratives, are premised on a concept of being Black in Britain which is not reducible to a bounded 'Black community' in any sociologically meaningful sense of the term.

The personal narratives of a few individuals who have successfully overcome structural constraints of their race and class positioning are not sufficient to counter the vast exercise in life world colonization of all British people – Black, White, Asian and other – that goes by the name of race relations. A few life stories are not sufficient to weigh in against this mega-structure, but I believe they are nonetheless necessary. Personal narratives can serve a pedagogical function ultimately, and this is the main way in which they have been utilized in the GPI Life Experience series.

Notes

1. The first series of talks has been published (White and Harris 1999), with more than 600 copies sold as of June 2001; at that time the second

series of talks was in the final stage of editing, on target for early 2002 publication.

2. The passages quoted in this and the following paragraph are taken from the short biographies and promotional flyers for each speaker's presentation.

3. 'Trinidad and Tobago' is the proper name of the twin-island nation state. There is strong identification with either island from those born there, so persons will refer to themselves as 'Trinidadian' or 'Tobagonian', respectively, even though they originate in the same nation state. A politically correct designation, used by some journalists and writers from Trinidad-Tobago is the term 'Trinbagonian', which is yet to go into widespread public usage.

4. Unless otherwise stated, the quotations are from my own notes and recordings made at the events; for those talks which I was unable to attend – Crooks, Brewster and McNish, I have not made any quotations, since part of my approach here is to place the texts into the contexts of the presentations.

5. Pearl is very light-complexioned.

6. I understand Prescod here to refer to ecstatic possession in Orisha and Shango ceremonies, which have been documented for Trinidad (Herskovits and Herskovits 1947).

7. Connotes a rustic, someone ignorant of modern and/or city ways.

8. Race and colour stratification is an enduring theme in the imaginative literature of the Commonwealth Caribbean. Sander (1988), studying colonial Trinidadian fiction, has noted that the pioneering novelists worked in the social realist paradigm; their concern to render faithful representations of ordinary people resonates with that of the classic ethnographer. Both Sander and Stewart (1989) argue that these novelists have provided rich insights into colour/class stratification in the colonial Caribbean. For a sample of this fiction see De Boissiére 1981; James 1971 [1936]; Lamming 1986; Mendes 1980 [1934]; Selvon 1952.

9. This sentence was punctuated by considerable laughter from the audience.

10. This is not to be taken to mean that Black assertiveness is only a feature of the post-1960s era: Marcus Garvey's movement suffices as the counter-example from earlier in the twentieth century (Martin 1976).

11. Connor-Mogotsi in fact presents herself as a Black woman; I read her narrating her family's colour tensions as a way of expressing her Black identity as not reducible to a determining African ancestry.

Evidence that her reading of her family's ethnicity was layered and complex is given by the following statement about her mother: 'She got a great deal done because she was considered white and received special privileges from the powerful high-brown people who represented colonial Trinidad'.

12. The references, in the same order Johnson names the texts: Williams 1964; Du Bois 1963 [1935]; Fanon 1967b.

13. To 'get licks' in the English of the south-eastern Commonwealth Caribbean means to be flogged. Corporal punishment looms large in the personal narratives of many adults of Caribbean heritage; it is widely, but by no means universally, believed in the English-speaking Caribbean that physical punishment is an effective method of disciplining children.

14. At this point there was much laughter from the audience and an air of anticipation.

15. The danger of ethnomethodological slippage – the researcher reflecting on him- or herself reflecting on his or her informants' reflections on . . . (!) – is real here as it remains for me in my engagement with the work of the circle.

16. Beryl McBurnie brought the hybrid Afro-European folk dances of Trinidad to respectability as 'art'. Kelshall and Pierre were left-wing lawyers intimately involved in workers' and anti-colonial politics. Laird is an English-born architect.

17. Politically-engaged intellectuals often claim to feel acutely a tension between the drive to learn and the urge to act. Marx and Gramsci both decried the bourgeois division between mental and manual labour; C.L.R. James often expressed suspicion of the motives of academics who engaged part-time in politics. In her autobiography, Angela Davis (1974) wrote that she was increasingly uncomfortable with staying on as a graduate student in Berlin in 1968 while there was intensifying anti-racist activity in the USA.

18. PC Blakelock was fatally stabbed on the Broadwater Farm estate in Tottenham, North London, in 1985, during the riots there which followed the death of Cynthia Jarrett, a Black woman who died in a struggle with police officers. A Black man was charged with the murder of PC Blakelock. The case polarized opinion along 'racial' lines.

19. John has researched and published several important studies on race, politics and community (John 1972; John and Humphry 1971; Humphry and John 1972).

20. As examples we have Malcolm X's (1968) prison conversion and self-education, or Angela Davis (1974) applying herself to the study of Marxism and European philosophy, and all the while trying to make the ideas inform her political work. Like Davis, Grace Lee Boggs was trained in academic philosophy and sought to turn this knowledge to activist work (Boggs 1998).

21. Fine writes: 'We narrate stories to help us process our experiences. As a result of our conversations, we build shared identification and rely on common emotional reactions that are easily called out' (Fine 1995: 134).

22. See, or rather, hear: 'Reggae Fi May Ayim', track 6 on Linton Kwesi Johnson, *More Time*, LKJ Records, 1996. LKJ CD 018.

23. From my field diary: Several of the more mature members present at Michael's talk (there were more than a dozen children and adolescents there, as well), such as Roxy Harris and Alex Pascall, nod heads in time with the music, smiles of pleasure – and reminiscence? – on their faces. The selections for that interlude were: 'Israelites' by Desmond Dekker; 'Blood and Fire' 'talking about rebellion and burning down, and an Al Green tune made into reggae'; the final one was by 'Big Youth' who was, according to Michael, 'a toaster (MC – Master of Ceremonies) who had gold teeth and locks and was the epitome of all that we wanted to be at that time'.

–6–

Radical Lifework

The life is illuminated by the work as a reality whose total
determination is found outside of it – both in the conditions
which produce it and in the artistic creation which
fulfils it and completes it by expressing it.

Jean-Paul Sartre[1]

I believe it is theoretically and morally indefensible to subsume individuals
and issues of individual agency within social structures. Yet, any social
study must seek to read, in ways that are historically and theoretically
explicable, the structures of constraints and possibilities in interaction
with which individuals and their projects exist and are realized or not, as
the case might be. When considered from this standpoint, the account
which you have just read shows that while the New Beacon circle are by
no means unique in their opposition to various forms of social and cultural
exclusion, especially as these impacted on Black people in Britain, they
were special in that they were able to mobilize considerable resources to
fight against race and class domination, police repression, streaming of
Black pupils into channels for the educationally sub-normal in schools,
and Eurocentric and sometimes racist narratives about the history of Black
and Asian people and their claims to belong to the British nation
(reconceptualised by the circle as multi-ethnic, multicultural society prior
to the arrival of blacks and Asians in large numbers).

Their activist work has required considerable personal commitment
spread over decades, in some cases. This meant in some cases following
relatively precarious occupations, subordinating career development to
activist work. While Roxy Harris and Irma La Rose, for example, had
stable salaried jobs in education, others like Janice Durham, Michael La
Rose and John La Rose had more precarious occupations. Sarah White
worked for years as a science journalist, then gave it up to work full time
in the bookshop and on circle projects. This occupational insecurity was
also the case with many other persons in allied organizations such as Race
Today and Bogle L'Ouverture (Roxy Harris, personal communication with
author). Many members of the circle paid a price in terms of deferring

their formal education for political work. If we recall the distinction made in radical humanist writing on education between schooling as formal training as against education as holistic development (Freire 1985 [1972]), we might consider that a significant number of core members of the circle did not have formal education and qualifications beyond school level, during the peak years of activism (1970s and 1980s). Roxy Harris explained to me:

> It would be fair to say that many members of the three allied organizations [New Beacon, Race Today and Bogle L'Ouverture] sacrificed formal education for activism for at least fifteen years. A number of them were left with personal crises, after the peak years of activism, concerning the ground they had lost vis-à-vis their non-activist contemporaries (personal communication).

This completely escaped my notice at first. I think because I first met most of these people at the New Beacon bookshop, I came to associate them most closely with literature and formal scholarship. This perception was further reinforced by my meeting them at a time in their collective life cycle when they were concerned with documenting their activities. The personal struggles and career insecurities of the peak period, as Harris puts it, were alluded to in interviews and conversations, but were not emphasized by any of my interlocutors. I have had to struggle to escape the easy empiricism of taking the members of the circle for what they at first appeared to be i.e. intellectuals first, activists second. Whole dimensions of their activist lives and work were completely outside my direct experience. I have had to attempt to recover these through life histories and documents.

It is neither circular nor banal to say that the circle were able to do what they did because of who they were: their social positions partly set the field for the conception and realization of their projects. But social structural analysis does not adequately address the issue of *why* they chose the kind of projects which they did – community organizing, bookselling, publishing, teaching – and not others. Such a question calls for a bio-graphically-informed approach, as argued by Sartre (1963) in the *Problem of Method*. No one is either entirely free or totally constrained, *but some people are more constrained than others*. My ethnographic-biographical method was intended to gain some purchase on the related interplay of agency/structure and life/work. My approach was intended to bring questions of biography, society and history into the kind of engagement called for by Mills's (1959) *Sociological Imagination*.

In building their cultural activist projects, in recognizing that culture was a potent space of political contestation, my interlocutors may be seen collectively to occupy the role of organic intellectuals vis-à-vis the Black and, for them, wider working class generally, principally in Britain. Gramsci saw intellectual activity as ubiquitous to social life:

> All men [*sic*] are intellectuals, one could therefore say: but not all men have in society the function of intellectuals . . . This means that, although one can speak of intellectuals, one cannot speak of non-intellectuals, because non-intellectuals do not exist (Gramsci 1971: 8).

Gramsci posited two types of intellectual. The traditional intellectual represents the interests of those in power. This is not to be taken to mean that traditional intellectuals are necessarily of the ruling class – indeed, Gramsci reminds us that many children of the peasantry become traditional intellectuals through the route of clerical training and office. By contrast, the organic intellectual represents the interests of the subordinate in society, variously defined; it must be noted that organic intellectuals need not have been born into a subordinate social class – what is pivotal is their political alignment with such a class. Such intellectuals counteract the hegemony of the ruling coalition of classes and class fractions. A defining characteristic of the organic intellectual is constant *engagement* with politics: such intellectuals do not only think and write, but they act. The organic intellectual is therefore also an activist. Writing on his own involvement in the development of cultural studies in Britain, Stuart Hall delineates two aspects to the work of the organic intellectual:

> On the one hand, we had to be at the very forefront of intellectual theoretical work because, as Gramsci says, it is the job of the organic intellectual to know more than the traditional intellectuals do: really know, not just pretend to know, not just to have the facility of knowledge, but to know deeply and profoundly . . . But the second aspect is just as crucial: that the organic intellectual cannot absolve himself or herself from the responsibility of transmitting those ideas, that knowledge, through the intellectual function, to those who do not belong professionally to the intellectual class (Hall 1996: 267–8).

The circle's emphases on holistic education and on knowledge in the service of social transformation lend strong support to the organic and movement intellectual theses. This is perhaps their area of greatest impact, where there is evidence of their having made a difference, in terms of expanding knowledge of newer literature in English, influencing an expansion of the range of literature taught in English schools and held in libraries, to include Caribbean, African and Asian works. Nowadays we tend to take this expansion of the literary canon for granted, and we sometimes forget the educational and activist work of an organization like the Caribbean Artists Movement, which helped to pierce the boundaries of the literary establishment. Through their publishing and bookselling the circle have helped to imagine and implement educational projects which were and are still at the cutting edge of processes that are nowadays termed 'multiculturalist'. An important part of their praxis is to mobilize biography as a political and cultural resource toward educational ends – we had one example of how they go about this at the GPI 'Life Experience with Britain' series.

As political actors the core members of the New Beacon circle appear to be hard-headed realists with respect to the power relations encoded in bourgeois cultural form and production, especially as these apply to the politics and political economy of schooling, writing and publishing, and to the political consequences of official categorization and policy-making predicated on ideas of race relations and bounded ethnic communities. Their realism is most vividly illustrated in their insistence on running the bookshop as a profitable business, and is also shown by their ongoing struggle to maintain financial autonomy, even if it means letting some projects close down. It is seen also in their plans to get their business and non-profit activities onto the Internet, and so keep pace with changes in communication technology.

There are problems which militate against effective organic activism – chiefly the issue of resource availability and mobilization, which is connected to the maintenance of relative autonomy from the existing structures of state and large civil institutions and of ensuring the long-term survival of the activist collective in question. The circle have been often confronted by a major drawback of the kind of autonomous activism in which they engage: as projects expand more broadly in the activists' terrain of engagement, there is increased pressure on human and other resources. The very autonomous standpoint of such activists then militates against rapid mobilizing of resources needed to meet increased organizational and technical demands. This was clearly at work behind the decision to discontinue the Book Fair. After political differences with the other two founders, New Beacon was left 'holding the can': with John La Rose's declining health and Sarah White's full-time engagement at the shop, there was a shortage of resources which could not easily be made up. The personal toll of the work was considerable. Roxy Harris explains:

> For my part what I actually did was exercise an exhausting super-commitment to activism which meant little or no leisure time . . . I can remember, for example during the New Cross Massacre campaign, working a full day then

driving to somewhere like Rugby for an evening meeting, returning to London in the early hours then being at work the next morning and working a full day (personal communication with author).

Another question which must be put to the circle is whether they have done enough to ensure that there will be a younger generation of activists to continue their work. Kinship links are important for the circle and through these we may trace lines of generational continuity. Michael and Keith La Rose were involved in the political milieux of their parents, John and Irma. Moreover, with peers they initiated their own activist projects, such as the Black Youth Movement and Peoples War sound System. Wole La Rose, the son of John La Rose and Sarah White, works occasionally for the bookshop. Remi Harris, daughter of Roxy Harris and Pat Harris, works on George Padmore Institute projects, including one to develop the Institute's website. Like her father had to before her, Remi must find time outside a regular salaried job (in the music industry in her case) to engage in activist work. Renaldo and Ramona La Rose, children of Michael La Rose and Janice Durham, have also given assistance, as has Roxy Harris Jr (the brother of Remi), though to my knowledge none was regularly involved in the four-year period of my own contact with the circle.

What will have to be confronted when thinking about the future of the work of the circle is whether in the so-called 'information age' and/ or with increasing electronic information-transfer, book publishing and bookselling will be as potent terrains for activism as they have been hitherto. This issue is of paramount importance in considering cross-generation continuity. An important part of that consideration must be concerned with what issues are politically motivating young people at the start of the third millennium. While cynics would see a late modernist triumph of lifestyle over political action, of narcissistic working on the self and a focus on consumption, we cannot overlook the many thousands of young people who have organized in virtually every country of the world around environmental issues and against global capitalism. The new millennium opened with heightened political activity suggesting that not everyone is content to lie back and enjoy late capitalism. The established political class in Western countries agonize over falling voter turnouts and bemoan young people's rejection of ballot-box politics. What that political class fail to see is that widespread disillusionment with their own brand of liberal democracy is accompanied by growing activity in the extraparliamentary political sphere. As C.L.R. James advocated, we need to look for the future in the present.

That future is open. The circle's ongoing project to establish the George Padmore Institute and eventually to have regular seminars, to promote research into the archival holdings on the circle's past projects, and to disseminate information over the Internet, all point to an awareness that the future must be planned for in concrete terms; they take the view that cultural politics will take on changed forms in the future. On the other hand, some elements of the circle's politics – especially their disdain for racial and ethnic nationalism, their socialist perspective on social transformation and their humanist universalism – put them at odds with currently widespread identity politics and politics of difference.

The circle and their projects existed and continue to exist in a context of considerable ideological and practical variation; sometimes the circle's activists are in alliance with other Black and radical groups, other times in contention. Perhaps the main reason why they remain tactically ecumenical even if strategically focused is that in the spheres of socialist, anti-racist politics and 'Black politics' there was, and is, neither a monolithic structure of ideas nor any one grand narrative of practice, in Britain or elsewhere. That having been said, it is also the case that the circle's articulation of race and class politics delineates a distinctive space in activism which has been relatively ignored by the fascination of cultural studies with postmodern identity politics, and disdain of many young scholars in cultural studies for projects of the 'Old Left', as well as older leftists. I question the faddishness and ageism of this point of view. Also, militant Black nationalism recently has occupied a large space in public perception of anti-racist politics in the UK; too large a space in my view. The New Beacon circle, in contrast, are living embodiment that the multi-ethnic socialist politics of the 1960s and 1970s is not dead.

The notions of *strategic universalism* and *transculturalism* can do useful work in translating the work of the circle back into sociology. Neither term is my own invention. The first is intended to represent a political design and standpoint which recognizes human differences but elects to try to find bases for coalition in organizing for remedies to problems seen to impact on people across human differences. It is of course the classical socialist strategy; but the way in which it was deployed by the circle was with an awareness of the need to recognize and adjust to non-class dimensions of social being, especially that of race; in so doing they at times constructed, in contrast to strategic universalism, a tactical *essentialism*. It is in terms of developing tactics within an overall strategy that we must understand the way the circle attached the signifier 'Black' to their projects. They formed, for example, a *Black* Parents Movement because there was a need to organize round a central antagonism – i.e. race – in a racist social and educational setting. Black was the means to an end and not the end in itself. Their Black activism is a tactical engagement which is subordinate to their strategic or transcendent vision for social transformation of oppressive relations. All political activists have a utopian vision: a radical democratic society is the circle's utopia. As they engage with present-day social antagonisms around race, they name some of their politics Black. Ultimately though, their activism is *against race* understood as the fundamental basis of identity and social organization. This style of Black activism deserves greater attention than it has been given.

The second term – transculturalism – is intended to suggest a way out of the main problem of multiculturalism: which is, how might we recognize cultural difference without essentializing it, such that we can account, for instance, for frequently documented instances of persons acting 'out of character' for their 'culture'. I do not suggest that these two terms as I use them represent theoretical or political solutions to the problems confronted by the activism I discussed in the book. Nor do I suggest that the people and ideas I wrote about have in any way 'solved' these problems in their political projects. I have written this book to make visible a conception of activism seen mainly through biographical narratives which may account in terms of new social-movement theory for ideas and projects usually understood reductively as Black politics conceived of and as an affair chiefly of concern to Black people.

Rather unfortunately, it seems as if it is enough for an activist grouping to be concerned with questions of race for it automatically to be excluded from candidateship for a new social movement. Writings on the new social movements are addressed to the coalitions of persons and projects that came out of 1968: student politics, workers' autonomy, a revitalized women's movement, environmentalism and lifestyle politics. Where writers on new social movements have engaged with questions of race as a site of struggle, they have often written about the actors in narrow and stereotypical terms, and appear uninterested in those activists who contest the dominant discourses of racial and ethnic signification. A few examples: in an otherwise illuminating reading of identity politics in the 1990s, Castells (1997a) frames Black politics in the USA only in terms of 'Black communities' and Black activists who accept the definitions of race that are constructed by mainstream US opinion; in an otherwise comprehensive treatment of social movements, della Porta and Diani (1999) bring up struggles over racial signification in a passing reference to Rastafarianism. With the exception of Eyerman and Jamison (1991), none of the major theorists of social movements pays much attention to Black radical political activity organized in 'mixed-race' collectives in modern Western societies. It is all-or-nothing for Black radicals, apparently. Black activism that rejects as part of its praxis conceptions of Black culture seen in terms of racial meanings is relegated to the margins of social-movement discourse, or omitted altogether.[2]

In Britain, many currently middle-aged and older Black activists, like many of their White counterparts, were engaged as young adults in the upheavals of the 1960s (exemplified by John La Rose and Sarah White first meeting each other in 1965 at a public meeting at the Nkrumah-funded Africa Unity House in London). Like many White activists too, some have adapted to the new social movements, others have been suspicious, while some have rejected them altogether. Given where the members of the circle worked, the nature of their work, and indeed the historical processes which framed the narratives I presented in this book, I find it surprising that the network of organizations of which the circle was a part does not get even passing mention in surveys of the cultural politics of the New Left in Britain (Chun 1993; Dworkin 1997). Surely the circle's venture into what is now termed multicultural literature, and indeed the formation of the Caribbean Artists Movement, are connected with the politicization of culture – '1968' – that has decisively impacted on society in Britain since that iconic year? But that question will have to be answered in another study. Still, my work as reported here suggests that the way in which the cultural politics of the New Left in Britain is conceived obscures a group of actors like the New Beacon circle.

The issue of *identity* is important here. We now generally hold, in the social sciences, that identities are socially constructed, and are thus not essential attributes of human beings, even though it is widely believed by many people that identities are somehow natural. We may think of identity as emerging in that zone where our own sense of who we are encounters others' conceptions of our self. This can be a zone of tension, and the struggles to name ourselves as subjects in the face of powerful social and cultural forces which may name us otherwise can shift depending on historical circumstances and whether the individual who is working at moulding identity is from a more or a less powerful social grouping. Castells (1997a) points out that identity is not role: roles are defined by norms structured by the institutions and organizations of society.[3] Identities are socially constructed, to a degree, and do depend on institutions, but they must be internalized as a source of meaning by individuals. Important questions which follow from this conception are: How, why, by whom and for what are identities constructed? Projects of identity are always unfinished, because both history and the individual life expressed as biography are in constant movement.

The New Beacon circle is an activist grouping comprised of Black and White members, inspired by and engaged with both old and new social movements. They maintain a classic class politics while making interventions into the spheres of culture – high and popular. They span the 1960s watershed that divides old from new social movements. They advocate a humanized history of the making of the modern Western world system, combining grand and personal narratives. This history is indissolubly connected to the overall development of the modern Atlantic world system. They mobilize joint efforts to narrate/write themselves and their political constituency into history as subjects. In so doing they begin by creating what Castells termed resistance identities, where the socially excluded turn away from the dominant social structure and seek to develop alternative institutions and systems of value. But the New Beacon circle do not stop there: they are mainly concerned with imagining and working toward a transformed society beyond the present reality. Their activism imagines a point in the future where contemporary social divisions and antagonisms are mediated, if not eliminated, by a more democratic and inclusive society. In this they are building a project identity, a collective sense of being in the world which is predicated on working for social transformation and thereby, self-transformation.

To paraphrase the Touraine (2000) epigram with which I began this book: we cannot live together in the global system if we hang on to our old essentializing identities. The circle have tried to create new, more inclusive, transcultural, *transracial* (Stephens 1999) social identities. I think that judging whether they have succeeded in this is less important that trying to understand how and why they made the attempt. In the circle's rejection of the stale categories and politics of 'race relations' we may read a critical awareness of the historical and social construction of race. In the praxis of the circle we may read an awareness that identities are constructed from social and cultural resources; we may also read an awareness that identities are made in conditions of social and economic constraint *and* opportunity; and that these constructions are sites of political contestation. Unlike many intellectuals and activists involved with identity politics, the circle's core members hold firm to the grand narratives of revolutionary and Marxian social history and political economy.

History is an important resource and terrain of imagination and action for the circle. In their work they instigate a conversation across time and space, reading the racialized politics of contemporary Britain through a radical history of anti-colonial struggle, working-class politics and politically committed intellectual artistic endeavours that span the Atlantic world system. In their work they have constituted a way of thinking about politics and identity, especially with regard to so-called ethnic minorities, that is radically different from dominant essentializing conceptions of these issues. Their sometime essentialism is tactical, strictly limited in scope to particular campaigns. A critical universalism is more typical of the circle's praxis. They are aware of the many obstacles to a fully inclusive politics, but still maintain inclusion as the ultimate goal of a transformed social reality. Going against the grain in much contemporary Black identity politics, the circle turn their backs on the allure of race, to borrow Gilroy's (2000) phrase.

In their publishing and bookselling and outreach activities, the circle are creating historical counter-narrative. By recovering and republishing little-known Black writing, by promoting radical black and third-world literature, by independent publishing and bookselling, the circle are imagining and placing themselves and their constituency in history. To elucidate how this imagining and placing worked I moved from description of their projects and relations to close reading of parts of their life histories. Personal narratives did double duty in the book. Life histories not only served to illuminate the work of people in the circle, but also are integral to the work of the members of the circle themselves: life history is part of their apparatus of representation, and is also part of the symbolic resource on which they build their activism.

The new type of subject that is constructed and engaged in much contemporary cultural politics is perhaps better understood in terms of *positionality*, of movement within and among different identity points none of which determines in the final instance, rather than in terms of position within stable structures of class or race or gender (Hall 1996; Hall 1996 [1989]). Contingency is the important notion here: social-structural positions do not determine identities – at any given point for any given person, identity is constructed, only contingently, at the intersection of various positions in discourse and social relations. These positions are in motion and so too is the identity that is temporarily made visible at their meeting points. This is not to say that persons cannot hold and act upon stable notions of themselves and their identities; they do, but are still not entirely free agents in this. History, geography and biography place limits on the possibility of play in identity, which I conceived in this book as made by persons, but always under conditions of constraint that it is the business of the sociologist to elucidate.

I consider, in passing, my own involvement during fieldwork in light of Touraine's (1977) technique of sociological intervention as an approach to the close study of activists involved in new social movements. For

Touraine, the sociologist must engage with the social-movement collective, must enter into dialogue with them, must observe and record their shared activity – with all of which I am in agreement. But Touraine goes on to argue that the purpose of the sociologist studying new social movements should be to inscribe the activists' ideas and analyses and then pass these back to them as the highest social meaning of their projects to affect social change – strong stuff indeed. I reject a strong version of Touraine's thesis in favour of a much weaker version. The fact of my interlocutors' extensive knowledge and experience of activism, and their having worked out in depth their own analyses of their action, implies to me that a Touraine-style intervention would have been inappropriate. Such an intervention would have perhaps even been absurd: for me to suggest to the circle that I could produce an analysis of their work that would uncover its 'highest social meaning' would have been arrogant and presumptuous.

In closing, I return to Gramsci's idea that the whole of society could be seen as having educational impact, in the sense that the existing political, social and economic arrangements of any society tend (Gramsci *must not* ever be read deterministically, tempting though it is here) to 'school' people into patterns of thought and behaviour appropriate – to a greater or lesser degree – to the maintenance of the existing order. How appropriate this schooling is to the existing hegemony depends on how secure is the grip of the ruling blocs. For Gramsci, education was a crucial site on which to wage struggles for social transformation (Adamson 1980; Gramsci 1971). Such a view resonates strongly with the ideas and practices discussed in this book.

For the New Beacon circle, education is perhaps the single most important process in bringing about the kinds of social transformation they desire: a life project of John La Rose and Sarah White was the setting up of the bookshop, international book service and publishing house; another early project was the setting up of the supplementary school; the Book Fair sought to disseminate literary culture with a particular political slant to as wide a potential as possible. All of these projects are educational. Related to this are two other recurrent themes concerning personal growth through education and engagement in political activity aimed towards social transformation. The people whose projects and personal narratives I wrote about here often talked of development in terms of learning about the world and applying and reflecting on that knowledge through acting on the world. What these individuals have in common is a choice of specific intellectual and cultural spaces as a terrain for pursuing politics. What seems to have sustained their commitment over years – in activities that have little financial reward, no guarantee of success, and which require considerable investment of time – is an ongoing collective articulation and practice of their brand of progressive politics, in which process they make and remake themselves as activists.

Notes

1. From *The Problem of Method* (Sartre 1963: 112). Sartre here is writing about the work in two senses: (1) a work as a product of the creative efforts of an individual artist, and (2) a work as the life of any person, seen as a project. Sartre rejects what he sees as the bourgeois division between artistic production and everyday life.
2. Black left-wing activists such as Angela Davis or C.L.R. James exemplify in biographical terms a radical politics that treats race as a central political antagonism without reifying it.
3. Castells (1997a: 6-10) offers a useful typology of identities. First there is *legitimizing identity*: this identity is produced by dominant institutions of society to extend and rationalize their domination vis-à-vis social actors (it fits many theories of authority and nationalism): it generates a civil society, and citizens. Second, we have *resistance identity*: generated by actors placed in stigmatized and delegitimated positions by the logic of domination; this type of identity formation is concerned with survival and resistance to the dominant institutions of society. It leads to formation of communes or communities. Castells terms the making of this type of identity the 'the exclusion of the excluders by the excluded'. Obvious examples are radical separatist feminism or ethnic nationalism. Then there is the *project identity*: using the cultural materials available to them, actors build a new identity that redefines their position in society and in so doing seek the transformation of the overall structure of society. This type of identity leads to formation of subjects; these subjects are not individuals but are instead the collective social actors through which individuals reach holistic meaning in their existence.

Appendix I
New Beacon Publications, 1966–1999

1966   *Foundations: a book of poems* by Anthony La Rose (John La Rose). O/P.

1967   *Marcus Garvey 1887–1940* by Adolph Edwards. Reprinted 1967, 1969, 1972 , 1987; French edition 1983.

        Tradition the Writer and Society: critical essays by Wilson Harris, Reprinted 1973. O/P.

1968   *Caribbean Writers: critical essays* by Ivan Van Sertima. O/P.

        New Beacon Review: collection one edited by John La Rose.

1969   *Froudacity: West Indian fables* explained by John Jacob Thomas. Reprint of 1889 edition with an introduction by C.L.R. James and biographical note by Donald Wood. O/P.

        The Theory and Practice of Creole Grammar by John Jacob Thomas. Reprint of 1869 edition with an introduction by Gertrud Buscher. Reprinted 1989.

1970   *Folk Culture of the Slaves in Jamaica* by Edward Kamau Brathwaite. Reprinted 1974; revised edition 1981.

1971   *Legends of Suriname* by Petronella Breinburg. O/P.

        How the West Indian Child is Made Educationally Sub-Normal in the British School System by Bernard Coard. Published for the Caribbean Education and Community Workers Association. Reprinted 1974. O/P.

        Minty Alley by C.L.R. James. Reprint of 1936 edition with an introduction by Kenneth Ramchand. Reprinted 1975, 1981, 1989, 1994. US edition 1997.

1972   *Georgetown Journal: a Caribbean writer's journey from London via Port of Spain to Georgetown, Guyana, 1970* by Andrew Salkey.

1973   *The Pond: a book of poems* by Mervyn Morris. New edition 1997.

1976   *The Poetry of Nicolas Guillen: an introduction* by Dennis Sardinha.

1977   *Labour in the West Indies: the birth of the workers movement* by Arthur Lewis. Reprint of 1948 edition with an afterword 'Germs of an Idea' by Susan Craig.

        Poems of Succession by Martin Carter.

1978   *A Quality of Violence* by Andrew Salkey. Reprint of 1959 edition.

        Eternity to Season by Wilson Harris. Reprint of 1954 edition with revisions by the author.

1979   *Fractured Circles* by James Berry. O/P.
       Shadowboxing by Mervyn Morris.
       For The Liberation of Nigeria by Yusufu Bala Usman. Reprinted
       1980.
1980   *Jane And Louisa Will Soon Come Home* by Erna Brodber.
       Reprinted 1988, 1993, 1998.
       East Wind In Paradise by Carl Jackson. French edition 1981.
       Pitch Lake by Alfred Mendes. Reprint of 1934 edition with
       introduction by Kenneth Ramchand.
1981   *Being Black: selections from Soledad Brother and Soul on Ice*
       edited by Roxy Harris.
1982   *Theatrical Into Theatre: a study of drama and theatre in the
       English-speaking Caribbean* by Kole Omotoso.
       Lucy's Letters and Loving by James Berry.
       Dreadwalk by Dennis Scott.
       World Without End: memoirs by John Wickham.
1983   *Barrel of a Pen: resistance to repression in neo-colonial Kenya*
       by Ngugi wa Thiong'o. O/P.
1984   *Petals of Thought* by Femi Fatoba.
       *Nigeria – the economy and the people: the political economy of
       state robbery and its popular democratic negation* by Edwin
       Madunagu.
       *History of the Voice: the development of nation language in
       anglophone Caribbean poetry* by Edward Kamau Brathwaite.
       Reprinted 1995.
       Black Fauns by Alfred Mendes. Reprint of 1935 edition with
       introduction by Rhonda Cobham.
       Jamaica Airman: a black airman in Britain 1943 and after by E.
       Martin Noble.
1985   *Bad Friday* by Norman Smith.
       New Beacon Review: number one edited by John La Rose.
       The Truthful Lie: essays in a sociology of African drama by Biodun
       Jeyifo.
       The Myth of Freedom and other poems by S. Anai Kelueljang.
       New Beacon Calendar 1986–1987: Black Children in Britain.
1986   *I Am Becoming My Mother* by Lorna Goodison. Reprinted 1995.
       New Beacon Review: numbers 2/3 edited by John La Rose.
1987   *I Am Becoming My Mother (cassette)* by Lorna Goodison.
       Notes Towards An Escape From Death by Dionyse McTair.
1988   *My Personal Language History* edited by Roxy Harris and Fou-
       Fou Savitzky.

Black Children in Britain: two year calendar 1989–1990.
Heartease by Lorna Goodison.
Myal by Erna Brodber. Reprinted 1992, 1995, 1999.
A Descriptive and Chronological Bibliography of the Work of Edward Kamau Brathwaite by Doris Monica Brathwaite.
Elma François: the NWCSA and the workers struggle for change in the Caribbean in the 1930s by Rhoda Reddock.
Smiles and Blood: the ruling class response to the workers rebellion in Trinidad and Tobago by Susan Craig.
For Bread Justice and Freedom: a political biography of George Weekes by Khafra Kambon.

1990　*Heroes Through The Day* by Ruel White.
Khoi by John Hendrickse.
Mas In Nottinghill: documents in the struggle for a representative and democratic carnival 1989/90 compiled by Michael La Rose.
Kaiso Calypso Music David Rudder in conversation with John La Rose

1991　*Foundations of a Movement* edited by Roxy Harris and Sarah White. Published on behalf of the John La Rose Tribute Committee.
Ghana: the struggle for popular power by Zaya Yeebo.

1992　*The Caribbean Artists Movement 1966–1972: a literary and cultural history* by Anne Walmsley.
Eyelets Of Truth Within Me by John La Rose.
Examination Centre by Mervyn Morris.

1994　*Louisiana* by Erna Brodber. US edition 1997.

1995　*The 1945 Manchester Pan-African Congress Revisited* by Hakim Adi and Marika Sherwood, with reprint of 'Colonial & . . . Coloured Unity (the Report of the 5th Pan-African Congress)' edited by George Padmore.

1997　*Trinidad Carnival* by Errol Hill. Reprint of 1972 edition with revisions.

1999　*Changing Britannia: life experience with Britain* edited by Roxy Harris and Sarah White. Co-published with George Padmore Institute.

Appendix II
Scope of the George Padmore Institute's Archive

It is expected that this archive will be ready for public access sometime in late 2003 or early 2004. Check *www.georgepadmoreinstitute.org* for updates.

- *Caribbean Artists Movement* – 1966 to 1972 – tapes, transcriptions, letters, interviews, photographs.
- *Black Education Movement* – from the late 1960s to the present – minutes, leaflets, campaign material, posters, tapes, photographs.
- *Black Supplementary School Movement* – from the late 1960s to the present – as above.
- *Black Parents Movement, the Black Youth Movement, the Alliance of the BPM, BYM and Race Today Collective* – 1975 to late 1980s – as above.
- *New Cross Massacre Action Committee* – 1981 – as above.
- *International Book Fair of Radical Black and Third World Books* – 1982 to 1995 – as above.
- *Carnival Movement* – 1970s to present – as above, plus costumes, designs.
- *European Action for Racial Equality and Social Justice* – early1990s – as above.
- *New Beacon Books* – 1966 to present.
- *Campaigns and Organizations.*
- *Rare journals and newspapers.*
- *Caribbean, African and African American materials* – relating to the interconnections between different communities of the Black diaspora
- *The Macdonald Inquiry into Racism and Racial Violence in Manchester Schools* (The Burnage Inquiry) – the complete body of evidence submitted to the Inquiry.

Appendix III
Activist Network centred around New Beacon

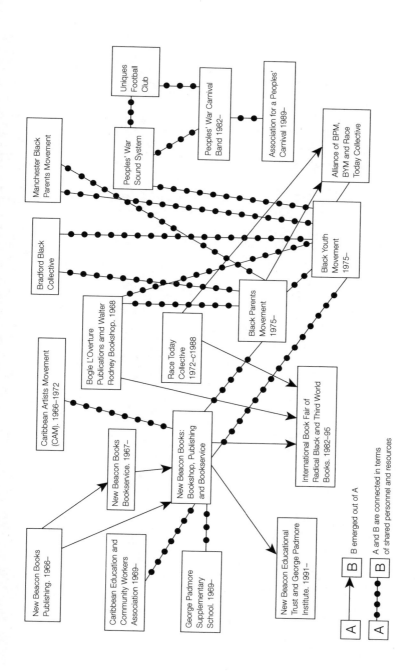

Bibliography

Abrahams, R. (1983), *The Man-of-Words in the West Indies: Performance and the Emergence of Creole Culture*. Baltimore: Johns Hopkins University Press.

Adamson, W. (1980), *Hegemony and Revolution: A Study of Antonio Gramsci's Political and Cultural Theory*. Berkeley: University of California Press.

Adi, H. and Sherwood, M. (1995), *The 1945 Manchester Pan-African Congress Revisited*. London: New Beacon.

Alexander, C. (1996), *The Art of Being Black: The Creation of Black British Youth Identities*. Oxford: Clarendon Press.

—— (2000), *The Asian Gang*. Oxford: Berg.

Ali, T. (1987), *Street Fighting Years: An Autobiography of the Sixties*. London: Collins.

Allen, H. (1987), *Justice Unbalanced: Gender, Psychiatry and Judicial Decisions*. Milton Keynes: Open University Press.

Alleyne, B. (1998a), 'Classical Marxism, Caribbean Radicalism and the Black Atlantic Intellectual Tradition', *Small Axe*, 3, 157–69.

—— (1998b), '"Peoples' War": Cultural Activism in the Notting Hill Carnival', *Cambridge Anthropology*, 20, 111–35.

—— (1999), Cultural Activism. Ideas, representation and practice. A study of the New Beacon Circle, Unpublished PhD dissertation, Department of Social Anthropology, University of Cambridge.

Alleyne-Ditmers, P. (1997), '"Tribal Arts": A Case Study of Global Compression in the Notting Hill Carnival', in J. Eade, ed., *Living the Global City: Globalization as a Local Process*. London: Routledge.

Althusser, L. (1984), *Essays on Ideology*. London: Verso.

Andrews, M. (1991), *Lifetimes of Commitment: Aging, Politics, Psychology*. Cambridge: Cambridge University Press.

Angrosino, M. (1989), *Documents of Interaction: Biography, Autobiography and Life History in Social Science Perspective*. Gainesville: University of Florida Press.

Ashcroft, B., Griffiths, G., and Tiffin, H. (1989), *The Empire Writes Back: Theory and Practice in Post-Colonial Literatures*. London: Routledge.

Back, L. (1996), *New Ethnicities and Urban Culture: Racisms and Multi-culture in Young Lives*. London: UCL.

Bakhtin, M. (1984 [1965]), *Rabelais and His World*. Bloomington: Indiana University Press.

Ballard, R. (1992), 'New Clothes for the Emperor?: The Conceptual Nakedness of the Race Relations Industry in Britain', *New Community*, 18, 481–92.

Beaton, N. (1986), *Beaton But Unbowed: An Autobiography*. London: Methuen.

Beck, U. (1992), *Risk Society Towards a New Modernity*. Theory, Culture & Society. [Special Issue]. London: Sage.

Beese, B. (1977), 'Race Today Interviews New Beacon', *Race Today*, 9.

Belgrave, T. (1993), 'Godfather of Pan', *The Vanguard*, 14, 2.

Benson, S. (1996), 'Asians Have Culture, West Indians Have Problems: Discourses of "Race" and Ethnicity Inside and Outside of Anthro-pology', in Y. Samad, O. Stuart, and T. Ranger, eds, *Culture, Identity and Politics*. Aldershot: Avebury.

Benton, T. (1984), *The Rise and Fall of Structural Marxism*. London: Macmillan.

Berglund, E. (1998), *Knowing Nature, Knowing Science: An Ethnography of Local Environmental Activism*. Cambridge: White Horse Press.

Besson, J. (1992), 'Reputation and Respectability Reconsidered: A New Perspective on Afro Caribbean Peasant Women', in J. Momsen, ed., *Women and Change in the Caribbean*, 15–33. Kingston, Bloomington and Indianapolis, London: Ian Randle, Indiana University Press, James Currey.

Besson, W., and Besson, J. (1989), *Caribbean Reflections: The Life and Times of A Trinidad Scholar (1901–1986)*. London: Karia.

Black Parents Movement (1980), *Independent Parent Power, Independent Student Power: The Key to Change in Education and Schooling*. London: Black Parents Movement.

Blackburn, R. (1988), *The Overthrow of Colonial Slavery, 1776–1848*. London: Verso.

Bloom, H. (1995), *The Western Canon: The Books and Schools of the Ages*. London: Macmillan.

Boggs, G. (1998), *Living for Change: An Autobiography*. Minneapolis and London: University of Minnesota Press.

Bogues, A. (1997), *Caliban's Freedom: The Early Political Thought of C.L.R. James*. London: Pluto Press.

Bolland, O. (1992), 'Creolization and Creole Societies: A Cultural Nationalist View of Caribbean Social History', in A. Hennessey, ed., *Intellectuals in the Twentieth-Century Caribbean*. London: Heinemann.

Bourdieu, P. (1986a), *Distinction: A Social Critique of the Judgement of Taste*. London: Routledge.

—— (1986b), 'The Forms of Capital', in J. Richardson, ed., *Handbook of Theory and Research for the Sociology of Education*, 241–58. New York: Greenwood.

——, and Wacquant, L. (1992), *An Invitation to Reflexive Sociology*. Cambridge: Polity.

Bourne, J., and Sivanandan, A. (1980), 'Cheerleaders and Ombudsmen: The Sociology of Race Relations in Britain', *Race & Class*, XXI, 331–52.

Bowring, F. (2000), *Andre Gorz and the Sartrean Legacy: Arguments for a Person-Centered Social Theory*. New York: St Martin's Press.

Boyle, J. (1994), *Critical Legal Studies*. Aldershot: Dartmouth.

Brah, A. (1996), *Cartographies of Diaspora: Contesting Identities*. London: Routledge.

Braithwaite, L. (1975), *Social Stratification in Trinidad*. Mona: Institute of Social and Economic Research.

Brasher, S. (1996), 'Influences: Linton Kwesi Johnson, Poet', *New Statesman*, 9 August.

Brathwaite, K. (1967), *Rights of passage*, London and New York: Oxford University Press.

—— (1970), *Folk culture of the slaves in Jamaica.*, London: New Beacon.

—— (1971), *The Development of Creole Society in Jamaica: 1770–1820*. Oxford: Oxford University Press.

Brereton, B. (1979), *Race Relations in Colonial Trinidad*. Cambridge: Cambridge University Press.

—— (1998), 'Gendered Testimonies: Autobiographies, Diaries and Letters by Women for Caribbean History', *Feminist Review* (59), 143–63.

Bridges, Y. (1980), *Child of the Tropics: Victorian Memoirs*. London.

Brodber, E. (1994), *Louisiana*. London: New Beacon.

Bryce, J. (1982), 'Black Writers, White Media', *The Leveller*, 16–29 April, 26–27.

Buhle, P. (1989), *CLR James: The Artist as Revolutionary*. London: Verso.

Cabral, A. (1973), *Return to the Source: Selected Speeches of Amilcar Cabral*. New York: Monthly Review Press.

Calhoun, C. (1982), *The Question of Class Struggle: Social Foundations of Popular Radicalism During the Industrial Revolution*. Oxford: Basil Blackwell.

Cambridge, A. (1971), 'Education and the West Indian Child – a Criticism of the ESN School System', *Black Liberator*, 1, 9–19.

Campbell, C. (1986), *Colony and Nation: A Short History of Education in Trinidad and Tobago*. Kingston: Ian Randle.

—— (1992), *Cedulants and Capitulants: The Politics of the Coloured Opposition in the Slave Society of Trinidad 1783–1838*. Port of Spain: Paria.

—— (1996), *The Young Colonials: A Social History of Education in Trinidad and Tobago 1834–1939*. Barbados, Jamaica, Trinidad and Tobago: The Press, University of the West Indies.

Caplan, P. (1997), *African Voices, African Lives: Personal Narratives from a Swahili Village*. London and New York: Routledge.

Carter, T. (1986), *Shattering Illusions: West Indians in British Politics*. London: Lawrence & Wishart.

Castells, M. (1996), *The Rise of the Network Society*. Oxford: Blackwell.

—— (1997a), *The Power of Identity*. Oxford: Blackwell.

—— (1997b), *Local and Global: The Management of Cities in the Information Age*. London: Earthscan.

Castles, S., and Kosack, G. (1985 [1973]), *Immigrant Workers and the Class Structure in Western Europe*. Oxford: Oxford University Press.

Caute, D. (1988), *Sixty-Eight: The Year of the Barricades*. London: Paladin.

Centre for Contemporary Cultural Studies (1982), *The Empire Strikes Back: Race and Racism in 70s Britain*. London and New York: Routledge.

Chun, L. (1993), *The British New Left*. Edinburgh: Edinburgh University Press.

Clarke, A. (1980), *Growing up Stupid Under the Union Jack: A Memoir*. Toronto: McClelland & Stewart.

Coard, B. (1971), *How the West Indian Child is Made Educationally Sub-Normal in the British School System*. London: New Beacon.

Cohen, A. (1993), *Masquerade Politics: Explorations in the Structure of Urban Cultural Movements*. Oxford: Berg.

Collingwood, R. (1994 [1946]), *The Idea of History*. Oxford: Oxford University Press.

Connerton, P. (1989), *How Societies Remember*. Cambridge: Cambridge University Press.

Connor-Mogotsi, P. (1995), 'Our Olympian Struggle', in *12th International Bookfair of Radical Black and Third World Books*. Camden Centre, London, England: The Author.

Cowley, J. (1996), *Carnival, Canboulay and Calypso*. Cambridge: Cambridge University Press.

Crapanzano, V. (1980), *Tuhami: Portrait of a Moroccan*. Chicago and London: University of Chicago Press.

Crick, B. (1995), 'The Sense of Identity of the Indigenous British', *New Community*, 21, 167–82.

Cudjoe, S. (1997), 'C.L.R. James and the Trinidad and Tobago Intellectual Tradition, Or, Not Learning Shakespeare Under a Mango Tree', *New Left Review*.

d'Anjou, L. (1996), *Social Movements and Cultural Change: The First Abolition Campaign Revisted*. New York: Aldine De Gruyter.

Davidson, A. (1977), *Antonio Gramsci: Towards an Intellectual Biography*. London: Merlin Press.

Davis, A. (1974), *An Autobiography*. New York: International Publishers.

De Boissière, R. (1981), *Crown Jewel*. London: Allison & Busby.

della Porta, D. and Diani, M. (1999), *Social Movements*. Oxford: Blackwell.

Denzin, N. (1989), *Interpretive Biography*. Newbury Park.

Dhondy, F. (1978), 'Teaching Young Blacks', *Race Today*, 10, 81–6.

Diani, M. (1995), *Green Networks: A Structural Analysis of the Italian Environmental Movement*. Edinburgh: Edinburgh University Presss.

Du Bois, W. (1963 [1935]), *Black Reconstruction in America: An Essay Toward a History of the Part Which Black Folk Played in the Atempt to Reconstruct Democracy in America 1860–1880*. New York: Russell & Russell.

Dworkin, D. (1997), *Cultural Marxism in Postwar Britain: History, the New Left, and the Origins of Cultural*. Durham, NC and London: Duke University Press.

Eco, U. (1984), *The Name of the Rose*. London: Pan.

Eyerman, R. and Jamison, A. (1991), *Social Movements: A Cognitive Approach*. Cambrige: Polity.

Fanon, F. (1967a), *Black Skin, White Masks*. New York: Grove.

—— (1967b), *The Wretched of the Earth*. London: Penguin.

Femia, J. (1981), *Gramsci's Political Thought: Hegemony, Consciousness, and the Revolutionary Press*. Oxford: Clarendon.

Fine, G. (1995), 'Public Narration and Group Culture: Discerning Discourse in Social Movement', in H. Johnston and B. Klandermans, eds, *Social Movements and Culture*, 127–43. London: UCL Press.

Fox, R. (1989), *Gandhian Utopia: Experiments with Culture*. Boston: Beacon Press.

Freire, P. (1985 [1972]), *Pedagogy of the Oppressed*. Pelican Books. Harmondsworth: Penguin.

Froude, J.A. (1888), *The English in the West Indies; or, The Bow of Ulysses*. New York: C. Scribner's Sons.

Fryer, P. (1984), *Staying Power: The History of Black People in Britain Since 1504*. New Jersey: Humanities Press.

Gandhi, M. (1983), *Autobiography: The Story of My Experiments with Truth*. New York: Dover.

Giddens, A. (1991), *Modernity and Self-Identity: Self and Society in the Late Modern Age*. Cambridge: Polity.

Gilroy, B. (1976), *Black Teacher*. London: Bogle-L'Ouverture Press.

Gilroy, P. (1991), *There Ain't No Black in the Union Jack: The Cultural Politics of Race and Nation*. Chicago: University of Chicago Press.

—— (2000), *Between Camps: Nations, Cultures and the Allure of Race*. London: Allen Lane, The Penguin Press.

Gomes, A. (1974), *Through a Maze of Colour*. Port of Spain: Key Caribbean Publications.

Goody, J. (2000), 'Introduction', in J. Goody, ed., *Multicultural Literature in the Classroom*, 1–2. Sheffield: National Association for the Teaching of English (NATE).

Gorz, A. (1999), *Reclaiming Work: Beyond the Wage-Based Society*. Cambridge: Polity.

Goulbourne, H. (1990), 'The Contribution of West Indian Groups to British Politics', in H. Goulbourne, ed., *Black Politics in Britain*, 95–114. Aldershot: Avebury.

Gramsci, A. (1971), *Selections from the Prison Notebooks*. New York: International Publishers.

Green, S. (1997), *Urban Amazons: Lesbian Feminism and Beyond in the Gender, Sexuality and Identity Battles of London*. London: Macmillan.

Guillaumin, C. (1995), *Racism, Sexism, Power and Ideology*. London and New York: Routledge.

Guillory, J. (1993), *Cultural Capital: The Problem of Literary Canon Formation*. Chicago and London: University of Chicago Press.

Habermas, J. (1972), *Knowledge and Human Interests*. London: Heinemann.

Hall, S. e. a. (1978), *Policing the Crisis: Mugging, the State, and Law and Order*. Basingstoke: Macmillan.

Hall, S. (1996 [1989]), 'New Ethnicities', in K. Chen and D. Morley, eds, *Stuart Hall: Critical Dialogues in Cultural Studies*, 441–9. London: Routledge.

—— (1996), 'Cultural Studies and Its Theoretical Legacies', in K. Chen and D. Morley, eds, *Stuart Hall: Critical Dialogues*, 262–75. London: Routledge.

Harman, C. (1988), *The Fire Last Time: 1968 and After*. London: Bookmarks.

Harney, S. (1996), *Nationalism and Identity: Culture and the Imagination in a Caribbean Diaspora*. London: Zed.

Harris, C. (1993), 'Post-War Migration and the Industrial Reserve Army', in W. James and C. Harris, eds, *Inside Babylon: The Caribbean Disapora in Britain*. London: Verso.

Harris, R. (1996), 'Openings, Absences and Omissions: Aspects of the Treatment of 'Race Culture and Ethnicity in British Cultural Studies', *Cultural Studies*, 10, 334–44.

Hart, R. (1998), *From Occupation to Independence: A Short History of the Peoples of the English-Speaking Caribbean Region*. London: Pluto.

Hebdige, D. (1987), *Cut 'N' Mix: Culture, Identity and Caribbean Music*. London: Methuen.

Herskovits, M. and Herskovits, F. (1947), *Trinidad Village*. New York: Knopf.

Herzfeld, M. (1997), *Portrait of a Greek Imagination: An Ethnographic Biography of Andreas Nenedakis*. Chicago: University of Chicago Press.

Hill, E. (1997 [1972]), *The Trinidad Carnival*. London: New Beacon Books.

Hobbs, D. (1988), *Doing the Business: Entrepreneurship, the Working Class and Detectives in the East End of London*. Oxford: Clarendon Press.

Hooker, J. (1967), *Black Revolutionary: George Padmore's Path from Communism to Pan Africanism*. London: Pall Mall Press.

Humphry, D. and John, G. (1972), *Police Power and Black People*. A Panther Original. London: Panther.

Hunte, J. (1986 [1966]), 'Nigger Hunting in England', *New Beacon Review*, 2/3, 22–37.

Illich, I. (1971), *Deschooling Society*. London: Calder & Boyars.

Ireland, P. and Laleng, P. (1997), *The Critical Lawyers' Handbook 2*. Law and Social Theory. London: Pluto Press.

James, C.L.R. (1933), *The Case for West-Indian Self Government*. London: L. and Virginia Woolf at the Hogarth press.

—— (1963), *Beyond a Boundary*. London: Stanley Paul.

—— (1971 [1936]), *Minty Alley*. London: New Beacon.

—— (1980 [1938]), *The Black Jacobins: Toussaint L'Ouverture and the San Domingo Revolution*. London: Allison & Busby.

—— (1980 [1961]), 'The Mighty Sparrow', in *The Future in the Present*, 191–201. London: Alison & Busby.

—— (1983), *Walter Rodney and the Question of Power*. London: Race Today Publications.

—— and Glaberman, M. (1999), *Marxism for Our Times: C.L.R. James on Revolutionary Organization*. Jackson: University Press of Mississippi.

Bibliography

Bibliography

John, A. (1972), *Race in the Inner City: A Report from Handsworth, Birmingham*, (2nd edn). London: Runnymede Trust.

John, G. (1986), *The Black Working-Class Movement in Education and Schooling and the 1985–86 Teachers Dispute*, London: Black Parents Movement.

John, G. and Humphry, D. (1971), *Because They're Black*. A Penguin Special. Harmondsworth: Penguin.

Johnson, A. (1996), '"Beyond the Smallness of Self"; Oral History and British Trotskyism', *Oral History*, (Spring), 39–48.

Johnson, B. (1985), *'I Think of My Mother': Notes on the Life and Times of Claudia Jones*. London: Karia Press.

Johnson, L. (1975), 'Jamaican Rebel Music', *Race and Class*, XVII, 397–412.

Jones, S. (1988), *Black Culture, White Youth: The Reggae Tradition from JA to UK*. Basingstoke: Macmillan Education.

Josselson, R. (1995), 'Imagining the Real: Empathy, Narrative, and the Dialogic Self', in R. Josselson and A. Lieblich, eds., *The Narrative Study of Lives: Interpreting Experience*. Thousand Oaks and London: Sage.

Kambon, K. (1988), *For Bread Justice and Freedom: A Political Biography of George Weekes*. London: New Beacon.

Kertzer, D. (1996), *Politics & Symbols: The Italian Communist Party and the Fall of Communism*. New Haven and London: Yale University Press.

Kohli, M. (1981), 'Biography: Account, Text, Method', in D. Bertaux, ed., *Biography and Society: The Life History Approach in the Social Sciences*, 61–75. Beverly Hills and London: Sage.

Koningsbruggen, P. v. (1997), *Trinidad Carnival: A Quest for National Identity*, London: Macmillan.

La Rose, J. (1966), *Foundations: A Book of Poems*. London: New Beacon Publications.

—— (1973), 'Back Into Time', in A. Salkey, ed., *Caribbean Essays: An Anthology*, 46–52. London: Evans Brothers.

—— (1985a), *Lessons of the Grenada Revolution*. London: Race Today Publications.

—— (1985b), *The New Cross Massacre Story: Interviews with John La Rose*. London: The Alliance of the Black Parents Movement, Black Youth Movement and the Race Today Collective.

—— (1986), 'The Changing Language of Riots in Britain', *Race Today*, January.

—— (1991), *Racism, Nazism, Fascism and Racial Attacks the European Response*. London: International Book Fair of Radical Black and Third World Books.

—— (1992), 'Everchanging Immanence of Culture' text of talk delivered at 1992 Conference on African Writers in Exile, London, March 27–28.

—— (1996), 'Unemployment, Leisure and the Birth of Creativity', *The Black Scholar*, 26, 29–31.

La Rose, M., Ed. (1990), *Mas in Notting Hill: Documents in the Struggle for a Representative and Democratic Carnival 1989/90*. London: New Beacon Books and Peoples War Carnival band.

—— (2000), 'Definitions, Roles and Responsibilities; Arts Funding Bodies and the Notting Hil Carnival'. London Arts Carnival Meeting. 2 Pear Tree Court, London EC1R 0DS: London Arts Board, 30 November.

Laclau, E. and Mouffe, C. (1985), *Hegemony and Socialist Strategy: Towards a Radical Democratic Politics*. London: Verso.

Lamming, G. (1986), *In the Castle of My Skin*. London: Longman.

—— (1992 [1960]), *The Pleasures of Exile*. Ann Arbor: University of Michigan.

Lemert, C. (1997), *Social Things: An Introduction to the Sociological Life*. Lanham, MD and Oxford: Rowman & Littlefield.

Leon, R. (1971), 'How the West Indian Child is Made Educationally Sub-Normal in the British School System: Critical Remarks on Bernard Coard's Book', *Black Liberator*, 1, 21–31.

Lewis, A. (1977 [1939]), *Labour in the West Indies*. London: New Beacon Books.

Lewis, O. (1968), *La Vida: A Puerto Rican Family in the Culture of Poverty – San Juan & New York*, London, Panther.

Linde, C. (1993), *Life Stories: The Creation of Coherence*. Oxford: Oxford University Press.

Lloyd, E. (1985), 'The International Book Fair of Radical Black and Third World Books: An Interview with John La Rose', *New Beacon Review*, no. 1, 27–41.

Lovelace, E. (1981), *The Dragon Can't Dance*. Harlow: Longman.

Martin, T. (1976), *Race First the Ideological and Organizational Struggles of Marcus Garvey and the Universal Negro Improvement Association*. Contributions in Afro-American and Africa Studies. Westport, Conn. And Canton, Mass.: Greenwood Press [distributed by] The Majority Press.

Bibliography

Mathurin, O. (1976), *Henry Sylvester Williams and the Origins of the Pan-African Movement 1869–1911*. Washington, DC.

Maxton, J. (1932), *Lenin*. London: P. Davies.

Maynard, O. (1992), *My Yesterdays*. Port of Spain: Granderson Brothers.

Melucci, A. (1989), *Nomads of the Present: Social Movements and Individual Needs in Contemporary Society*. London: Hutchinson Radius.

Melucci, A. (1996), *Challenging Codes: Collective Action in the Information Age*. Cambridge Cultural Social Studies. Cambridge: Cambridge University Press.

Mendes, A. (1980 [1934]), *Pitch Lake*. London: New Beacon.

Miles, R. (1982), *Racism and Migrant Labour*. London: Routledge.

Miller, D. (1994), *Modernity: An Ethnographic Approach. Dualism and Mass Consumption in Trinidad*. Oxford: Berg.

—— and Slater, D. (2000), *The Internet: An Ethnographic Approach*. Oxford: Berg.

Mills, C. (1959), *The Sociological Imagination*. Oxford: Oxford University Press.

Mirza, H.S. and Reay, D. (2000), 'Spaces and Places of Black Educational Desire: Rethinking Black Supplementary Schools as a New Social Movement', *Sociology*, 34/3, 521–44.

Moodie-Kublalsingh, S. (1994), *The Cocoa Panyols of Trinidad: An Oral Record*. London: British Academic Press.

Moody, G. (2001), *Rebel Code: Linux and the Open Source Revolution*. London: Penguin.

Mostern, K. (1999), *Autobiography and Black Identity Politics: Racialization in Twentieth-Century America*. Cambridge: Cambridge University Press.

Murray, J. (1999), 'The C.L.R. James Institute and Me', *Interventions: International Journal of Postcolonial Studies*, 1/3, 389–96.

Negri, A. (1989), *The Politics of Subversion: A Manifesto for the Twenty-First Century*, Cambridge: Polity Press.

Nettleford, R. (1992), 'The Aesthetics of Negritude: A Metaphor for Liberation', in A. Hennessey, ed., *Intellectuals in the Twentieth-Century Caribbean*. London: Macmillan.

Nietzsche, F. (1967 [1886, 1888]), *The Birth of Tragedy and The Case of Wagner*. New York: Vintage.

Okely, J. (1986), *Simone de Beauvoir: A Re-Reading*. London: Virago.

Oxaal, I. (1968), *Black Intellectuals Come to Power: The Rise of Creole Nationalism in Trinidad and Tobago*. Cambridge, Mass.: Schenkman.

Padmore, G. (1955), *Pan-Africanism or Communism? The Coming Struggle for Africa*. London: Dennis Dobson.

Patterson, S. (1963), *Dark Strangers: A Sociological Study of the Absorption of a Recent West Indian Migrant Group in Brixton, South London*. London: Tavistock.

—— (1969), *Immigration and Race Relations in Britain, 1960–1967*. London: Institute of Race Relations.

Peach, C. (1969), *West Indian Migration to Britain*. London: Institute of Race Relations.

Philippe, J. (1996 [1826]), *Free Mulatto*, Amherst: Callaloux.

Phillips, M. and Phillips, T. (1999), *Windrush: The Irresistible Rise of Multi-Racial Britain*. London: HarperCollins.

Plummer, K. (2001), *Documents of Life 2: An Invitation to a Critical Humanism*. London: Sage.

Poster, M. (1984), *Foucault, Marxism, History*. Cambridge: Polity.

Pryce, E. (1990), 'Culture from Below: Politics, Resistance and Leadership in the Notting Hill Gate Carnival: 1976–1978', in H. Goulbourne, ed., *Black Politics in Britain*, 130–48. Aldershot: Avebury.

Radin, P. (1925), *Crashing Thunder: the autobiography of an American Indian*, New York, Appleton.

Ramchand, K. (1983), *The West Indian Novel and Its Background*. London: Heineman.

Ramdin, R. (1982), *From Chattel Slave to Wage Earner: A History of Trade Unionism in Trinidad and Tobago*. London: Martin Brian & O'Keefe.

—— (1987), *The Making of the Black Working Class in Britain*. Aldershot: Gower.

Rapport, N. (1997), *Transcendent Individual: Towards a Literary and Liberal Anthropology*. London: Routledge.

Reddock, R. (1994), *Women, Labour and Politics in Trinidad & Tobago: A History*. London: Zed.

Rex, J. and Tomlinson, S. (1979), *Colonial Immigrants in a British City*. London: Routledge & Kegan Paul.

Rifkin, J. (2000), *The End of Work: The Decline of the Global Work-Force and the Dawn of the Post-Market Era*. London: Penguin.

Rigby, P. (1996), *African Images: Racism and the End of Anthropology*. Oxford: Berg.

Rodney, W. (1972), *How Europe Underdeveloped Africa*. London: Bogle-L'Ouverture.

—— (1981), *A History of the Guyanese Working People*. Baltimore: Johns Hopkins University Press.

—— (1990), *Walter Rodney Speaks: The Making of an African Intellectual*. Trenton, NJ: Africa World Press.

Rohlehr, G. (1990), *Calypso and Society in Pre-Independence Trinidad*, Port of Spain: The Author.

Roussel-Milner, D. (1996), 'False History of Notting Hill Carnival: A Review of Professor Abner Cohen's "Masquerade Politics"', *Newsletter of the Association for a People's Carnival*.

Salkey, A. (1967), *Caribbean Prose: An Anthology for Secondary Schools*. London: Evans Bros.

—— (1971), *Havana Journal*. Harmondsworth: Penguin.

—— (1977), *Writing in Cuba Since the Revolution: An Anthology of Poems, Short Stories and Essays*. London: Bogle-L'Ouverture.

Sander, R. (1988), *The Trinidad Awakening: West Indian Literature of the Nineteen Thirties*. New York: Greenwood.

Sartre, J. (1963), *The Problem of Method*. London: Methuen.

Selvon, S. (1952), *A Brighter Sun*. London: Allan Wingate.

Sherwood, M. (1999), *Claudia Jones: A Life in Exile*. London: Lawrence & Wishart.

Shore, C. (1990), *Italian Communism: The Escape from Leninism*. London: Pluto.

—— (2000), *Building Europe: The Cultural Politics of European Integration*. London: Routledge.

Singh, K. (1994), *Race and Class Struggles in a Colonial State: Trinidad 1917–1945*. Calgary and Mona, Jamaica: University of Calgary Press and The Press, University of the West Indies.

Smith, M. (1965), *The Plural Society in the British West Indies*. Mona, Jamaica: Institute of Social and Economic Research.

Solomon, P. (1981), *Solomon; An Autobiography*. Port of Spain: Inprint.

Solomos, J. and Back, L. (1995), *Race, Politics and Social Change*. London: Routledge.

Starr, A. (2000), *Naming the Enemy: Anti-Corporate Movements Confront Globalization*. London: Pluto Press and Zed Books.

Stephens, G. (1999), *On Racial Frontiers: The New Culture of Frederick Douglass, Ralph Ellison, and Bob Marley*. Cambridge: Cambridge University Press.

Steumfle, S. (1997), *The Steelband Movement in Trinidad: The Forging of a National Art in Trinidad and Tobago*. Bridgetown, Kingston, and Port of Spain: The Press, University of the West Indies.

Stewart, J. (1989), *Drinkers, Drummers and Decent Folk: Ethnographic Narratives of Village Trinidad*. Albany: State University of New York.

Tarrow, S. (1998), *Power in Movement: Social Movements and Contentious Politics*. Cambridge: Cambridge University Press.

Thomas, J. (1969 [1869]), *The Theory and Practice of Creole Grammar*. London: New Beacon.

—— (1969 [1889]), *Froudacity: West Indian Fables by James Anthony Froude*. London: New Beacon.

Thomas-Hope, E. (1992), *Explanation in Caribbean Migration: Perception and the Image: Jamaica Barbados, St Vincent*. London: Macmillan.

Thompson, P. (1978), *Oral History: The Voice of the Past*. Oxford: OUP.

Tiffin, H. (1995), 'Cricket, Literature and the Politics of de-Colonisation: The Case of CLR James', in H. Beckles and B. Stoddart, eds, *Liberation Cricket: West Indies Cricket Culture*. Manchester: Manchester University Press.

Torres-Saillant, S. (1997), *Caribbean Poetics: Toward an Aesthetic of West Indian Literature*. Cambridge: Cambridge University Press.

Touraine, A. (1977), *The Voice and the Eye: An Analysis of Social Movements*. Cambridge: Cambridge University Press.

—— (2000), *Can We Live Together? Equality and Difference*. Cambridge: Polity.

Toynbee, P. (2001), *'It's the Poor That Matter'*, The Guardian Online <http://www.guardian.co.uk/Archive/Article/0,4273,4198867,00.html> (Accessed 06/06/2001).

Trotman, D. (1986), *Crime in Trinidad*. Knoxville: University of Tennessee Press.

Vertovec, S. (1993), 'Indo-Caribbean Experience in Britain: Overlooked, Miscategorized Misunderstood', in C. Harris and W. James, eds, *Inside Babylon: The Caribbean Diaspora in Britain*, 165–78. London: Verso.

Walch, J. (1998), *The Internet: An Activist's Guide*. London: Zed.

Walmsley, A. (1992), *The Caribbean Artists Movement 1966–1972: A Literary and Cultural History*. London: New Beacon Books.

Watson, J. (1979), *Between Two Cultures: Migrants and Minorities in Britain*. Oxford: Oxford University Press.

Webster, W. (1998), *Imagining Home: Gender, 'Race' and National Identity, 1945–64*. Women's History. London: UCL Press.

White, S. and Harris, R. (1999), *Changing Britannia: Life Experience with Britain*, S. White, and R. Harris, eds. London: New Beacon Books and George Padmore Institute.

Williams, E. (1964), *Capitalism and Slavery*. London: André Deutsch.

—— (1969), *Inward Hunger: The Education of a Prime Minister*. London: André Deutsch.

Bibliography

Williams, R. (1977), *Marxism and Literature*. Oxford: Oxford University Press.

Wilson, P. (1973), *Crab Antics: The Social Anthropology of English-Speaking Negro Societies in the Caribbean*. New Haven and London: Yale.

Witherford, N. (1994), 'Autonomous Marxism and the Information Society', *Capital & Class* (52), 85–125.

Wolf, E. (1982), *Europe and the People Without History*. Berkeley and London: University of California Press.

Worcester, K. (1996), *CLR James: A Political Biography*. Albany: State University of New York.

X, M. (1968), *The Autobiography of Malcolm X*. London: Penguin.

Young, M.F.D. (1971), *Knowledge and Control: New Directions for the Sociology of Education*. Open University Set Book. London: Collier Macmillan.

Yourcenar, M. (1955), *Memoirs of Hadrian*. London: Secker and Warburg.

Index

activism, 2, 3, 5, 14
  elective affinity, 14
  resource mobilization, 174
Africa, 64, 120
  colonialism, 150
Africa Unity House, 178
African National Congress, 23
Afro-Caribbean, 16
  community, 17
amnesia,
  mainstream British society and, 158
anthropologists, 8
apartheid, 162
  White liberals and, 163
Apollonian/Dionysian aesthetic contrast, 72
archival practice, 102
archivists, 103
Aries, 89, 90
Arima, 115–8 *passim*
Assembly of Caribbean Peoples, 111, 112
Association for a Peoples Carnival (APC), 73, 74
Atlantic world system, 179
audience,
  for personal narratives 163–4
autobiography, 11, 158
autonomous socialism, 126
  see also socialist autonomy
Ayim, May, 165

Bandung, 127
Barbados, 32
Barette, Jim, 122
Battle Front: Paper of the Black Parents Movement, 55
BBC, 157
  Caribbean Voices, 32
Beacon, 41–2, 115
  circle, 121

Besson, William, 144n15
Beyond a Boundary, 150
biographical narrative, 2, 12
  and activism, 177
biographical representation, 15
biography, 10, 11
Birmingham school of cultural studies, 6
Bishop, Maurice, 55
Black activism,
  Britain, 27–31
  rejection of racialized culture, 178
  tactical engagement, 177
Black Atlantic, 42
Black Britishness, 167
Black children,
  schooling in Britain, 43
Black community,
  boundedness, 167
  in Britain, 164
Black immigrants, 28
Black Jacobins, The, 121
Black Liberator Collective, 155
Black Londoners, 157
Black Panther Party
  British 58
  policy on dealing with arrests, 156
Black Panther youth movement, 152
Black Parents Movement (BPM), 21, 40, 51–7, 84, 132, 176
  legal defence campaigns, 92, 93
Black People's Day of Action, 57, 64
Black politics, 16, 28
  anti-racism and, 176
  Black people and, 177
  Britain and, 40
  socialism and, 176
Black Power,
  Britain, 29
  1960s, 29
  uprising in Trinidad, 158
  USA, 39–40

Index

Black radicalism, 30
  new social movements and, 178
Black struggle,
  class and, 163
Black Youth Movement (BYM), 21, 51–7,
  71,72
Blair, Tony, 129
Blakelock, PC, 156
Boggs, Grace Lee, 170n20
Bogle L'Ouverture Books , 58
Bogle L'Ouverture, 63, 171
  see also Bogle L'Ouverture Books
Book Fair,
  decision to terminate, 174
  see also International Book Fair of
    Radical Black and Third World Books
Bookmarks, 63
bookselling,
  business in Britain, 45
Bovell, Dennis, 146
BPM *see* Black Parents Movement
Bradford, 57
Brathwaite, Doris, 37
Brathwaite, Edward, 33, 37, 124
Brewster, Yvonne, 147, 153
British empire, 28
  emancipation and, 42
  white supremacy and, 42
British Council of Port of Spain, 121
British Communist Party,
  see Communist Party of Great Britain
British Cultural Studies (BCS), 8
Brixton, 9, 29, 58, 156
Broadwater Farm, 169n18
Burke, Aggrey, 22, 147, 149, 158, 161
Burnham, Forbes, 56
Busby, Margaret, 59
BYM
  see Black Youth Movement

C.L.R. James Institute, 81
calypso, 73
CAM
  see Caribbean Artists Movement
canon, 34
  formation of, 34–5
  Western Civilisation and, 136
capital,
  see cultural capital, economic capital,
    social capital, symbolic capital

Capitalism and Slavery 121
Caribbean Artists Movement, 21, 31–40,
  44, 51, 121, 124, 174, 178
Caribbean Creole, 165
Caribbean Educationists Association, 52
Caribbean Education and Community
  Workers Association (CECWA), 52
Caribbean, 7, 16, 17, 64, 124
  folk dances, 161
  unemployed, 129
  war contribution, 159
Caribbean-heritage, 17
Caribbean-heritage children,
  education and, 52
carnival, 122, 129
  history in Trinidad, 115
  law-and-order, 73
  Lent, 66
  music, 69
  Notting Hill, 66, 67, 72, 100
  Trinidad, 66
carnival masquerade, 74
  see also masquerade
carnival movement, 56
Carter, Trevor, 30
Castro, Fidel, 100
Centre for Creative Arts, 38
Césaire, Aimé, 100
childhood,
  early schooling in personal narratives,
    151–4
Cipriani, Andrew, 122
Clarke, Sebastian *see* Saakana, Amon
  Saba
class politics,
  culture and, 179
class struggle,
  colonial Trinidad and, 115
Coard, Bernard, 53
cognitive praxis, 15, 79, 91, 98, 106
colonialism, 43
Comintern, 138
Committee for the Release of Political
  Prisoners in Kenya, 55
Committee Against Repression in
  Guyana, 56
Commonwealth Caribbean, 17, 38
Commonwealth Literature, 35
communication technology 81, 174
Communist China 127

Index

Communist Party 97
Communist Party of the Soviet Union 99
Communist Party of Great Britain 23, 30
Communist Party of the USA 99
Community Relations Councils 28
Congo village 150
Connor, Edric 161
Connor-Mogotsi, Pearl, 146, 148, 150, 151, 153, 155, 156 158, 161, 162, 163, 165
cosmology, 106
counter-hegemony, 65
counter-narrative, publishing and bookselling as producing, 180
Craig, Susan, 112
Creation for Liberation, 38
Creole stratified society, 114
Creole, 114
  intelligentsia, 135, 138, 139
  linguistics, 121
creolization, 33
critical humanism, 9–10
critical universalism, 180
Crooks, Garth, 146
Cultural Correspondence, 81
cultural politics, 4, 5, 35
  alienation and, 4
  exploitation and, 4
cultural activism, 71
cultural politics and 1960s, 4
cultural capital, 83, 166
cultural autonomy, 65
cultural studies, 8
  see also British Cultural Studies
culture,
  social transformation and, 74
curriculum,
  George Padmore Supplementary School and, 54

Davis, Angela, 158
de Beauvoir, Simone, 99
desktop publishing, 81, 89
dialogical model of research, 10
discrimination, 30
Durham, Janice, 22, 23, 24, 45, 46, 89, 90, 175

East Germany, 62
East Indians, 117

Eastern Europe, 25
economic capital 82
education,
  colonial subjects and, 161
  radical sociology of, 53
  social transformation and, 181
  value for radicals, 161
Educationally Sub-Normal (ESN), 52
Edwards, Adolph, 37, 42, 43
empiricism, 10, 172
epiphany, 154
essentialism, 176
ethics, 13
ethnic communities, 6, 7
  culturalism and, 6
ethnographic-biographical method, 172
EU, 62
Eurocentricism, 42
Europe, 64
  New Left and, 36
European Union, 62

Fanon, Frantz, 36, 100
Festival of Britain, 67
Finsbury Park, 1
Forum Statement, 91, 92
Foundations, 37
France, 62
François, Elma, 143n9
Friere, Paulo, 74
Froude, James Anthony, 42

Garvey, Marcus, 43, 100, 122
Gayelle, 38
gender ideology,
  colonial Trinidad, 139
George Padmore Institute, 24, 27, 21, 79, 100–5, 132, 145, 176
  archive, 102–4
  archive committee, 102, 103
George Padmore Supplementary School, 21, 52, 53, 85
Ghana, 100
Giuseppi, Neville, 121
global capitalism,
  resistance to, 175
Goody, Joan, 54
Gorz, André, 132
GPI,
  see George Padmore Institute

Index

GPI series,
  see Life Experience with Britain
GPI talks,
  see Life Experience with Britain
Gramsci, Antonio, 13, 65, 99, 181
grass-roots methodology, 64
Greater London Council, 156
Grenada, 24, 55
Griffiths, Courtenay, 146, 148, 151, 152,
  153, 156, 162, 165
Guevara, Ernesto 'Che', 36, 99
Guyana, 36

Hall, Stuart, 173
Harlem, 156
Harris, Wilson, 42
Harris, Pat, 22, 175
Harris, Remi, 105, 175
Harris, Roxy, 9, 22, 89, 171, 174, 175
Harris, Roxy Jr, 175
Havana Journal, 36
Havana Cultural Congress, 36
hegemony, 65
heroic generation, 8, 147
Hibiscus Club, 68
Hindi, 117
history,
  as resource, 179
Howe, Darcus, 29
humanism, 9
humanist Marxism, 74
humanistic document,
  life story as, 142
    see also critical humanism
Huntley, Eric, 58
Huntley, Jessica, 58

identity, 178, 179, 182n3
  contingency, 180
  Creole , 117
  Black roots and, 150
  positionality, 180
identity politics, 176
  new social movements and, 177
imagination, 12
immanent critique,
  colonial society, of, 140
Imperial College, 23
imperialism, 127

independence,
  English-speaking Caribbean, 36
indigenous culture, 139
information technology, 90
  bookselling and, 88–91
  publishing and, 89–91
  wage labour and, 130
Institute of Race Relations, 58, 162
intellectual,
  types of, 173
International Book Fair, 27, 121
    see also International Book Fair of
    Radical Black and Third World
    Books
International Youth Festival, 25
International African Service Bureau, 100
International Book Fair of Radical Black
  and Third World Books, 57–66
internationalism, 100
Internet, 88, 89, 90, 104, 174
IQ testing, 52
Island Scholarship, 115, 137, 143n14
  women and, 139
Islington Town Hall, 58, 60
Italian Communism, 99
Italian Communist Party (PCI), 99

Jamaica, 32, 36, 69, 158
James, C.L.R., 13, 28, 29, 32, 36, 41, 43,
  56, 88, 100, 111, 113, 121, 124, 127,
  134, 135–7, 150, 162, 175
  African ancestry, 150
Jeanetta Cochrane Theatre, 37
John, Gus, 22, 55, 101, 146, 149, 158
Johnson, Linton Kwesi, 146, 153, 156,
  160, 162, 165
Jones, Claudia, 28–9, 100, 160

Kelshall, Jack, 155
Kenya, 55
King, Christina, 143n9
Kingston, 151

La Rose, Irma, 22, 25, 52, 53,171
La Rose, John, 1,16, 22, 23, 33, 36, 37,
  41, 43, 46, 52, 53, 57, 62, 91, 93, 96,
  101, 111–35, 171, 174, 178, 181
  self-representation, 133
La Rose, Keith, 22, 51, 175

La Rose, Michael, 22, 24, 45, 51, 67, 71,
   146, 148, 151, 152, 157, 160, 165, 171,
   175
La Rose, Ramona, 175
La Rose, Renaldo, 165, 175
La Rose, Wole, 175
Labour Party, 133
Laird, Colin, 155
Laird, Christopher, 38
Lamming, George, 33, 111, 135
League of Coloured Peoples, 28
left-wing activists, 28
left-wing politics, 29–30
Lenin, 127
Lewis, Arthur, 122
Life Experience with Britain, 145,
   146–67 *passim*, 174
life history, 11
life stories,
   cultural capital and, 166
   social capital and, 166
life story,
   late modern societies, 147
   narrating of, 164
   resource in maintaining the self, 166
life-project, 13
literature,
   Caribbean, 98
   English Caribbean, 35
   taught in English schools, 173
   Western literary canon, 98
London,
   Book Fairs, 57
   Caribbean writers, 33
London Book Fair, 89
London carnival,
   disputes over history of, 160
   see also Carnival, Notting Hill
Lovelace, Earl, 118

Macdonald, Ian, 22
McBurnie, Beryl, 155
McDaniel, Cliff, 51
McNish, Althea, 146
Mais, Roger, 33
Malcolm X, 170n20
Manchester Black Parents Movement, 55
Manchester, 57
Manhattan Brothers, 162

Mansfield, Michael, 156
Marley, Bob, 99
Marx, Karl, 126–7
Marxism, 13, 140
   autonomous wing of, 129
   strands of, 126
masquerade, 70, 71
   see also carnival
Matthews, Marc, 39
Maxton, James, 121
Maynard, Olga Comma, 139
migration, 5, 6
Mills, C.W., 12, 74, 160
Minshall, Peter, 155
Minshall, Wilson, 155
Miranda, Carmen, 155
Mobil Oil, 25
Mogotsi, Joe, 162
Moody, Harold, 28
Morris, Garry, 101
multicultural literature, 53, 178
multiculturalism, 177
multiform capital, 106
Murray, Jim, 81
music,
   Caribbean heritage and, 68
   Jamaican, 68
   Black Diaspora and 72
   Black youth and, 71

Naipaul, V.S., 33
nationalism,
   Third World and, 35–6
Negro Welfare Cultural and Social
   Association (NWCSA), 122, 123
network society, 80
New Beacon circle, 1, 2, 21, 22, 28, 31,
   40, 66, 145, 162, 171, 181
   close associates, 22
   core members, 22, 174
   leadership, 132
New Beacon Publishing House, 21, 41, 47
New Beacon Books, 1, 27, 41, 44–7, 52
New Beacon bookshop, 21, 145, 172
New Beacon book service, 21
New Beacon Educational Trust, 101
New Cross, 57, 64
New Cross Massacre Action Committee,
   57

Index

New Cross Massacre campaign, 174
New Left, 30, 36, 92
  in Britain, 178
New Statesman, 29
New Left Review, 37
New Scientist, 23
New Labour, 128, 129, 133, 134
New York, 156
New Commonwealth, 7
new social movements, 2, 3, 177
Nietzsche, Friedrich, 72
Nigeria, 55
Nigerian Society of Creative Artists, 38
North London West Indian Association, 52
Notting Hill, 9
  and riots, 28, 52
Notting Hill carnival, 31
Nuñez, George, 159

Obeah, 148
objectivity,
  autobiography and, 158
Oilfields Workers Trade Union 57, 111, 112
Old Left, 30, 128
online commerce, 90
Open University, 26
oral history, 12
organic intellectuals, 173–4
organizational strategy, 106
Orisha, 168n6
Oxford,
  migrant communities, 158

Padmore, George, 88, 99, 138, 140
Pan African Conference (1900), 28
Pan-African Congress (Manchester), 100
Pan-Africanism, 154
Panama, 151
Pascall, Alex, 146, 157, 160, 164, 165
Patterson, Orlando, 37
Peoples War Carnival Band, 66, 69–73
Peoples War Mas camp, 69
Peoples War Sound System, 66, 68–9, 72, 157
personal narrative, 10–13, 158
  as cultural and political resource, 166–7

as 'document of interaction', 145
as humanistic document, 167
as performance practice, 164–5
humanistic model of research and, 141
political engagement and, 154–8
political value of, 161
personal computer, 81
Peru, 127
Philippe, Jean-Baptiste, 140
physical punishment,
  discipline of children and, 169n13
Pierre, Lennox, 122, 123, 155
poetry,
  performance of, 165
police,
  bias, 98
  courtroom procedure and, 95
  encounter with, 156
politics,
  extraparliamentary sphere, 175
  of difference, 176
  poststructuralist-inspired critiques of, 65
  transcendent orientation to, 96
    see also transcendence
  transient orientation to, 96
    see also transience
popular music, 71
Port of Spain, 119, 129
positionality,
  contemporary cultural politics, 180
post-war migration, 5
Powell, Enoch, 18n2
praxis 2, 40, 180
  mobilization of biography, and, 174
Prescod, Colin, 146, 148, 150, 152, 154, 160, 162, 164, 165
Presentation Boys College, 151
progressive-regressive method, 13
project, 12
  individual life and, 13
public school education, 162
publishing, 65
  New Beacon, 47

Queen's Royal College, 119, 136, 137

race, 6
  migration and, 6

Race, 162
Race and Class, 162
race relations, 6
 life-world colonization and, 167
Race Relations Act, 28
Race Relations Board, 28
Race Today, 29, 38
Race Today, 63, 171
 see also Race Today Collective
Race Today Collective, 56, 58
racial discrimination, 158
racist discourses, 161
radical democratic politics, 21, 74
radical mas', 73
 see also masquerade
radical humanism,
 views on education and schooling, 172
radical sociology, 160
Ramchand, Kenneth, 37, 43
Rastafarianism,
 new social movement, 177
rave culture. 160
reggae, 68, 165
reggae artists,
 as poets, 161
Rennie, Alexis, 147, 152
reputation, 134
respectability, 134
Rights of Passage, 37
Rodney, Walter, 56, 100, 158
Romania, 25
Royal Academy of Dramatic Arts, 165
Rugg, Akua, 22

Saakana, Amon Saba, 39
Salkey, Andrew, 33, 36, 124
Sartre, Jean-Paul, 13, 74, 132, 171
Savacou, 34, 40
Savannah,
 Arima, 116
scholarship,
 social transformation and, 138
schooling,
 sense of self and 161
self,
 class and race aspects, 162–3
 domination and, 158
 performance, 158–60 *passim*, 163–5
 vindication of, 140, 158, 159

self-government,
 West Indian territories 32
self-history, 164
self-representation 117
 methodological approach to, 126
 racialization and, 162
 roots and origins, 148
 symbolic universe as underlying, 167
Selvon, Sam (Samuel), 33, 118
serious mas', 73
 see also masquerade
Shango, 148
Shepherd, Claire, 104
slow builders and consolidators, 105
soca, 73
social capital, 82, 166
social construction, 6
 cultural difference and, 7
 ethnicity and, 7
 race and, 7
social memory, 166
social movements, 2
social transformation 13
 culture and, 129
 education and, 181
 John La Rose's vision of, 135
 of oppressive relations, 177
 politics and, 129
socialism,
 strands of , 126
socialist autonomy, 127
socialist politics, 123
Socialist Workers Party (SWP), 63, 87, 97
Sociological Imagination, 172
sociological imagination, 12, 160
sociological object, 14
sociological intervention, and study of
 social movements, 180
sociologists, 8
sociology of reggae music, 160
Solomon, Patrick, 144n15
sound system, 69
South Africa, 56, 158, 162, 163
South East London Parents Organisation,
 38
Southall 31
Southeast Caribbean, 71
Soviet Union, 127
Soviet Weekly, 128

Index

Spain, 127
St Joseph's Convent, 151
St Lucia, 156
St Mary's College, 119, 138
Stalin, 127
steel bands, 122
Steelband, 129
  see also steel bands
strategic universalism, 176
strategic essentialism, 133
Stroud Green Road, 1, 44, 56
subjecthood, 158
subjects,
  vindication and, 158
submerged knowledge, 61
supplementary schools, 53
SUS, 31
symbolic capital, 98

Teddy boys, 153
Third World, 36
Thomas, John Jacob, 42, 115, 140
Thomas, J.J., 121
  see also Thomas, John Jacob
Tobago, 151
Tobagonian, 168n2
Touraine, Alain, 1, 180
Toynbee, Polly, 128
trade unions, 92
transcendence, 73
transculturalism, 176, 177
transformation of work, 129–30
transience, 73
Trinbagonian, 168n2
Trinidad, 32, 41, 57, 93, 99, 111, 114,
  125
  colonial civil service, 115
  colonial social structure, 114–5, 140
  ferment against colonial order, 123
  war contribution, 159
Trinidad, 41–2
Trinidadian, 168n2
Trinidad All Steel Percussion Orchestra
  (TASPO) 67
Trinidad and Tobago, 36
  independence, 156
Trinidad and Tobago Youth Movement,
  155
Trinidad Labour Party, 122
Trinidad Working Men's Association, 122

Trinidad Youth Council, 25
Trotskyists, 127

Uniques, 56
United States, 127
University of Essex, 155
University of Hull, 155
University of the West Indies, 38
University of London, 26
US Communist Party, 28
USA,
  Afro-American community, 39
USSR, 128, 133
utopia, 177

Van Sertima, Ivan, 42
vanguard,
  politics, 130–3
Venezuela, 25, 123, 124, 148, 151
Victoria, Queen, 116
Vienna, 25
Viet Cong, 125
vindication,
  narratives of, 161

wage labour, 130
Walcott, Derek, 156
Walter Rodney Bookshop, 58
West Indian Standing Conference, 52
West Indian Gazette, 28–9
West Germany, 62
West Indian Standing Conference, 28
West Indies, 17
  African ancestry in colonial times, 149
West Indian Independence Party, 123
White, Sarah, 1, 22, 23, 37, 45, 62, 89,
  90, 101, 124, 171, 174, 175, 178, 181
Wilberforce, William, 116
Williams, Eric, 112, 121, 122, 137–8
Williams, Henry Sylvester, 28
Wilson, Peter, 134
Wood, Wilfred (Bishop), 146, 157
Workers Freedom Movement, 123
Working Peoples Alliance, 56
World Federation of Trade Unions, 25
World Federation of Trade Unions
  Congress, 123
world system, 3

Zapatistas, 99